Proving

Zechariah Sitchin

and the Ancient Sumerian Texts

Published by Mindstir Media, LLC
45 Lafayette Rd | Suite 181| North Hampton, NH 03862 | USA
1.800.767.0531 | www.mindstirmedia.com

Printed in the United States of America
ISBN-13: 978-1-7344892-5-5
Library of Congress Control Number is on file with the publisher

Proving
Zechariah Sitchin
and the Ancient Sumerian Texts

By Donald M. Blackwell

MINDSTIR MEDIA

Table of Contents

Acknowledgments:

First and foremost is Zechariah Sitchin, for here is a man who dedicated 30 years of his life, educating himself, learning to speak six different languages which enabled him to read, speak, interpret, write, comprehend, analyze and explain the ancient texts: Then and only then did he write his first book! His "Earth Chronicles" books, translated into 26 different languages worldwide are, in my opinion, the most profound writings ever made available to mankind. Zachariah Sitchin was intellectually honest. He had a very high abstract IQ which equates to nothing less than him being brilliant. He gave me a gift for which I can never repay him. He gave me, through his writings, "Food for Thought," and that food for thought was laid out before me like a great King Arthur banquet and I being the only indulgent. That said, in the future, I will always have his food to eat, for which I will be forever grateful and indebted.

Donald M. Blackwell

Introduction To Zechariah Sitchin And The Ancient Sumerian Texts

The necessity for writing this book is long overdue. For decades I have tolerated the arrogance, hubris and blatant denial of empirical evidence offered by the Sumerian, Akkadian, Babylonian, Ugaritic, Assyrian and Phoenician texts, Stale, cylinder seals, etc., that is prevalent and permeates almost every facet of our scientific world. Whether it be Cosmology, Astrophysics, Genetics, Archaeology, Mathematics, Engineering or other fields of applied science, etc., I find that our highly educated scientific world, in almost every endeavor, push their intelligent, abstract knowledge aside and slide into a supercilious, pseudo-intellectual cul-de-sac of groupthink, denying that which is in reality.... history!

The use of "Sumerian Text" in the title of this book is purposely inclusive of all ancient texts written, some of which are mentioned above. I point this out because there are those who inanely state, that if any of the ancient texts do not start out by identifying the title as being the "Sumerian Text," that invalidates it as being an ancient text. A simile to that would be saying, that if any of the writings of Zechariah Sitchin were not immediately identified as *The Earth Chronicles, that would make them invalid.* That kind of thinking, in today's world, is prevalent and it is also patently absurd!

The big question is why? Why does the scientific community, along with intelligent and knowledgeable people, suborn the truth and walk a deviant path? I believe the answer is that the scientific community adamantly believes that they are, as of this current date, or any future date, will be the epitome, the apex, the pinnacle of scientific knowledge. There is little, to no acceptance, as to what has been written, *sometimes in stone, m*any millennia past

When we read the ancient texts we should realize that since they were written, millennia passed, *there has not been one word that has changed!* If our scientific community, and current ancient astronaut theorists proffer a theory, they can change, modify, alter or delineate their writings and ideas and theories to correct their previously written and/or stated words. The ancient text, as previously stated, cannot change one word of what was written in the past, yet, I challenge anyone in any scientific field of endeavor, to prove that the ancient texts are false. The Ancient Texts are referred to as myth or legend. Certainly, legend can be gleaned from the written words of the Anunnaki, but there is no myth relating to the Ancient Texts, *it is simply written history!*

The entire world owes a debt of gratitude to Zechariah Sitchin, the author of *The Earth Chronicles.* Here is a man who dedicated himself totally for *30 years of studying and researching the ancient texts,* **before** putting one word into print, so his intent had absolutely nothing to do with writing books with a profit motive, it had everything to do with an exposé of the ancient texts. His writings are about expression, not an impression. His *Earth Chronicles* are the result of one man's insatiable curiosity, joined at the hip with his intellectual pursuit of truth.

What Zechariah Sitchin has accomplished with his writings has resulted in the simplification, edification, and elucidation of a rather difficult subject matter referred to as the *Ancient Text.* His 14 books, *"The Earth Chronicles,"* give to the world, in my opinion, *the empirically written words of the Ancient Text on a silver platter.* And for this, to Mr. Sitchin, I will be eternally grateful.

When we watch programs like National Geographic, the Ancient Alien series, articles and read books relating to the ancient text, the word Zechariah Sitchin is almost never used. The reference to his *Earth Chronicle books is never mentioned! The word, Anunnocki* is rarely mentioned and when they are, they are almost never associated with Zechariah Sitchin's books, or the writings of the ancient texts The pseudonyms they use are, *extraterrestrials or ancient astronauts,* when it can be proven that the subject matter they are discussing or writing about, is 95% of the time, *related directly and only to the Anunnaki!* That begs the question as to why they fail to attribute to Zechariah Sitchin, the ancient texts and the Anunnaki, that which solely belongs to Zechariah Sitchin, the Ancient Texts and the Anunnaki! I believe the answer to be, that ***almost every question, they are asking has already been answered by Zechariah Sitchin can be empirically vetted by "reading" the ancient text!*** That being the truthful case, if the ancient astronaut theorists relied on, and accepted the Ancient Texts for verification, they would have very little to talk about, very little to surmise, , there would be very little to write about; they would have to drastically reduce their pseudo-hypotheses and theories; not to mention the number of television programs and the number of books written would be numerically reduced ***because their questions would have already been answered!***

My objective here is to put before the reader and the public, what I believe to be, irrefutable empirical evidence of the ancient texts. I will inform the reader, by placing the information I have obtained, in print, using primarily the ancient text! I will fully identify the ancient text, the volume number and/or the page number so that anyone can verify what I'm writing is not simply my opinion. I want the reader to *trust and then verify* the written word of the ancient texts so that the readers of this book will be able to decide for themselves, what is the truth, what is history and what is factual. I have been reading, studying and analyzing the ancient texts for more than a quarter of a century, therefore I offer to every field of science and ancient theorists, to provide me with your written documented refutation of anything that is written in this book or anything that is written in the Ancient Texts.

What I find currently, prior to writing this book, leaves me quite dismayed. I have e-mailed six Universities, two in my state of Florida and the remaining four out-of-state. I wanted to provide them with specific ancient text subject matter, the same as I will do here for you, the reader. I wanted them to read the designated, specific areas of the ancient texts and asked them for a response to either verify and agree with or refute that specific text. The ancient text information would relate specifically to their scientific area of knowledge ie, Astrophysicist, Geneticist, Biologist, Astrology, Cosmology, etc. After three months of searching, I have only received one response, from the scientific community, "He is on vacation." My response to them is, that is probably true, in more ways than one. Therefore I will, myself, have to do the "layman's analysis of the ancient text.

In my hometown of Hudson, Florida, in the spring of 1994, my wife and I were coming home from shopping. We were passing a yard sale consisting of nothing but books. There were boxes, upon boxes, upon boxes, of thousands of books filling the empty lot. Being an avid reader since childhood, I could not resist the temptation. After spending more than an hour, I had about a half a dozen books in hand. The gentleman selling the books was sitting in a chair in back of a small table. I placed the books on the table and paid him for those books. The seated gentleman said, "May I recommend a book for you to read?" I said, "Please do." The gentleman said, "Based on the books that you have purchased, I would recommend Zechariah Sitchin's, " The 12th Planet." I animated "I don't read many fiction books anymore, I'm more into history and biographies." The gentleman stated, "Again based on the books that you have purchased, *if you read it, you will know it is not fiction!*" In retrospect, that was one of the most profound statements ever made to me in my lifetime!" The result of which is the book you're about to read.

Donald M. Blackwell

Introduction to the Anunnaki – A Synopsis

In order to have a better understanding of the ancient texts, and the book you are about to read, succinct synopsis of the ancient texts and the Anunnaki, is necessary. Most of you have never had the opportunity to read one ancient text, never mind thousands that are available and in print, nor even one of Zechariah Sitchin's 14 books, "The Earth Chronicles," hence the following as written in the ancient texts:

The ancient texts tell us that the Anunnaki, a highly advanced civilization, came to this planet around 445,000 years ago. At that time and prior, the Anunnaki were having a problem with the depleting, protective atmosphere on their planet, Nibiru. They tried the extreme measures of dropping nuclear weapons into their volcanoes, hoping to raise particles into the upper atmosphere to enhance planetary protection. This methodology was not successful. The Anunnaki leadership knew the value of gold and its potential use in protecting their atmosphere. That goal was noncorrosive and once placed into orbit, atmospherically around the planet it would provide an infinite, interminable solution. The problem is that gold was a rare commodity on their planet Nibiru. They tried mining gold that they had detected on some of the larger orbiting stones of the Asteroid Belt. That too was unsuccessful and eventually abandoned, due to a constant loss of lives and spacecraft.

Alalu, once reigning King on Nibiru, after physically fighting Anu, another high-ranking Anunnaki, for the Kingship of their planet Nibiru, and losing; was forced to forever leave the planet Nibiru. This became a very fortunate incident for the Anunnaki and planet Nibiru as Alalu in his spacecraft came upon this beautiful planet, having snow-caps on its northern and southern areas.

Landing his craft in the area of today's Persian Gulf Area, south of where the Tigris and Euphrates River joined together, with his Crystal instrument he discovers gold. He then contacts the planet Nibiru to inform the Anunnaki of his findings. Anu, the newly established king of Nibiru, sends his first son Ea (Enki) and 20 other Anunnaki men from the planet Nibiru to Earth (Ki) to evaluate Alulu's discovery of gold.

From this period of time, (445,000 years ago) onward, the Anun-

11

naki's main and only function on Earth is to mine gold and return the payloads to the planet Nibiru. The Anunnaki increased their numerical strength on Earth and the rank and file were assigned the laborious task of mining. The Igigi, numbering 200, remained in orbit around the Earth. Their primary function was to transport the mined gold from Earth to Mars and then to the planet Nibiru.

When massive amounts of gold were discovered in southeast Africa, referred to by the Anunnaki as the Abzu, Ea, (Enki) was assigned that specific area to mine gold. Enki's son Viracocha, (Adad) at a later date, was sent to South America (later called Cuzco) and created the Andean civilization Tiahuanacu, near the southern shores of Lake Titicaca, (Bolivia) and his sole purpose there was to mine gold.

Quetzalcoatl (Enki's firstborn son Thoth) was sent to Mesoamerica. That specific date was stated in the ancient text, as 3113 BC. Also his sole purpose of creating a civilization there was, to mine for gold. Along the banks of the Amazon River, to this day, remain there what has been determined to be sluice's for mining gold, in short, the Anunnaki were assigned all over the world for one single purpose, to save their planet by mining gold, wherever they could find it.

The Anunnaki rank-and-file, during the 12th Sar, who had been mining the gold for thousands of years rebelled. Enki, their chief scientist, and Ninhursag, their chief medical officer, then fashioned a "Being" by genetically manipulating the native ape to serve the Anunnaki as slave labor. After repeated failures of splicing ape genes with Homo erectus genes, continued trial and error, inevitably led to merging Homo genetic genes with that of Anunnaki genes, which, through more trial and error, produced Homo erectus i.e. the genetically bicameral species Homo sapiens, a hybrid that could not reproduce. With the demands of slave labor constantly increasing, they genetically manipulated the existing Homo sapiens, resulting in what is better known as US. That scientific genetic "fashioning," answers the question of, "the Missing Link."

The Homo sapiens were then able to reproduce as a stable genetic stock. The day and night, frequent conjugations, became numerically uncontrollable and Homo sapiens were cast out all of the cities and metropolitan areas to fend totally for themselves From Mesopotamia, the Anunnaki left their footprints literally all over the world.

The promiscuous Anunnaki, whose sexual exploits did not exclude their own sisters, half-sisters, nieces, etc. and the female human being became very attractive to the Anunnaki as sexual partners, resulting in additional children of Anunnaki blood.

Enlil, the top Anunnaki commander of Earth, in summoned counsel, decided that they would no longer be responsible for the Homo sapiens on earth. They provided them with nothing, no food, no clothing, no anything to ensure their survival As Enlil stated in the ancient text, "Let them eat grass!"

It is often stated by authors, historians and those who have read the ancient text, that the Anunnaki intended to destroy mankind by, they themselves, creating a worldwide flood. That simply is not true. The, "Let them eat grass," era according to the ancient text, happened three Sars, or 10,800 years **prior** to the great Deluge The Anunnaki had absolutely no control of the slippage of the ice sheet from the landmass of the South Pole which was increasing with each orbit and the resulting gravitational pull of Nibiru, accompanied by 11 moons.

Prior to the great Flood, Enki, our most benevolent extraterrestrial Anunnaki, having been involved directly with the genetic manipulation and creation of the human race, felt a deep commiseration. To save at least a small segment of mankind, he instructed Ziusudra, (from the original Sumerian version of the Deluge tale) or Utnapishtim (from the latter Acadian version of the Deluge) to build a submarine type craft in which they could survive the oncoming Deluge.

After that the great flood, which some human beings survived, they again experienced their numerical increase on Earth. From 10,500 BC (in my opinion, the date of the great Deluge) to around 3800 BC the human race proliferated, which accounts for the surprise and sudden appearance of the first historical and documented civilization called Sumer.

At this juncture in time (3800 BC) the Anunnaki realize that they needed humankind to primarily do one thing, to provide them with food by growing grains and vegetables and providing them with meat, through animal husbandry. (Ka'in and Abael)

The first step in Sumeria was to create a strain of humans which would be genetically advanced by being given more of the Anunnaki genes. A specific bloodline related closely to the Anunnaki, that would be given a higher degree of intelligence and then taught from almost all technological areas known to the Anunnaki. From that bloodline came the Kings and hierarchy of Sumeria through which the Anunnaki communicated their wants and desires to be disseminated to the king, he to the priest and on down the line of rank-and-file. What was established as a line of hierarchy and authority, to facilitate, enhance and maintain a properly functioning social structure. The Anunnaki were never worshiped, nor was there anything that we could directly or indirectly describe as religion. In all my readings of the Sumerian text, religion, with the Anunnaki, in Samaria, or Egypt the word religion did not exist!

From the beginning, some 445,000 years ago, until her departure from this Earth (Nasca) around 600 BC, the Anunnaki established the first civilization known to man as Sumer. Enlil and Enki, with their respective sons, demonstrated a very humanistic trait, the desire for power. From this power contest, for the control of Earth, the Anunnaki chose to war against each other, resulting in the use of seven "named" nuclear weapons.

This entire book can be documented and proven by using the written word of the "Historical Sumerian Texts, of which, I provide the reader of this book by specific identification of chapter and verse, each and every ancient Sumerian Texts I use in this book.

Chapter 1: VA 243 The Sine Qua Non of the Ancient Texts

This one cylinder seal depiction, shown to exist more than 4500 years ago is responsible for launching me on a decade's long insatiable quest for knowledge relating to the Ancient Texts. In January 1994, when I first read, "The 12th Planet," by Zechariah Sitchin my first thoughts relating to chapter 7, The Epic of Creation was, this depiction of VA 243 simply cannot be true and my intent was to prove this `Sitchin fella' wrong. The more I read, the more anxious I became. My computer shows me a picture of Vorderasiatische Abteilung 243. After about a period of about 10 to 15 minutes, I am asking myself, "How can this possibly be a depiction of our solar system?" This simply cannot be true and my next step was to make a solid effort and void Sitchin's credibility.

I did find something `negative' relating to Mr. Sitchin. One man, whose name I do not recall, criticized Mr. Sitchin, relating to his conjugation of two Akkadian verbs. Now there is a big woop! I continued on the computer for hours looking for anyone to critique Mr. Sitchin. I found no one else.

Going back to the picture of VA 243, I judged that the location, distance between the depicted planets and their size were apparently accurate excepting two planets, Pluto and another planet which Mr. Sitchin refers to as Niburu. Pluto was depicted as being positioned between the planets Saturn and Uranus. Aha! I've got you now Mr. Sitchin! And I held that attitude for approximately six months….. Until I read Enuma Elish. Enuma Elish revealed that Niburu, on the second retrograde orbit into our solar system, picked up Pluto as a satellite and during its orbit, heading toward its apogee, out of our solar system, repositioned Pluto to orbiting outside the orbit of Neptune. From here I accepted a higher degree of credence relating to VA 243.

My next thoughts were to somehow measure the distances between planets, their relative size and position as depicted in VA 243. I found an expanded picture of VA 243 which would allow more accurate measuring. Next, I found the distances from the Sun to all the planets in our solar system and obviously the distance between the earth and our moon. Then I needed to know the radius of each of the planets. One could not describe this approach as being scientific however it seemed to me to be a practical approach that might either satiate some of my questions or instill more doubts.

THE CURRENTLY KNOWN DISTANCE FROM THE SUN OF THE PLANETS IN OUR SOLAR SYSTEM

Mercury- 38.98 million miles   Radius-1,516 miles

Venus-27.24 million miles   Radius 3,760 miles

Earth-92.96 million miles   Radius-3,959 miles

Mars-146.6 million miles   Radius-2,106 miles

Jupiter-483.8 million miles   Radius-43,441 miles

Saturn-890.7 million miles   Radius-36,184 miles

Uranus-1780 4 billion miles   Radius-15,759 miles

Neptune-2.793 billion miles   Radius-15,299 miles

Pluto-3.67 billion miles   Radius-738.4 miles

So let's apply some math to our VA 243, numerical solar system which renders the following:

1. Mercury is 2.61 times smaller than Earth

2. Venus is only .95% smaller than Earth

3. Mars is 1.88 times smaller than Earth

4. Jupiter is 10.79 times larger than Earth

5. Saturn is 9.14 times larger than Earth

6. Uranus is 3.98 times larger than Earth

7. Neptune is 3.86 times larger than Earth

8. Pluto is 5.36 times smaller than Earth

The math completed, we can now apply the latest scientific information, relating to distance, size, and scale of our solar system to that of the Akkadian cylinder seal VA 243.

Using nothing more than a simple visual perusal of the drawn diagram we can ask:

1. Is Mars smaller than Venus but larger than Mercury?

2. Is Mercury larger than our Moon?

3. Is Mars larger than Pluto?

4. Is Jupiter somewhat larger than Saturn?

5. Are Uranus and Neptune relatively close in size?

6. Is the planet Nibiru very close to the size of Neptune?

The answer to all six is a definitive YES! Therefore one can logically conclude that **VA 243 IS AN EMPIRICAL DEPICTION OF OUR SOLAR SYSTEM!**

Relating back to question number six, is the planet Nibiru very close to the size of Neptune? We know that Neptune has a radius of 15,299 miles, and if we divide Earth's radius, 3, 959 miles, into the radius of Neptune we get 3.87. Therefore Neptune is approximately four times the size of Earth and we can, therefore, determine that **NIBIRU IS APPROXIMATELY FOUR TIMES THE SIZE OF EARTH!** What is significant about that is that our "modern-day theorists," tell us that Planet X, a.k.a. Planet Nine is estimated to be about 17 times the size of the earth. As I previously explained, there may be a Planet X or Planet Nine out there, orbiting our solar system, however; I can definitively tell you that it is not Nibiru, as Nibiru, having been mathematically established, is about four times the size of Earth.

Further, Planet X is orbiting in a normal counterclockwise plane. Nibiru, *as established by NASA, and Enuma Elish,* orbits in retrograde, which is clockwise. When knowledge ends, speculation begins. I think I'll stick to my more prosaic approach.

Back in 1994 when I was first evaluating VA 243 it was my opinion that the cylinder seal depiction was either one hundred percent right or one hundred wrong. My "gotcha Mr. Sitchin," moment came when I saw, according to VA 243, that the planet Pluto was located between Saturn and Uranus. I found it inexplicable and very confusing. When, months later, reading Enuma Elish, which relates to the reader that when the planet Nibiru entered our solar system, Gaga (Pluto) was a satellite moon of Saturn. I asked myself why would VA 243 include something as insignificant as a moon of Saturn? I have determined the answer to be thus: VA 243 depicts our solar system beginning with the initial entry of Nibiru into our solar system and depicts Gaga accurately was an innocuous insignificant moon of Saturn. Then gaining a better understanding and comprehension of Enuma Elish, (a somewhat difficult read) it reveals that during the second orbit of Nibiru, into our solar system, Gaga was gravitationally separated from Saturn as its moon, placing it temporarily as a moon of Nibiru and then Nibiru, heading towards its perigee in outer space, Gaga was then gravitationally removed from the planet Nibiru and fell into orbit around Earth. Therefore the pictorial aspect of showing Gaga in VA 243.

Fortunately, I recently found on Karel Donk's Blog, that they had taken basically the same approach that I did in evaluating VA /243 and here are some of their conclusions:

Can it be, just mere coincidence that the relative sizes of all of the 12 globes on cylinder seal VA/ 243 happen to closely match with the relative sizes of the heavenly bodies in our solar system on a logarithmic scale? Can it be just mere coincidence that the diameters of the globes on the cylinder seal happen to be chosen so perfectly relative to each other and to scale, to closely match the dimensions in reality? Or must we conclude that the artist who drew the globes most likely made a conscious decision to draw them in their relative sizes based on the knowledge he had? What are the odds that this could happen just by chance-- that the artist just randomly placed 12 globes on the cylinder seal that just happen to be most precisely to scale compared to our solar system?

If what I've shown above is correct, then it leads to the following conclusions:

*Zechariah Sitchin was right to point out that the globes on the cylinder seal VA/243 depict our solar system.

*Apparently the Sumerians knew about our complete solar system all the way back in the third millennium B. C. Not only did they know how many planets there were, but they also knew their relative sizes (possibly even their exact sizes). And if Sitchin is correct they also knew details about the colors and compositions of the planets.

*Apparently the Sumerians knew how to use some form of logarithmic scaling to be able to depict the **planets and their relative sizes very close to accurate. Rather than linearly scaling the solar system** down to a smaller size in the drawing – which would have made certain planets so small in relation to the sun that they would be hard to see – they did it logarithmically. A clever solution, it's a smaller fractal representation of the whole.

*Apparently the Sumerians thought that Pluto was indeed a planet. If it's not Pluto then it has to be a heavenly body the size of Pluto that they found significant enough to include.

*It's not clear to me why the artists chose the positions he did for all the planets. If the relative sizes were done on purpose, it's likely that the positions were also chosen on purpose.

*If the Sumarian depiction of our solar system is accurate, then what else is? Could that be **everything** they wrote about is accurate and based on scientific and historical fact? Certainly, Sitchin, who spent decades of his life researching this, thought so.

*It appears that it's highly likely that planet Niburu exists and that astrophysicist John Matese and Daniel Whitmire could be proven correct with regard to the estimated size of the planet.

The above analyzation of VA/243 is about 95% correct. The lone exception being is his diameter measurements of the earth (12,756 km) in relation to planet X (Niburu) which is shown as 226,973 km. cannot be accurate. Dividing earth kilometers into Niburu's kilometers gives the answer that Niburu is 17.79343 times the size of the earth. Even a casual visual perusal of VA/243 comparing the Earth's size to Niburu's size, one could easily determine that Niburu is approximately four or five times larger than Earth and certainly not 17 times the size of earth!

I believe the discrepancy here can be answered by stating definitively that their **Planet X is not the planet Niburu!** It very well may be that Planet X exists and is 17 times larger than Earth but **the planet Niburu is approximately only four times the size of the Earth.**

I do have what I consider to be a very reliable source of scientific information. That source I will not reveal because that person could lose their "position." I believe the information that I have received will, in fact, prove itself over time. My source, whom I will in the future refer to as *Existential Tabulate,* relates to me**, not only is Niburu part of our solar system,** *there are two additional planets that are part of our solar system!* One of those two additional planets is estimated to be 17 times the size of **Nibiru.** The way it was explained to me, by my source, is that the other planet is a blue planet. That planet is very much in size like the ice planet orbiting Jupiter and it is not Titan! That leaves only one "planet" that it could be, namely Ganymede an ice moon of Jupiter. Albeit a moon of Jupiter, Ganymede is the seventh-largest "planet" in our solar system.

What is absolutely amazing relating to VA 243, is not the size of Earth relating to the size of Niburu, it is the pictorial cylinder seal evidence that **there is another planet in our solar system that we are not aware of.** And let me correct that statement to say *we know empirically that Nibiru is a member of our solar system and have known that for more than two decades!* Our scientific community is simply in a state of denial due to an overdose of scientific hubris. If the scientific community came forth and admitted that there was another planet in our solar system, they would be admitting to the validity of VA 243, being an empirical depiction of our solar system. They would be admitting the historical knowledge and value of the Ancient Samarian Texts. They would be admitting that those people that lived in ancient times, going back at least to 4500 years ago, that had no telescope, they had no Hubble, they had no Mariner 1 and 2, no Voyager1 and 2, no Kepler telescope, no Sadaru telescope in Hawaii, etc. so how could they possibly have more scientific knowledge than we have today. And let me put it in colloquial slang, "Day ain't gonna do dat!"

Dunks Blog expresses my sentiments this way:

"Perhaps it's time that we start paying more attention to all those ancient writings in order to see what we can learn from them. Scientists and all their arrogance have continued to downplay the significance of these ancient writings, often dismissing them as "Myths." But as others, such as Sitchin, have pointed out, the ancients don't waste so much of their time writing hundreds of clay tablets and making cylinder seals just to write down fantasy stories or chocolate chip cookie recipes. They are recording history and preserving knowledge for future generations."

We like to think that we're the height of human civilization; that we know all and that ancient civilizations were primitive and believed in made-up gods. But a lot of the knowledge and technology we think is new today is just being rediscovered and reinvented. This fact will continue to become more apparent in the future. Meanwhile, if you're a smart scientist and especially if you are in the field of genetics, (and I'll add astrophysics, astrology, geology, Astrogeology, etc. etc.) you want to study the Samarian writings for any clues you can find.

In 2005 I attended a Zechariah Sitchin seminar in Dallas Texas. There were about 200 people in attendance, including a very special guest by the name of Amnon Sitchin, the brother of Zechariah Sitchin. Mr. Amnon Sitchin has a couple of Ph.D.'s after his name, and I am certainly not saying that in a trite manner, one being an astrophysicist. He was at that time and could still, employed by NASA. During that seminar what was revealed by Mr. Amnon Sitchin, Ph.D. is that _**NASA was fully aware that Niburu existed as a planet in our solar system!**_ That was 13 years ago! So NASA has known about Niburu for something more than two decades.

Over the past two decades, being interested in the planet Nibiru and its questioned existence, I have cut out several newspaper articles describing the discovery of the 10th planet, here is just one of them.

A 10TH PLANET MAY ORBIT SUN
Tuesday, October 12, 1999, Knight Ritter Newspapers.

WASHINGTON- Our solar system may have a new, strange and very distant member, two teams of astronomers think.

It may be a big 10th planet hidden far beyond Pluto, a hitchhiker that joined the solar system later than the rest of the planets. Or it could be a burned-out ministar, called a brown dwarf, a long lost twin to our sun.

Whatever it is, it's really, really far away: 3 trillion miles, give or take a few billion, the scientist figure.

But it's still part of our solar system and big enough – probably three times the size of Jupiter – that it is warping the orbits of some far traveling comets. Patterns in the distortion of their paths led separate teams of scientists in Louisiana and England to conclude something else is out there.

Other astronomers are skeptical. They want to see something, and that's part of the problem. The object – informally nicknamed "the perturber" – is so distant and dark that telescopes can't see it. What these two teams of scientists "see" is a gravitational push-pull of this mysterious neighbor on about three different comets.

It's not unusual for astronomers to see the effects of a planet before they see the planet itself. That's what happened earlier this century before Pluto was first observed in 1930.

And that's what's happening now. John Murray, a planetary scientist at the Open University in Milton Keynes, England said he was looking at the paths of 13 comets whose huge orbits bring them into this part of the solar system once every few million years or so. He found that their paths showed a similar distorting pull. After two years of rejections and more noted scientific journals, Murray's findings were published in Monday's Monthly Notices of the Royal Astronomical Society.

At Louisiana University in Lafayette, physics professor John Matese found warping in about one-quarter of 82 other comets that generate from the Oort Cloud, a comet breeding ground far past Pluto. He and physicist Daniel Whitmire used a different type of analysis from Murray's but reached similar conclusions. Their paper will appear in the Journal *Icarus* next month.

The two groups differ on the precise orbit of the object, its origins and what exactly to call it.

"We prefer brown dwarf," Whitmire said. "It's how it formed. We don't think it formed like a planet. We believe it formed like a star."

Whitmire's group theorizes that when the solar system formed, there were two stars: the sun and a small twin. The theoretical twin shrank and cooled. If it can be observed at all, it is in the infrared spectrum of light, he said.

Murray, the British researcher, prefers to call the object a planet, "because something orbiting the sun is a planet unless it glows." He thinks the object moved into our solar system after the solar system formed.

Astronomers have long suspected something works comets' paths – everything from a theoretical anti-son called Nemesis to passing stars – but many are dubious about a 10th planet or a brown dwarf.

"I'm quite a bit skeptical," said Brian Marston associate director of the Harvard Smithsonian Center for Astrophysics. "But there might be something to it."

"You don't have enough numbers of comets to feel comfortable that this is really convincing evidence," added Renu Malhotra, a scientist specializing in planetary dynamics at the Lunar and Planetary Institute of Houston.

Whitmire hopes that a new NASA infrared telescope, scheduled to launch in 26 months, will find the inner heat of this mysterious object, confirming its existence.

For purposes of showing progress toward the discovery of the planet Nibiru, I will include one more news article, dated Sunday, July 31, 2005, from the Tyler Courier-Times-Telegraph.

ASTRONOMERS CLAIM DISCOVERY OF 10TH PLANET IN SOLAR SYSTEM.

Los Angeles (AP) – Astronomers announced Friday that **they have discovered** *a new planet larger than Pluto in orbit around the sun. (There is nothing ambiguous about that statement.)*

The discovery in the outlying regions of the solar system was made with the Samuel Oschin Telescope at the Palomar Observatory, planetary scientist Mike Brown of the California Institute of Technology said in a statement.

Details were being released in a conference call with reporters on Friday.

The unnamed planet would be the 10th in the solar system, although there are scientists who dispute the classification of Pluto as a planet.

The discovered object is the farthest known object in the solar system, Caltech said in a statement.

Brown made the discovery with colleagues Chad Trujillo of the Gemini Observatory and David Rabinowitz of Yale University.

The object was first photographed on October 31, 2003, but it was so far away that its motion was not detected until data was analyzed again this past January. The scientists have since studied the object over the past seven months.

The above-mentioned newspaper article was Sunday, July 31, 2005. During the Zechariah Sitchin seminar in Dallas Texas, Amnon Sitchin revealed to the audience through his brother Zechariah Sitchin, that NASA already knew that Niburu existed as a member of our solar system, was on May 2005.

> Realize what we have many highly advanced scientific instruments today, already mentioned in the above paragraphs. One of the most important and the most technologically advanced, in my opinion, is the Hubble space telescope. I have seen pictures taken by Hubble, showing so many **galaxies**, so close together in one picture, that unless you were told differently you would think you were looking at **stars!**' So please don't tell me that NASA is not fully aware of the existence of the planet Niburu. They know the size, they know its' orbit. The question now becomes, how does NASA currently handle the situation? The answer is obsequious, with the obvious intent to make the subject matter obviate.
>
> Let me give you some examples: if you were to Google, planet X or Niburu what you're going to read is NASA saying, in one area of print, that Niburu does exist as part of our solar system. Another NASA release will say that Nibiru does not exist as a member of our solar system. And I say both statements are intentionally misleading. Here is their press release dated 06: 32 EDT, 13 October 2017, and note, they refer to the planet Niburu as Planet Nine.
>
> "It has been widely debated among the science community for years but now **NASA** claims that Planet Nine does exist. The space agency highlights five different lines of evidence pointing to the existence of the mysterious world and says that imagining that Planet Nine does not exist, generates more problems than you solve.

*NASA highlights five different lines of evidence of the existence of Planet 9.

Go to dailymail.com to get the **picture** of six objects orbiting in the Kuiper belt and the orbit of Planet Nine as determined by Caltech in 2016, by Dr.Batygin.

"In 2016, the researchers examined the orbits of six objects in the Kuiper Belt – a distant region of icy bodies stretching from Neptune outward toward interstellar space. His findings revealed that the objects to all had elliptical orbits that point in the same direction and are tilted 30°' downward' compared to the plane in which the 8 Planets circle the sun.

The Planet Nine is shown having an elliptical orbit **around our solar system.** There very well may be a Planet Nine orbiting our sun yet, the reason Planet Nine cannot be the planet Niburu as depicted in VA 243 simply because the planet Niburu comes in retrograde and passes very close to the Asteroid Belt **and `between the planets Jupiter and Mars'.** Planet Nine's shown orbit does not come within a measured distance of three of our solar systems to our sun.

So scratch Planet Nine is being Niburu. Scratch any planet that is said to be five times larger than Earth. Scratch any planet that does not come in retrograde and scratch any planet that doesn't come into our solar system and pass very close to the asteroid belt between the planets Jupiter and Mars. Scratch any planet that does not complete its orbit in approximately 3600 years. And scratch any planet that is not the home planet of the Anunnaki!

No one has more right to express themselves on this matter than Zechariah Sitchin. In his book, `Genesis Revisited', page 17 – 19 he writes:

"The ancient explanation regarding the origin of Pluto reveals not just factual knowledge but also great sophistication in matters celestial. It involves an understanding of the complex forces that have shaped the solar system, as well as the development of astrophysical theories by which moons can become planets, and planets in the making can fail and remain moons. Pluto, according to Sumarian cosmology made it; our Moon, which was in the process of becoming an independent planet, was prevented by celestial events from attaining the independent status."

Modern astronomers moved from speculation to the conviction that such a process has indeed occurred in our Solar System. That observations by the Pioneer and Voyager spacecraft determined in the past decade that Titan, the largest moon of Saturn, was a planet-in-the-making whose detachment from Saturn was not completed. The discoveries at Neptune reinforced the opposite speculation regarding Triton, Neptune's moon that is just 400 miles smaller in diameter than Earth's Moon. It's peculiar orbit, its 'volcanism, and other unexpected features have suggested to the JPL scientists, in the words of the Voyagers projects chief scientists Edward Stone, that "Triton may have been an object sailing through our Solar System several billion years ago when it strayed too close to Neptune, came under its gravitational influence and started orbiting the planet."

How far is this hypothesis from the Sumerian notion that planetary moons could become planets, shift celestial positions, or failed to attain independent orbits? Indeed, as we continued to expound the Samarian cosmology, it will become evident that not only is much of modern discovery merely a rediscovery of ancient knowledge but that ancient knowledge offered explanations of many phenomena that modern science has yet to figure out.

Even at the outset, before the rest of the evidence in support of this statement is presented, the question and evidence mentally arises: how on earth could the Sumerians have known all that so long ago, at the dawn of civilization?

The answer lies in the second difference between the Sumarian depiction of the Solar System (VA 243) and our present knowledge of it. *It is the inclusion of a large planet in the empty space between Mars and Jupiter.* We are not aware of any such planet; *but the Sumarian cosmological, astronomical, and historical texts insist that there indeed exist one more planet in our solar system-- it's 12th member:* they included the Sun, the Moon (which they counted as a celestial body in its own right for reasons stated in the texts), and 10, not nine, planets. It was the realization that a planet in the Sumarian texts called **NIBIRU ("Planet of the Crossing")** Was Neither Mars nor Jupiter, as some scholars have debated but another planet that passes between them every 3, 600 years that gave rise to my first book's title, *The 12ᵗʰ Planet--- the planet which is the "12ᵗʰ member" of the Solar System (although technically it is, as a planet, only the 10ᵗʰ).*

It was from that planet, the Sumerian texts repeatedly and persistently stated, that the **ANUNNAKI** came to Earth. The term literally means "Those Who from Heaven to Earth Came." They are spoken of in the Bible as the *Anakim,* and in Chapter 6 of Genesis, they are also called Nefilim, which in Hebrew means, in essence, the same thing: "Those Who Have Come Down", from the Heavens to Earth.

Comment: Whether one uses the word Anakim or Nefilim, the reference is still to the one and only Anunnaki! The word Anakim is used in the Bible, is plural for Anak and meaning " giant." And any time you see that word used in the Bible, it literally means Anunnaki. In the original Hebrew Nefilim translated means, "Those who came down." The exact Sumarian translation of Anunnaki, according to Enki, an Anunnaki god, translates to "Those who from heaven to Earth came. As for me in any literal or verbal circumstance, I will always use the word Anunnaki! Period.

If one accepts the validity, that VA 243 is an actual representation of our solar system, which I most certainly do, then the Anunnaki, in their writing of their Sumarian text, must have had a far more superior knowledge of our solar system, *then we do today!* Enuma Elish is a prime example, clearly demonstrating their scientifically advanced knowledge.

The Anunnaki's scientific knowledge, demonstrates that empirical knowledge, rather ubiquitously throughout the ancient texts and here I will provide a small example from "The Lost Book of Enki," THE FIRST TABLET STARTING AT PAGE 30:

To remedy the afflictions ways he thought; of Nibiru's

heavenly circuit he made many studies.

In its loop, of **the Sun's family five members** it embraced planets of dazzling beauty.

For the cures to the afflictions, **their atmospheres he caused to be examined**.

Comment: If you're going to examine the atmospheres of the Sun's five family members, me thinketh thou shalt needeth a spacecraft.

To each (Planet) he gave a name, ancestral forefathers he honored; as heavenly couples he then considered.

Comment: Here are the names and Sumerian translation of the names, allocated to each planet by the **Anunnaki:**
Sun – Apsu, "one who existed from the beginning."
Mercury –Mammu, counselor and emissary of Apsu.
Venus – Lahamu, "lady of battles."
Mars – Lahmu, "deity of war."
Jupiter – Kishar, "foremost of firm lands."
Saturn – Anshar, "foremost of the heavens."
Pluto – Gaga, counselor and emissary Anshar.
Uranus – Anu, "he of the heavens."
Neptune – Nudimmud (Ea), "artful creator."

Note that Pluto is listed between Uranus and Saturn as one of Saturn's moon. This is exactly how VA 243 represents our solar system. The question that keeps coming to mind is, why is a moon of Saturn even depicted in VA 243? Could it be that at the time the original cylinder seal, VA 243 was conceived, *that that, was the current, initial status of our solar system and the Anunnaki knew that Pluto would be gravitationally repositioned into an orbit, which could only then be defined as a plane? The trans-positioning of Pluto from being a moon of Saturn to its current orbital pattern is a plaintively described happening in Enuma Elish, during Nibiru's second entrance into our solar system* I am sure if I keep reading the ancient texts as I have done the last two decades, I will find more answers.

An and Antu, the twin-like planets, he called it the first two to be encountered.

Beyond in Nibiru's circuit were Anshar (Saturn) and Kishar, (Jupiter) in their size the largest.

As a messenger of Gaga (Pluto) among the others coursed, **sometimes first** Nibiru to meet.

Comment: In the above sentence the word "sometimes" connotes scientific knowledge.
The reason being that Pluto (Gaga) *sometimes orbits inside the orbit of the planet Neptune!*

Five in all were Nibiru's heavenly greeters as the Sun it circled.

Beyond, like a boundary, the Hammered Bracelet (The Asteroid Belt) the Sun encircled;

As a guardian of the heavens forbidden region with havoc, it protected.

Other children of the Sun, **four** in number, (Mercury Venus Earth and Mars) from intrusion the bracelet shielded.

The atmospheres of the five greeters (Pluto, Neptune, Uranus, Saturn, and Jupiter) Enshar set out to study.

In its repeating circuit, the five in Nibiru's loop carefully were examined.

What atmospheres they possessed by observation and with celestial chariots intensely were examined.

Comment: As I have already mentioned if you're going to

observe the atmospheres of those planets, you are going to need a *celestial chariot!*

The findings were astounding, the discoveries confusing.

Comment: Astonishing, yes! Especially when we realize that all this scientific information was written in "The Lost Book of Enki," starting exactly on the Date of, *February 2, 2017, B. C.* It was from the Anunnaki, the Sumerians explained--- as though they had anticipated our questions--- that they had learned all they knew. The advanced knowledge we find in Sumerian texts is thus, in effect, the knowledge that was possessed by the Anunnaki who had come from Nibiru; and theirs must have been a very advanced civilization because as I have learned from the Sumerian texts, the Anunnaki came to Earth about 445,000 years ago. Way back then they could already travel in space. Their vast elliptical orbit made a loop--- this is the exact translation of the Sumerian term--- around all the outer planets, acting as a moving observatory from which the Anunnaki could investigate all those planets. No wonder that what we are discovering now, what was already known in Sumerian times.

When it becomes scientifically undeniable that Nibiru exists in our solar system, then the Anunnaki themselves will become undeniable; whereby our World, by necessity, will be forced to admit and then confirm that there are superior beings existing, not only within our universe but within our own solar system.

THE CASE OF THE LURKING PLANET

"Far beyond the solar systems nine <u>known</u> planets, a body as massive as Mars may once have been part of our planetary system-- and it might still be there;"

The lead paragraph in a science fiction script?
The lead paragraph from an article by Zechariah Sitchin about Nibiru?

No. It is the lead paragraph in a report in <u>Science News</u> of April 7, 2001, headlined "A Comets Odd Orbit Hints at

Donald M. Blackwell

Hidden Planet."

The article reports the conclusions of an international team of astronomers who have studied an unusual comment discovered last year, designated 2000 CR/105. It follows a vast elliptical orbit around our Sun--an orbit that takes it way out to some 4.5 billion km from the Sun, and brings it back at its closest to the Sun, to the vicinity of Neptune; it is in orbit whose period "takes roughly 3300 years" (according to Sky and Telescope News of April 5, 2001).

"Such an oblong orbit is usually a sign that an object has come under the gravitational influence of a massive body," wrote our: in Science News. Was this the gravitational pull of Neptune? In a study to be published in the Journal Icarus, the team of astronomers (led by Brett Gladman of the Observatoire de la Cote d'Azur in Nice, France), after analyzing all the possibilities, do not think so. An alternative solution, they say, is that "the comet's orbit could be the handiwork of an as yet unseen planet" --as massive as Mars-- "that would have to lie some 200 AU from the Sun," in the so-called the Kuiper belt of cometary and other planetary debris. This would also explain "why many members of the Belt have orbits that angle away from the plane in which the nine known planets orbit the Sun."

"Undoubtedly, something massive kicked the hell out of the Belt," Harold F Levison of the Southwest Research Institute in Boulder, Colorado, told the magazine. "The question is whether it is still there now.

"Comet's Course Hints at Mistry Planet," was how the Journal Science headlined the discovery news in its issue of 6 April 2001. The special report, written by Dutch astronomer Govert Schilling, summed up the findings in the following lead paragraph:

"A Super Comment following an unexpectedly far-flung path around the sun suggest that an on identified planet

once lurked in the outermost reaches of the solar system, an international team of astronomers reports. What's more, the mysterious object may still be there."

Now, As the Sumerians Said...

Readers of my books may well join me now in saying: So what else is new?

Ever since the publication of my first book (The 12ᵗʰ Planet) in 1976 I have asserted that Sumerian and other ancient Near Eastern texts and depictions showed familiarity with a complete Solar System that included, besides the Sun and the Moon, ten (not nine) planets-- the tenth planet (or 12ᵗʰ member of the Solar System) having a vast elliptical orbit the lasts 3600 years. Its Sumerian name was Nibiru.

"I have suggested that Sumerian/Akkadian texts such as Enuma Elish (also called the Babylonian Epic of Creation) were not mythological tales, but records of sophisticated advanced knowledge. Establishment scientists and scholars (see a previous article, **The Case of the Misplaced Teapot,** as an example) resist such an inevitable conclusion because it requires the acceptance of the ancient claim that Earth had been visited by Extraterrestrials, the ANUNNAKI ("Those Who from Heaven to Earth Came") of Sumerian lore."

"According to the ancient texts as interpreted by me, Nibiru was a planet ejected from some other planetary system in outer space that was captured into our Solar System as it passed near Neptune. It became involved in a collision with a pre-existing planet where the debris of the Asteroid Belt Are Now. As a result of that collision, some 4 billion years ago, the Earth and the Moon came to where they are now."

"And, what do you know? In an article titled Neptune Attacks! In the 7 April 2001 issue of the magazine New Scientist, Ivan Semeniak wrote thus:"

"There is new evidence that a sudden barrage of deadly debris crashed against the Earth and the Moon 3.9 billion years ago... What triggered this onslaught? Something in the structure of the Solar System must have changed."

The "something," I am more certain than ever, was Nibiru.

C- Z. Sitchin 2001

Planetary Discoveries

The assertion that the Anunnaki came from a planet (Nibiru) whose orbit extends far out in our solar system has repeatedly lead to the question: How could life exist so far away from the Sun, where it is extremely cold and everything freezes?

My answer has been that we need not go that far out to freeze to death, just rising above Earth's surface would do the trick. It is the planet's atmosphere that retains the warmth, be it warmth obtained from the Sun, or from an internal source of heat. The crucial issue for the Anunnaki, I explained, was to prevent the loss of Nibiru's atmosphere; they sought to do that with a shield of gold particles, and that they came here to obtain the goal.

Now comes the news that made headlines worldwide: WATER GUSHERS ON THE SATURN MOON HINT LIFE POSSIBILITY.

The exciting news came from a report in the Journal Science (10 March 2006), in which NASA revealed that its Cassini spacecraft discovered that Saturn's fourth moon, Enceladus, spouts water geysers-"which hints at pockets of **liquid water** under the surface." For that, the temperature below the surface must be above freezing. In fact, even the moons above-surface temperature turned out to be 100° warmer than what he had expected!

While planets generate internal heat from radioactive materials in their cores, the Saturn moon, it is now theorized, maybe warmed by magnetic reactions as it orbits Saturn. One way or another, the astounding discovery corroborates scientifically the information that I have reported based on Sumerian writings: Yes, even that far away from the Sun, it can be hot enough for water to flow in life to emerge!

THE CASE OF THE EARTHLIKE PLANET

An exciting planetary discovery, just reported, spilled over from the scientific publications to the general media. Radio and television stations announced in headline news that "Another planet like Earth discovered"; The New York Times presented the news more accurately: SEARCH FINDS FAR-OFF PLANET AKIN TO EARTH.

The excitement stemmed from a report in the British scientific journal Nature (issue of 26 January 2006), in which 73 astronomers, working in three teams, disclose the tracking-- since July 11, 2005-- Of an "Earthlike" planet orbiting a distant star. The bottom line implication or hint is that it, therefore, might harbor life.

Astronomers have held for centuries that our solar system came into being due to extraordinary circumstances, with Earth happening to emerge in a "habitable zone" by the sheerest of chances. It is barely a decade since astronomers-with initial disbelief-began to find "extrasolar" planets in orbit around other stars; but even with some 170 such planets found to date, they all seem to be giant like and to close to their suns, and thus (so the notion goes) unsuitable for life.

As both the original scientific paper and follow-up news reports explained, the latest find is different; It is of a planet just three times (or slightly more) the mass of Earth and only about three times as far from the sun as Earth is from ours; the discovered planet-- orbiting a star in our own galaxy!--- is thus "Earthlike" in key aspects.

Donald M. Blackwell

AS I WAS SAYING...

The news, I can tell my readers, put me in a philosophical mood of wonderment.

It was 30 years ago (yes, 30 years!) Since my first book, The Twelfth Planet, was published. In it, I brought to life the 6000-years-old cosmology of the Sumerians. They wrote, I said, that soon after our solar system began to form, a planet thrust from another solar system passed near ours, was attracted inward, collided with a planet called Tiamat, broke her up to create Earth and that the asteroid belt, and itself was captured into a great orbit around our Sun to become the planet Nibiru. It Is so "Earthlike" that the Seed of Life began there, was transferred to Earth during the collision

At that time, the established view abhorred the idea of catastrophic celestial events (now it is accepted). The notion of planets elsewhere in the cosmos was deemed nonsense (now 171 such planets are listed). All that I said that the Sumerians had known has been proven true. And you know what? The mass of the newfound planet is akin to the estimate of Nibiru, and its distance from its Sun is about the same as Tiamat was...
It does make you wonder.

C- Z. Sitchin 2006

THE NAMING OF NIBIRU

Astrophysicists, Astrologists, and Cosmologists **along** with the other germane scientists plainly state that when a new planet is discovered, the individual who discovered that planet has the right to name it: so I offer this, a letter to The Planetary Society, sent to them on January 31, 1983.

Ms. Charlene Anderson
The Planetary Society
110 S. Euclid

Pasadena, CA. 91101

In view of very recent reports in the press concerning the intensified search for the 10th planet, I am forwarding to you copies of my exchanges on the subject with Dr. John D Anderson.

According to the New York Times of this Sunday (see enclosure)
"Astronomers are so sure of the 10th planet, they think there's nothing left but to name it."

Well--- the ancients have already named it: *Nibiru* in Sumerian,
Marduk in Babylonian; and I believe I have the right to insist that it so be called.

Sincerely,

C- Z. Sitchin

The impact will be especially profound in two areas: The first being religion and the second being military. I am adamantly convinced that it is not a question of "*if*" Nibiru will be found, the question is "**when**" **Nibiru is found! And that will be, based on the ancient text, approximately 800 years from now!**

Chapter 2: Enuma Elish

My personal interpretation of Enuma Elish based on my readings of, The Seven Tablets of Creation by Leonard William King, George Smiths' and E.A.Wallis Budges' "The Babylonian Legends of Creation" (Between the 18th and 16th century B.C.E.) and Zechariah Sitchin's' chapter 7 of "The 12 Planet."

Most often the names of a specific Sumerian, Akkadian, Babylonian, Ugaritic, Assyrian texts, etc., are determined by the first few words written of that ancient text. So be it with.....

Enuma elish la nabu shamamu
When in the heights Heaven had not been named
Shaplitu ammatum shuma la zakrat
And below, firm ground [Earth] had not been called

This ancient Babylonian story describes the very early stages of the evolution of our Solar System. The planet Nibiru was drawn into our solar system by the planet Neptune. Neptune at that time being the outer and the last planet in our solar system and further being pulled into our solar system, by Saturn, and then by Jupiter. The new planet can be definitively described as coming into our solar system, Retrograde. That set a new course for the planet Nibiru into what is its current orbit between Mars and Jupiter. On the first pass, orbit, one of the moons of Nibiru collides with the planet Tiamat. On the second pass or orbit, the planet Nibiru itself collides with Tiamat creating the Asteroid Belt, Comets and gravitationally taking the now planet Pluto, a moon of Saturn at the time and leaving it in its current position as our last planet.

This Babylonian story relates very clearly from the beginning of our Solar System naming each planet as it coalesced into a planet and gave each planet a Babylonian name. The names of the planets created in numerical sequence are of significant value as they empirically describe our fully established Solar System! **One must understand that Enuma Elish, providing the following information was "in cuneiform print" more than 3600 years ago!**

Sun (Apsu) ("one who exists from the beginning")
Mercury (Mummu) ("counselor and emissary of Apsu")
Tiamat ("maiden who gave life")
Mars ("Lahmu") ("God of War")
Venus (Lahamu) (Goddess of Both Love and War)
Jupiter (Kishar) ("foremost of the firm lands")
Saturn (Anshar) ("foremost of the heavens")
Pluto (Gaga) ("counselor and the emissary of Anshar")
Uranus (Anu) ("he of the heavens")
Neptune (Ea) ("artful creator")

The first that is created, after coalesced matter explodes, that later develops into a Solar System is a Sun. Ours was given the apt Babylonian name Apsu, meaning, the first to exist.

The first formed planet Mercury, the Babylonian Mammu, counselor or emissary of Apsu. simply stated, Mercury orbits the Sun.

Tiamat, maiden who gave life, relates to two different factors. Tiamat was a planet with vast amounts of water. One knows, where you have water, you have the potential for life. That water was transferred to our Earth, when, in its second orbit into our solar system, the planet Nibiru collided with Tiamat. This imparted the "biological soup of life," (DNA) to our planet.

Kishar, Foremost of the firm lands. The largest planet in our Solar System.

Anshar, Foremost of the heavens. The second-largest planet in our Solar System.

Gaga, counselor and emissary of Anshar. When the planet Nibiru entered our Solar System, Enuma Elish relates that Gaga was then a Moon of Saturn, hence, counselor or emissary.

Anu, he of the heavens. The ancient Sumerian Texts tells us that Anu was the leader of the Anunnaki with the highest rank of 60. His sons Enlil and Enki had a numerical ranking of 50 and 40 respectively. The two of them literally, lived here on Earth, Anu, never did live on

Donald M. Blackwell

Earth and came to Earth only when Nibiru was nearing its perigee to Earth when Anu would authorize the imparting of knowledge from to his two sons to the "Earthlings." Nibiru's collision with Tiamat created the asteroid belt, referred to in the ancient texts as "the hammered out bracelet." The hammered out bracelet was the location that the Anunnaki referred to as Heaven, where Nibiru passed in its 3600-year orbit, between Mars and Jupiter. The Sumerian word, "Anunnaki," literally means, "Those who from heaven to earth came." Hence the reference to Anu, as he of the heavens. Also, note the **anu** in Ur**anu**s.

Ea, artful creator. Enki had several epithets. I recall at least seven different epithets. For example, in the Egyptian pantheon, he was known as Nudimmud, which means "The Artful Creator," and/or the "Fashioner of Mankind."

On the second orbit of Nibiru, the millennia-old Sumerian epic explains the phenomena of how our Asteroid Belt and Comets were created. The planet Nibiru itself collides with planet Tiamat, the shattered half becomes the Asteroid Belt (Hammered Bracelet), referred to by the Anunnaki as "Heaven." Currently, our comets are established and set in a retrograde orbit of our Sun.

One might ask the question, relating to the above cosmology, "Where is the Earth?" Being a simple man, I will explain it as simply as I can.

On the second entry into our Solar System, referred to in the Sumerian Text as a Shar, now in a fixed elliptical orbit of 3600 years, Nibiru returns to the now battered planet Tiamat, which is located in the same orbital plane as our now established Asteroid Belt, located between Jupiter and Mars.

The Babylonian text relates:

The Lord (Nibiru) paused to review her lifeless body.

To divide the monster (Tiamat) he then artfully planned.

Then, as a muscle, he split her into two parts.

39

Recall on the first Shar or orbit of Nibiru, Tiamat collides with two of Nibiru's moons. Nibiru now collides with the subdued planet, Tiamat's upper part. It is important to remember that the planet Nibiru is coming into our solar system retrograde or clockwise. The planet Tiamat is in orbit traveling counterclockwise. From the impact of the collision, the separated half of Tiamat then collides with one of Nibiru's moons, referred to in the ancient texts as a satellite of Nibiru, called the North Wind. This places the separated half into another orbit closer to the Sun. Along with the separated half of Tiamat, is the gravitationally attached chief moon of Tiamat named Kingu, which we now identify as our Moon. The Anunnaki, now name this established orbital planet "Ki." Ki in Sumarian means Earth.

I firmly believe that that the Sumerian epic, Enuma Elish provides its' reader with a very sophisticated cosmology describing the creation of our solar system dating back to roughly 3.6 billion years. I would ask anyone in our scientific community this question of profundity: How could Enuma Elish have been written without empirical knowledge of the subject matter? I submit to all, that it is my **unwavering and most adamant contention, that it could not have been written without the Anunnaki having that empirical knowledge**!

I would also submit that the writer of Enuma Elish was the Anunnaki god Enki. I believe I can establish a degree of credibility here as several pages of "The Lost Both of Enki" duplicate some of the same information written in Enuma Elish and list the specific day, month and year that the ancient Sumerian Text was written. That date being February 2, 2017 BC., derived from the following.

"In the seventh year after the Great Calamity, in the second month, on the 17th day, I was summoned by my master the Lord Enki, great God, benevolent fashioner of Mankind, omnipotent and merciful.

Those who have read and studied the ancient texts know that the "Great Calamity" refers to a nuclear explosion which occurred in the year 2024 BC. The nuclear event happened south of the joining of the Tigris and Euphrates rivers. Therefore the seventh year after the Great Calamity equates to a date of February 17, 2017 BC.

It should be noted and highlighted, that within the last decade, scientists have agreed that there was a nuclear explosion south of the joining of the Tigris and Euphrates rivers around 2024 BC. How they arrived at that conclusion is explained in the chapter, "Proof – Nuclear Weapons." More importantly, what is clearly demonstrated here is precisely the purpose of this book; modern-day science continues to *prove the ancient knowledge of Sumerian Texts!*

During my readings of the Sumerian Text, and of particular Enuma Elish, one outstanding question kept coming to mind, which was perplexing, frustrating and for the longest time unanswerable, – the question being, how did Nibiru become a member of our solar system? Was Nibiru always a member of our solar system, coming to fold in a normal cosmological manner as did the other planets? Did it have a more normal elliptic orbit or was it perpendicular to the elliptic? Did Nibiru take it's established orbit, as the other planets did, in our solar system somewhere in space past the Oort cloud or beyond? Or… did it come to us from another solar system?

For the longest period of time, not having anywhere near the qualifications of an astrophysicist or cosmologist, I reasoned: even with the most abnormal orbit, to the extreme, Nibiru could not have come from another solar system as the nearest star/solar system (Alpha Centauri) was 12 trillion miles away or 4.4 million light-years away. Therefore Nibiru, even though it had an extremely abnormal orbit, had to be part of our normal cosmological formation as were the other planets. And I was wrong!

Meghneel Gore, the Senior Android Engineer at Tonal Incorporated, answered the question, "Could a rogue planet enter the solar system?" He answered, "Absolutely! There's nothing stopping a rogue planet from entering our solar system." He continues: "The planet can be captured in a highly elliptical orbit like a comet and pass through the Solar System then not seen for hundreds, or thousands of years before it makes its way back into the orbits of the current planets in the Solar System.

Isn't this exactly what Enuma Elish tells us? That Nibiru was captured by the planet Neptune into a highly elliptical orbit, *like a comet,* which travels retrograde, as does the planet Nibiru, taking thousands of years to complete its orbit, referred to in the Ancient Text as a Shar, taking 3, 600 years.

Further, does it make scientific sense that Neptune could pull Nibiru into our solar system? The answer is yes. We know from reading

Enuma Elish that at the point of time that Nibiru was pulled into our solar system, *Neptune, not Pluto, was the outermost planet of our solar system.* Then understanding the physics of gravity, Neptune would necessarily have to be larger than Nibiru exerting its net pull of gravity inward. We also know that Neptune is 17 times the size of Earth and that Neptune, based on the measurements of VA 243, Nibiru is between 3 to 5 times the size of Earth. So if we pick the number four, the middle size of Nibiru, divide four into 17 the size of Neptune we can easily determine that Neptune is approximately 4.25 times the size of Nibiru, which again makes scientific sense.

Mr. Gore also tells us "The planet could go into an egg-shaped elliptical orbit (*almost any orbit it could take would be elliptical*) in the outer solar system where it is *outside the orbit of the planets.*" Is this not what Enuma Elish tells us?

"The planet could have a near-miss with one of the other planets and throw one or both of them out of orbit so we lose a planet from the solar system."

Enuma Elish also tells us that during its second orbit into our solar system, from its gravitational pull, Nibiru takes Pluto, which was at that time a moon of Jupiter, and as it is exiting toward its apogee, in its clockwise/retrograde orbit, it deposits Pluto to be orbiting outside the existing orbit of Neptune.

"The planet could impact one of the planets. So long as the planet is not Earth, the results will only be devastating as the planetary impact will throw vast quantities of material into space...."

Again Enuma Elish tells us that on Nibiru's first entry into our solar system, two moons of Nibiru collided with Tiamat, a watery planet orbiting between Jupiter and Mars. During its second entry orbit into our solar system, Nibiru itself collided with Tiamat, the end result being the Asteroid Belt. Mr. Gore's last sentence above is very descriptive, "the planetary impact will **throw vast quantities of material into space**. Again Enuma Elish makes scientific sense and moreover it provides us with what I consider to be.... A sophisticated cosmology!

Astrologists, in general, agree that an exploding star could be responsible for dispelling matter and planets from its solar system. A planet, orbiting its exploding sun/star, then has nothing to keep it in a destined orbit. Without "destiny" a planet would travel in a straight line into the void of space and would continue on that straight line forever, or until some celestial body exerted its gravitational effect. Mr. Gore explains it this way:

"Any planet traveling close to that star/solar system would either pass on through or become a member of that solar system."

With any given statement that a scientist or a professional makes, you can bet on the fact that there will be those who will dispute their statements and argue against them. After decades of studying the Ancient Texts, I place my trust in them. Time and time again the ancient texts scientifically prove themselves. In this particular case, I'll place my trust in the historical Enuma Elish.

In 2010 we lost Mr. Zechariah Sitchin and that was a short period of time after he lost his beloved wife Freda. I don't think I will ever forget the story that he told to me and a crowd of more than 200 people in Dallas Texas in 2005; that being, he had stretched out on the couch, not to take a nap, but to think, a method he often used to analyze a specific subject matter. The subject matter on that particular day was VA 243. He instantly jumped to his feet when he realized the orb depicted in VA 243, located between Mars and Jupiter, had to be another planet in our solar system.

He halfway ran into the kitchen where Freda was working and his exciting words continue to flow. Half talking to himself, and half talking to Mrs. Sitchin, the words poured out like a verbal Niagara Falls. The more he talked and conveyed his thoughts to Freda, the more he realized what he had discovered.

Freda, realizing Zechariah's uncommon excitement upon entry into the kitchen, had seated herself to simply listen. When Zechariah's words, and animated body motions, finally slowed, he looked to her for a response, which was, after a long silence........... STOP TALKING AND START WRITING! That writing was his first book in 1976, The 12th Planet.

I will incorporate, into different chapters of this book, some of Zechariah Sitchin's writings from his website: On the Trail of "Planet X"

THE CASE OF THE FRENCH ASTRONOMER

In ancient Sumer, the highlight of the new year celebration was the public reading of Enuma Elish, the "Epic of Creation." Scholars have treated the long text (inscribed on seven clay tablets) as an allegory of a struggle between good and evil, between a benevolent celestial god and a celestial monster.

In my books, I treated the ancient text as a sophisticated scientific cosmology about the formation of our solar system, and a celestial collision in which a planet named "Tiamat" was destroyed by the invading planet "Nibiru," bringing about the Earth and the Moon. Nibiru (renamed "Marduk" by the Babylonians) itself was caught into a permanent elongated orbit around the Sun, becoming the 12th member of our Solar System (the Sumerians counted the Sun, the Moon, and- with Nibiru- 10 planets).

The Unavoidable Collision

Many Astronomers and Astrophysicists, Struggling to Explain the Asteroid Belt (between Mars and Jupiter) and the origin of our moon, find it unavoidable to include a celestial collision in their explanatory theories.

The British weekly New Scientist devoted to the cover of a recent issue to "The Planet That Stalked the Earth." The long lead article offers theories about a "rogue planet" involved in the collision. What I found most fascinating in the article's suggestions is it's calling the enigmatic planet THEIA-without explaining why. Was someone thinking of Tiamat?

A `Phantom Planet'

Last year, in France, a pending discovery-- an astounding discovery- was announced in the pages of the prestigious monthly Science Et Vie ("Science and Life"). In its issue of February 2003, it published an update on the planetary makeup of our Solar System in light of recent discoveries in the "Kuiper Belt" (a zone in the Solar Systems fringes). Titled "PLANETS- But How Many Are There in Our Solar System?" The long article, by the journals Valerie Greffos, made a sensational announcement: there is one more, unknown planet in our Solar System-

"A 'PHANTOM PLANET' WHOSE POSSIBLE ORBIT IS TOO ELONGATED TO BE SEEN"

The assertion was based on statements made to the Journal by Alessandro Morbidelli, an astronomer at France's Observatory at Cote d' Azur. The Solar System, he explained, was chaotic in the beginning. There was a celestial collision involving a "supplementary planet" that had existed where the Asteroid Belt is now. It happened about 3.9 billion years ago, and those events explain the unusual long elliptical orbit of the "Phantom Planet."

"I expect that one day we will discover a new, Mars-sized planet!" He told the Journal with certainty, a planet whose orbital period is "several thousand years." He provided the Journal with a sketch of the planets elongated elliptical orbit and even indicated in the sketch where the "Phantom Planet" is probably now:

"It's Sitchin's Drawing!"

The article in Science Et Vie, with its sensational statements by the French astronomer, was brought to my attention (regrettably relatedly) by a fan in France, who could not resist writing on the photocopy, above the sketch: "It's Sitchin's drawing!"

Now, were the French astronomer merely suggesting the existence of one more large planet far out from the Sun, his announcement would have been just one more addition to the decades-long discussions by astronomers regarding a planet "planet X" beyond Uranus, Neptune and Pluto. I, for one, would have welcomed such an additional affirmation, especially from a French observatory known for its interest in the subject.

But the statements by this astronomer went well beyond a mere suggestion of one more planet; he added details that could have come only from reading my books, especially The 12th Planet (1976) and Genesis Revisited (1990) concerning NIBIRU, the home planet of the Anunnaki "gods" of the Sumerians:

*At the beginning of the Solar System was "chaotic" (my exact words);

*There had been a "supplementary planet" where the Asteroid Belt is now (= Tiamat of the Samarian texts);

*A celestial collision,` rearranged' the Solar System (the essence of Enuma Elish if treated as a cosmology);

*Based on findings on the Moon, the collision occurred circa 3.9 billion years ago (my exact conclusion);

*In the aftermath of the collision, the Solar System acquired the "Phantom Planet" (= Nibiru/Marduk;

*Its orbit is elliptical and not circular (a major aspect of my conclusions);

*At its perigee (closest to the Sun) it passes between Jupiter and Mars (a key unorthodox conclusion in my writings);

*The orbit lasts thousands of (Earth-) years (I applied it to the Sumerian Sar= 3600).

Moreover, the sketch that an Alessandro Morbidelli provided to the French journal is not just similar to sketches in my books of Nibiru's orbit, but is exactly a copy of the sketch in Genesis Revisited (Fig. 107) where I indicated Nibiru's probable position now:

So What Did They Have to Say?

My French fan (himself an author of books on UFOs) lost no time writing Alessandro Morbidelli at the Cote d'Azur Observatory, pointing out the similarity. But months past without a response. He has also written to Science Et Vie but never received an answer....

I asked my editor at Edition Carnot in Paris, Who Was Preparing a French Translation of Genesis Revisited, to take up the issue with Science Et Vie. "I think that an intervention would be more powerful if it comes not from someone in New York but from a respected French publisher, like Carnot," I wrote to him (oh so naïvely...).

I finally heard from him about the results of his`intervention'.

"I talked to the author of the SEtV article, Mrs. Valerie Greffos.

She told me She Doubted Alessandro Morbadelli could have been inspired by your books."

Just like that!

She gave me SEtV's phone numbers, saying it would be useless to try to write to them.

So I never did.

And to this day I wonder: Should I be pleased that a respected astronomer at a leading French observatory adopted my conclusions regarding Nibiru and the Sumerian cosmology-- or should I be upset that my life's work was "appropriated" without any acknowledgment and credit to me?

C- Z. Sitchin 2004

WHEN ASTRONOMERS NEED RETHINKING, SITCHIN SMILES

Two recent discoveries by astronomers In the fast-expanding field of Extrasolar Planets "challenge scientists to rethink current theories," according to the published reports.

In both instances, a smiling Zechariah Sitchin says, "The Sumerians did tell you so!"

The latest buzz in the scientific community and the media concerns a discovery, reported in the journal Science of 11 July 2003, of "a giant planet amid a cluster of primitive stars." The discovery, Science reported, "is challenging one of the astronomers 'test notions." "It's a big shock," said the leader of the team of astronomers, astrophysicists Stein Sigurdsson of Pennsylvania State University. "The discovery, based on measurements by the Hubble space telescope, challenges scientists to rethink theories of how, when and where planets form," explaining science editor of The New York Times.

Nicknamed "Methuselah planet," the newly discovered planet is "almost 3 times as old as Earth." It is the oldest extrasolar planets 04 discovered; it is almost as old as the universe itself, and this discovery unsettles current theories about how and when planets could form around stars (suns).

THE REAL ISSUE: WHEN AND WHERE LIFE BEGAN

But why is it so shocking (especially since other findings, reported in May 2003, had already suggested that planets began to form earlier than astronomers believe)? To find out why the shock effect extends beyond the astrophysical community one has to read the scientists' conclusions:

"This implies... that planet formation is more widespread and has happened earlier than previously believed." **"What's more," 'Sigurdsson noted, "ancient planets would mean that life has had 5 billion or 6 billion years longer to appear than astronomers expected."**

That life "happened" out there much before than on earth-- that is a shocking part of the new discovery...

ANCIENT KNOWLEDGE COOPERATED

This admission is music to my ears. In my very first book the 12th planet and then in Genesis Revisited, I asserted that the well-known Sumerian/Akkadian Epic of Creation (Enuma Elish) has to be treated not as a mythical allegory but as a sophisticated cosmology; and that the challenger that appeared at the edge of our solar system, coming from outer space, was a planet ejected from another distant solar system. This entailed recognition by the authors of the ancient text that there are other solar systems in the universe with their own planets-a notion held impossible by astronomers until a few years ago. It entailed the notion that stars and their planetary systems could explode, ejecting a planet to journey in space - another revolutionary astronomical aspect only recently accepted; and it entailed the even more challenging idea, that life exists elsewhere in the universe and could have and did evolve earlier than on Earth.

The "seed of life"- but we now called DNA- was brought into our solar system by the invader (Nibiru in Sumerian, Marduk to the Babylonians) and was transmitted to Earth during the collision with Tiamat (of which Earth is the remnants).

All those three incredibly advanced and sophisticated cosmological- scientific aspects of ancient knowledge are now corroborated by the just-announced findings.

A "Tiamat" Discovered?

The below paragraph should be written in normal type, couldn't correct on my computer.

According to Enuma Elish, as interpreted by me, Sumerian cosmology (or rather the Anunnaki who had told the Sumerians) held that our planetary system began with a messenger planet near the Sun ("Mercury") and a larger planet called Tiamat. That orbited where the asteroid belt is now. In the next phase, the two inner planets that we call Mars and Venus formed between Tiamat and the Sun; and after that, the outer planet formed in pairs; Jupiter and Saturn, Uranus and Neptune.

Drawn into the center of that early solar system, the invader Nibiru/Marduk was fated to collide with Tiamat. One half of her was shattered and became the Asteroid Belt; the other more intact half was thrown into a new orbit and became the planet Earth.

A week before the announcement by the U Penn team (described above), a team of British, Australian and American astronomers announced the discovery of a solar system similar to ours in the constellation Puppis. "There, and what is the closest resemblance to Earth's solar system yet found in outer space, a Jupiter-like planet circles a sun-like star and an orbit that corresponds to one-half way between Mars and Jupiter in our solar system."

The New York Times (7 July 2003) accompanied the report with a diagram showing the positions of the Earth, Mars, and Jupiter in our solar system compared to a superimposed sketch of the newfound solar system with a planet, in a circular orbit, between Mars and Jupiter.

Astronomers and reporters found a discovery exciting because the findings suggest that the solar system might also include "an Earthlike planet."

I find it exciting because, as my readers know, in our solar system, there indeed was a planet precisely between Mars and Jupiter: TIAMAT; and were it not for the collision, it would still be there.

Once again, what the Sumerians learned from the Anunnaki is proven right.

ZECHARIAH SITCHIN

C- Z. Sitchin 2003

Chapter 3: Ancient Genetic Manipulation

To understand the' how' of the Anunnaki's genetic manipulation, one should understand the 'why': The Anunnaki came to this planet for one simple reason, gold! Gold was discovered on this planet by Alalu, an Anunnaki King from the planet Niburu. He relayed this information back to his home planet. A scouting force was sent to the planet Earth led by Ea. (Enki)

To search for gold, which was urgently needed to supplement their planets' dwindling atmosphere, they first had to sustain themselves. They built housing structures and looked for edible foods, resulting in the first city on earth for the Anunnaki, which they called Ur.

They found the most prolific area to mind vast quantities of gold to be the Abzu, or what we now know to be southeast Africa. That discovery required a workforce consisting of lower-ranked Anunnaki. As more gold was discovered at different geographical locations on earth, more of a workforce that was required and as explained by Zechariah Sitchin in his book the 12th planet....

The story of the toil and the ensuing mutiny of the Anunnaki informs us that "for 40 periods they suffered the work, day and night"; the long years of their toil are dramatized by repetitive verses.

For 10 periods they suffered the toil;
For 20 periods they suffered the toil;
For 30 periods they suffered the soil;
440 periods they suffered the toil;

The ancient text uses the term ma to denote "period." And most scholars have translated this as "year." But the term had the connotation of something that completes itself and then repeats itself." To men on Earth, one year equals one complete orbit of the earth around the sun. As we have already shown, the orbit of the Nephilim's (Anunnaki) planet equaled 1 Shar or 3,600 Earth years.

Forty Shars, or 144,000 Earth years, after their landing, the Anunnaki protested "No more!" (The laborious mining of gold) If the Nephilim first landed on Earth, as we have concluded, some 450,000 years ago, then the creation of Man took place some 300,000 years ago!

The evolution of Homo erectus took millions of years, then suddenly about 300,000 years ago Homo sapiens (wise) appear. Their appearance is enigmatic and unexplainable and cannot be is contributed to evolution, as the Homo sapiens appear and many millions of years too soon. There is no fossil evidence to bridge the gap between Homo erectus and Homo sapiens. Scientists referred to the evolutionary gap as "the missing link."

The "missing link" is defined as a hypothetical form of animal assumed to have constituted a connecting link between the anthropoid apes and man.

And our opinion, the Anunnaki, figuratively speaking, are the "missing link" for it is they who **did not create, but " Fashioned"** mankind.

So explicitly, the reason that mankind was "Fashioned" was as a substitute laborer replacing the Anunnaki workers who had toiled for 144,000 years.

The Lost Book of Enki - Tablet Five Page 125

Ever since Earth's heat has been rising, the toil is excruciating, unbearable that is!

A solution is possible! Enki was saying:

let us create a Lulu, a Primitive Worker, the hardship work to take over,

Let the Being the toil of the Anunnaki carry on his back!

Astonished were the besieged leaders, speechless indeed they were.

Whoever heard of a Being a fresh created, a worker who the Anunnaki's work can do?

They summoned Ninmah, one who of healing and succor was much knowing.

The task is unheard of! She to Enki said. All beings from a seed have descended,

One being from another over eons did develop, none from nothing ever came.

Comment: Clearly the Anunnaki are telling us, *they evolved on the planet Nibiru!* All beings from a seed have descended. One being from another over eons did develop.
The Being that we need, it already exists!
All that we have to do is put on the mark of our essence, (DNA)
Thereby a Lulu, a Primitive Worker, shall be created! So did Enki to them say.
Let us hereby a decision make, a blessing to my plan give:
To create a Primitive Worker, by the mark of our essence (DNA) to fashion him!

The Lost Book of Enki Tablet Six Page 129-139

To create a Primitive Worker, by the mark of our essence to fashion him!

The Being that we need, it already exists!

Thus did Enki to them a secret of the Abzu (South East Africa) reveal.

Creatures in the Abzu there are, Enki was saying, that walk erect on two legs,

Their forelegs they use as arms, (Great Apes) with hands they are provided.

They eat plants with their mouth, they drink water from lake and ditch.

Shaggy with hair is their whole body, their head hair is like a lion's;

No creature like that has ever in the Eden (southern Iraq) been seen! Enlil, disbelieving, said.

Eons ago, on Nibiru, or predecessors like that might have been! Ninmah was saying.

It is a Being, not a creature!

Male and female they are! Enki was saying; Malehoods and female-hoods they have.

Ningishzida, my son, their Fashioning Essence (DNA) has tested;

Akin to ours it is, like two serpents it is entwined;

When theirs' with our life essence shall be combined, our mark upon them shall be.

Comment: Our scientists repeatedly try to determine how 'The Seed of Life' got on this planet? Meteorites and comets represent a viable probability. However, something else of prime importance should also be considered; which is revealed to us clearly in the ancient text, *Enuma Elish*. The story relating to the creation of our solar system, tells us that the planet Nibiru collided with the planet Tiamat, resulting in placing Earth into its current orbiting position closer to the Sun. In our opinion, although there are competing interests and theories, that collision would be my first choice, implanting on this Earth, "The Seed of Life".

The Anunnaki God Enki, based on his writings of Enuma Elish and the readings of the Sumerian "*Atra Hasis,* reasoned and then concluded that the collision between Nibiru and the planet Tiamat, deposited the "seed of life" first on the planet Nibiru and later gave rise to life on planet Earth.

To the House of Life Enki lead them; in strong cages there were some of the beings.

They were grunting and snorting; no words were they speaking.

Like us, from Nibiru coming, they are procreating.

Ningishzidda, my son, their Fashioning Essence has tested;

Akin to ours it is, *like two serpents is entwined;*

When their, with our life essence shall be combined, our more upon them shall be,

A Primitive Worker shall be created! Our commands will be understood.

Our tools he will handle, the toil in the excavations he shall perform;

To the Anunnaki in the Abzu relief shall come!

So was Enki with enthusiasm saying, the excitement his words came forth.

Enlil at the words was hesitating: The matter is one of great importance!

On our planet, slavery had long ago been abolished, tools are the slaves, not other beings!

A new creature, before nonexisting, you wish to bring into being;

Creation in the hands of the Father of All Beginning (Sun) alone is held!

So was Enlil in opposing saying; stern were his words.

Enki to his brother responded: Not slaves, but helpers in my plan!

The Being *already exists!* Ninmah was saying. *To give more ability is to plan.*

Not a new creature, but one existing more in our image made! Enki

with persuasion said,

With little change can be achieved, *only a drop of our essence is needed!*

A grave matter it is, it is not to my liking! Enlil was saying.
Against the rules of from planet to planet journeying it is,

To obtain gold was our purpose, to replace the Father of All Beginning it would not!

Comment: It is clearly described above that these ancient astronauts obviously had the ability to do DNA testing and the statement "like two serpents is entwined" gives us a clear mental picture of the symbol of medicine that we use today, the Caduceus.

Let us with wisdom new tools fashion, not new beings create,

What knowledge we possess, its use cannot be prevented! Ningishzidda was saying.

If gold must be obtained, let the Being be fashioned! the Council decided.

Until the Being is achieved, to the toil willingly you must return! he said

There was disappointment; rebellion there was not; to the toil the Anunnaki returned.

To put the matter before Anu they decided; Anu before the Council the matter presented.

Let Anu forsake the rules of planetary journeys, let Nibiru be saved!

In the clean place Ningishzidda to Ninmah the life essence secrets were explaining,

How the essence from two kinds combined can be, he to her was showing.

How the essences to combine, how much of this, how much of that to put together,

In which womb conception to begin, in which womb should the birth be given?

By a male inseminating a female are the essences transmitted,

The two entwined strands separate and combine an offspring to fashion.

Let a male Anunnaki a two-legged female impregnate, let a combination of offspring be

born! Thus did Ninmah say.

That we have tried, with failures it resulted! To her Enki responded.

There was no conceiving, there was no birth!

Now, this is the account of how the Primitive Worker was created.

Another way of admixture to attain it must be tried, Ninmah was saying.

How the strands of essences to combine (Double Helix) another way must be found,

Which from the Earth is the portion must not be harmed.

To receive our essence in graduations it must be shaped,

In a crystal vessel Ninmah an admixture was preparing, the oval of a female two legged she
gently placed,

With ME Anunnaki seed containing, she the oval (a female reproductive gland) impregnated;

That oval back into the womb of a two legged female she inserted.

Comment: This is evidence of in vitro fertilization!

This time there was conceiving, a birth was indeed forthcoming!

The allotted time arrived, there was no birth-giving!

In desperation Ninmah the cutting made, that which was conceived with tongs she drew out.

Comment: This is evidence of Cesarean Birth.

A Living Being It Was!

In her hands Ninmah the newborn held, with joy she was not filled:

Shaggy with hair all over was the newborn, his four parts like of the Earth creatures were,

His hind parts to those of the Anunnaki more akin they were.

Fast was the newborn growing, what on Nibiru a day was, a month and the Abzu was.

Taller the Earth child grew, in the image of the Anunnaki he was not;

His hands for tools were not suited, his speech only grunting sounds was!

We must try once more! Ninmah was saying. The admixture needs adjusting;

With the Enki and Ningishzidda assisting, they repeated the procedures,

The essences of the ME's Ninmah carefully considered,

One bit she took from one, one bit she took out from another,

Then in the crystal bowl the oval of theEarth female she insemi-
nated.

Comment: This is just a `classic description' of in vitro fertilization!

Ancient text continued:

This one more in the likeness of the Anunnaki was;

Appealing he was by his looks, his hands to hold tools were shapen;

His senses were tested, they found them deficient:

The Earth child could not hear his eyesight was altered.

Again and again Ninmah rearrange the admixtures,

One Being had paralyzed feet, another his semen was dripping,

One had trembling hands, a malfunctioning liver had another;

One had the hands too short to reach the mouth, one had lungs for
breathing unsuited.

Enki by the results was disappointed.

What is good or is bad in this Being by trials I am discovering!

Once more an admixture she made, once more the newborn most
efficient.

Perhaps the shortfall is not in the admixture! Enki to her was saying.

Perchance neither in the females' oval nor in the essences is the hindrance?

Of what the Earth itself is fashioned, perchance that is what is missing?

Not of Nibiru's crystals use the vessel, of the clay of Earth make it!

Perchance what is curse on admixture, of gold and copper, is required!

Thus was Enki, he who knows things, prompting her to use clay of the Abzu

As a purifying bath she shaped the vessel, within it to make the admixture.

Gently into the clay vessel the oval of an Earth female, the two legged, she put,
The life essence of an Anunnaki's blood extracted she in the vessel placed.

Then the oval thus fertilized into the womb of the Earth female she inserted.

There is conception! Ninmah with joy announced. The allotted birth-giving time they
awaited.

In her hands she held the child, his image she examined; it was the image of perfection.

From month-to-month the newborn progressed, from a baby to a child he was becoming.

His limbs for tasks were suited, speech he knew not, grunts and snorts were his utterings!

Into the womb of the Earth female the fertilized oval was always inserted;

Perchance this is the remaining obstruction! Thus was Enki saying.

Of who the fertilized oval nurturers, the birth giving carries;

In our image and after our likeness to be, perchance *an Anunnaki womb is required!*
In the House of Life there was silence; words never before heard Enki was uttering!

They gazed at each other, about what in each other's mind they were thinking.

Wise are your words, my brother! Ninmah long last was saying.

Per chance the right admixture in the wrong womb was inserted;

He was turning to depart when Ninmah put her hand on his shoulder:
I shall be the one the Anunnaki womb to provide, for good or evil face-to-face.

The oval of an Earth female with Anunnaki male essence they put together;

The fertilized egg into the womb of Ninmah by Enki was inserted; there was conception!

The pregnancy, by and add mixture conceive and, how long will it last? To each other they wondered.

Will it be nine months of Nibiru, will it be nine months of Earth?

Longer than on Earth, quicker than on Nibiru, travail came; to a male child Ninmah birth was giving!

Enki the boy child held in his hands; the image of perfection he was.

He slapped the newborn on his hind parts; the newborn uttered proper
!
He handed the newborn to Ninmah; she held him up in her hands.

My hands have made it! Victoriously she shouted.

Comment: The question to be asked here is, how can anyone present this kind of genetic manipulation, so accurately, many millennia ago, without having an empirical relationship with the stated subject matter? The answer is _they did have an empirical relationship with the written material, as has been presented in the ancient texts!_

GENETICS: SO WHAT ELSE IS NEW?

The January 26, 2004 issue of Newsweek magazine, featuring photos of babies on its cover illustrating the main story on "The New Science of Sex Selection"-advances in genetic and fertilization technologies that made it possible to pre-determine the sex of one's baby; not just to find out the baby's sex once pregnancy is in progress, but to decide ahead of time whether the baby should be a male or a female to begin with.

That indeed sounds like a New Science, as the magazine calls it.

But a detail in the ten-page long report caught my eye; it sounded like a line out of millennia-old Sumerian texts, inscribed on clay tablets, which described how the gods created Man!

Seven and Seven

Newsweek's report begins with the story of a couple from Gillette, Wyoming, "who always wanted a baby girl, but the odds seem stacked against them." They kept having boys. Then they found out about a fertility Institute in California that developed and in vitro fertilization technique called PGD-Pre-Implementation Genetic Diagnosis. "By creating embryos outside the womb, then testing them for gender, PGD could guarantee, with almost 100% certainty, the sex of the baby.

Then came the eye-catching detail:

> "Last November Sharla's eggs and Shane's sperm were mixed in a lab dish, producing 14 healthy embryos, seven males and seven females.

The lab transferred three of the female embryos into Sharla's uterus, where two implanted successfully. If all goes well, the run of the Miller boys will end in July with the arrival of twin baby girls.

The Sumerian Creation Texts

"""" """" In my very first book, The 12th planet, in 1976, I dealt at length with the Sumerian creation texts which provide a highly sophisticated scientific narrative dealing with the creation of our solar system, the formation of the earth, the evolution of life on earth, the coming of Earth of the Anunnaki from their planet Nibiru, and their employment of genetic engineering to fashion Homo sapiens from a primitive human species. In The 12th Planet and later in Genesis Revisited (1990) I showed how the Bible summed up that very scientific tale in the book of Genesis; and how modern science was only catching up with ancient knowledge.

"In a chapter titled "The Creation of Man" I quoted passages from various clay tablet texts that provided details of the Creation of Man process- How Enki, the chief scientist of the Anunnaki, suggested that an already existing being could be upgraded by mixing Anunnaki genes with the humanoid ones; now minty, the chief medical officer of the Anunnaki (and Enki's half-sister) performed the gene mixing; and how the resulting "clay" was used to impregnate fourteen "birth goddesses," to become pregnant with seven males and seven females!

Using the "essence" of a young male Anunnaki (extracted in a "purifying bath") to prepare the proper "mixed clay,"

> Ninti ripped off 14 pieces of clay;
> Seven she deposited on the right,
> Seven she deposited on the left....

The Wise and Learned,
Twice- seven birth- goddesses had assembled.
even brought forth males,
Seven brought forth females…
In pairs they were completed,
In pairs they were completed in her presence.
The created ones were People-
Creatures of the Mother Goddess.

While many other aspects of similarities between in-vitro and other genetic engineering procedures now developed and what the ancient texts describe have been dealt with in my writings, the precise number of 14 sperm/embryos divided into seven male, seven female is- to say the least- an amazing coincidence.

ZECHARIAH SITCHIN

One might ask, when did the current existing Homo sapien, sapiens, discover DNA? Two scientists, Rosalyn Franklin, and Maurice Wilkins studied DNA using x-rays. Franklin produced an x-ray photograph that allowed two other researchers, James Watson and Francis Crick to work out the 3-D structure of DNA. The structure of DNA was found to be a double helix. The year of discovery was the early 1950s.

Currently, we are unable to decipher 95% of our genetic material. It is difficult to understand, that in a single cell, our DNA stores more information than all of the supercomputers known to mankind.

We now know that early humans not only coexisted with other primitive humanoids, they also mated with them. The results of a study by Max Planx and biologist Savanti Paabo, at the Institute for Evolutionary Biological Anthropology in Lepzig, Germany (2010) tells us with astonishment that they may have **found another unidentified species represented in human DNA** which would had to be the **direct result of interbreeding.** I would like to change the wording of the last sentence to read, and change, "*they may have found*" too, and our opinion" *they have found*" as I firmly believe that **proof lies in the Ancient Text,** part of which you have already read in this chapter, but there's more….

Dr. John Hawkes an Anthropologist at the University of Wisconsin did a study analyzing the human DNA going back to the DNA of humans 5000 years ago or 3000 B.C.

Comparing the B. C. DNA, to today's DNA and mapping the human genome, Dr. Hawkes found **a progressive change of 7%.** So what happened in the last 5000 years that caused a progressive genome percentage change that was greater than any time in the history of mankind? The only explanation for the astonishing and monumental changes to our DNA can be explained, as the Ancient Texts points out repeatedly, that **humans interbred with extraterrestrials! Those extraterrestrials were the Anunnaki!**

The "Book of Enoch" tells us that 200 *men* came down to Earth and bread with human females. "The Autobiography of the Extraterrestrial God Enki, tells us most definitively that those 200 *men* were Anunnocki, whose name in the Ancient Text was the **Igigi.**

The Lost Book of Enki - The Ninth Tablet Page 200

Now, this is the account of how the Igigi the daughters of the Earthlings abducted,

And how afflictions followed and how Ziusudra was born.

In a great number did the Igigi from Lahmu (Mars) to Earth came,

Only one-third of them on Lahmu stayed, **to Earth came two hundred.**

To be with their leader Marduk, his wedding celebration to attend, was their explanation;

Unbeknownst to Enki and Enlil was their secret: To abduct and have conjugation was their plot.
Unbeknownst to the leaders on Earth, a multitude of the Igigi on Lahmu got together,

What to Murdoch permitted is from us too should not be deprived! to each other they said.

Enough of suffering and loneliness, of not offspring ever having!

was their slogan.

During their comings and goings between Lahmu and Earth,

The daughters of the Earthlings, the Adapite Females as them they called,

They saw and after them they lusted; and to each other the plotters said:

Come, let us choose wives from among the Adapite Females, and children beget!

(Lower middle page of 201)
By a signal prearranged Shamgaz to the others a sign gave

An Earthling maiden each one of the Igigi seized, by force they them abducted,

To the Landing Place in the Cedar Mountains the Igigi with the females went,

Into a stronghold the place they made, to the leaders a challenge they issued:

Enough of deprivation and not having offspring! The Adapite daughters we wish to marry.

Your blessing to this you must give, else by fire all on Earth destroyed we will!

THE LOST BOOK OF ENKI 11th TABLET Page 248

In the beginning the Earthlings in our image and after our likeness we made,

Now the Anunnaki offspring in the image and likeness of the Earthlings became!
Then it was Ka'in who his brother killed, now a son of Marduk is

his brother's killer!

For the first time ever, and Anunnocki offspring from Earthlings an Army raised,

THE LOST BOOK OF ENKI - NINTH TABLET Page 197

A bride I wish to choose, to have a spouse it is my desire!

So did Marduk to his father Enki say.

Your words happy make me! Enki to Marduk was saying. Your mother too shall rejoice!

Is she one of the young ones who heal and succor give? Enki went on to ask.

A descendant of Adapa **she is, of Earth, not Nibiru, is she!** Marduk softly whispered.

With a puzzled look, Enki was speechless; then uncontrolled words he shouted:

A Prince of Nibiru, a Firstborn to succession entitled, **an Earthling will espouse?!**

Not an Earthling, **but your own offspring!** to him Marduk said.

A daughter of Enkime (biblical Enoch) who to have been was taken she is, Sarpanit is her name!

Step by step on this planet a Primitive Being, one like us to be, we have created,

In our image and in our likeness Civilized Earthling is, except for long life, **he is we!**

The Ninth Tablet Page 202

Upon the Landing Platform in the Cedar Mountains were the Igigi and their females secluded,

Children there to them were born, Children of the Rocket Ships they were called.

Marduk and Sarpanit his spouse also had children, Asar and Satu (Egyptian god Seth) were the first two sons called.

Comment: Prof. Sir Alex Jeffries invented DNA fingerprinting at the University of Leicester on September 10, 1984.

Now let's take a look at mitochondrial DNA: All people alive today can trace their genetic heritage to their mothers back to one woman. Scientists hypothesize this 'Ancient' woman's existence by looking within the cells of living people and analyzing short loops of genetic code known as mtDNA. The DNA is only traceable back to the female as mammalian sperm are usually destroyed by the egg cell after fertilization.

One must conclude, without doubt, from evaluating the printed words of the Ancient Texts **that you and I and all of humanity, are related to the Anunnaki goddess Ninmah!**

The Attestation of Endubsar The Sixth Tablet

Now this is the account of how Adamu by name was called.

The newborns visage and limbs the leaders carefully examined:

Of good shape were his ears, his eyes were not clogged,

His limbs or proper, hind parts like legs, foreparts like hands were shaped.

Shaggy like the wild ones he was not, dark black his head hair was,

Like dark red blood was its color, like the clay of the Abzu was its hue

They looked at his malehood: Odd was that shape, by a skin was its foreparts surrounded,

Unlike that of the Anunnaki malehood it was, a skin from its foreparts is hanging!

Let the Earthling from us Anunnaki by his foreskin be distinguished! So was Enki saying.

The newborn to cry was beginning; to her chest Ninmah closely drew him;

Her breast to him she gave; the breast he began to suckle.

Perfection we did attain! Ningishzidda with elation was saying.

Enki at his sister was gazing; a mother and son, not Ninmah and a Being, he was seeing.

A name will you give him? Enki inquired. A Being is, not a creature!

Adamu I shall call him! Ninmah was saying. One Who like Earth's Clay Is, that will be his name.

Comment: From the name Adamu, the Bible relates that he is Adam, of the Garden of Eden. In fact, as we read on from the ancient text, what is clearly stated, is that Adamu was "A model for Primitive Workers. From his model, numerous primitive workers were made to slave in the mines and replace the lower-ranked Anunnaki workers. Adapa, later created by the Anunnaki, was the first Homo sapien, and it was he and his similarly created spouse Titi, who were the *Bible's usurped representation* of Adam and Eve.

A model for Primitive Workers we have indeed attained! Enki was saying.

Now a host of workers like him are needed! Ningishzidda his elders reminded.

A model indeed he shall be; as for himself, like a Firstling he shall be treated,

From toil himself shall be protected, *his essence alone as a mold shall be!*

From her city Shurubak Ninmah female healers summoned, the task required to them she explained,

To the crib of Adamu she led them, the newborn Earthling to perceive.

To perform the task is not commanded! Ninmah to them was saying; your own wish is the decision!

Of the female Anunnaki assembled, seven stepped forward, seven the task excepted.

Their task is heroic, by them a race of Primitive Workers shall come into being!

Earthlings in their wombs to conceive and bear, Primitive Workers to create.

In seven vessels of the clay of the Abzu made, Ninmah ovals of the two legged females placed,

The life essence of Adamu she extracted, bit by bit in the vessels she it inserted.

Then in the male part of Adamu an incision she made, a drop of blood to let out;

Let this a Sign of Life be; That Flesh and Soul have combined let it forever proclaim!

In this clays admixture, Earthlings with the Anunnaki shall be bound!

To a unity shall the two essences, one of Heaven, (Nibiru) one of Earth, together be brought.

In the wombs of the birth giving heroines the fertilized ovals are inserted.

At the allotted time, birth givings were occurring!

At the allotted time, seven male Earthlings were born,

Seven Primitive Workers have been created! Ningishzidda was saying,

Let the procedure be repeated, seven more the toil to undertake!

Female ones we have to fashion! Enki was saying, for males counterparts to be.

Let them know each other, as one flesh the two to become,

Let them by themselves procreate, on their own the childbirthing make,

To Primitive Workers by themselves give birth, Anunnaki females to relieve!

For a counterpart to Adamu to be fashioned, in a womb of an Anunnaki female conception is needed!

Enki at Ninmah his gaze directed; before he could speak, he raised his hand.

Let me this time Ninki my spouse summon! With strong voice he said,

They showed her Adamu, all that matters to her they explained,

By the task, Ninki was fascinated. Let it be done! he then said,

By the ME formulas Ningishzidda adjusting made, by the admixture was an oval fertilized,

Into the womb of his spouse Enki it inserted; with much care he did it.

There was conception; in the allotted time Ninki was in travail; a birth there was not.

Ninki the months counted, Ninmah the months counted;
The tenth month, a month of evil fates, they began to call.

Ninmah, the lady whose hand wombs have opened, with a cutter an incision made.

Her head was covered, on her hand's protections she wore;

With dexterity the opening she made, her face at once was brightened:

That which in the womb was from the womb came forth.

A female! A female birth was given! To Ninki with joy she shouted.

The newborn's visage and limbs were carefully examined,

Of good shape were her ears, her eyes were not clogged;

Her limbs were proper, hindparts like legs, foreparts like hands were shaped;

Shaggy she was not, like beach sands was the hue of her head hair,

Her skin smooth was, as that of the Anunnaki in smoothness and color it was.

Ninmah the girl child held in her hands. She slapped her hind parts;

Proper sounds the newborn appeared!
To Ninki, the spouse of Enki, she the newborn handed, to be suckled, nourished, and raised.

In your image she is and after your likeness,

Perfectly she is fashioned, **a model for female workers you have attained!**

Ti-Amat let her name be, the Mother of Life! Ninki was saying.

From her wombs life essences other birth givers shall be molded,

To a multitude of Primitive Workers she thereby life will be giving!

Thus was Ninki saying; the other words of concurring uttered.

Now this is the account of Adamu and Ti-Amat in the Eden,

After Ti-Amat in the womb of Ninki was fashioned,

In the seven vessels of the clay of the Abzu made Ninmah ovals of the two legged females placed.

The life essence of Ti-Amat she extracted, bit by bit in the vessels she it inserted.

In the vessels of the clay of the Abzu made, Ninmah the admixture formed;

In the wombs of the birth-giving heroines the fertilized ovals were inserted;

At the allotted time, seven female Earthlings were born.

Thus were seven female counterparts of the Primitive Workers created;
After the **Earthlings were thus created,**

Let the males the females inseminate, *let the Primitive Workers* by themselves offspring beget!

Plentiful will be the Primitive Workers' numbers, **the toil of the Anunnaki they shall bear!**

As for Adamu and Ti-Amat from the toil of the excavations they shall be protected

Let us them to the Eden bring over, to the Anunnaki therein our handiwork display!

The circuits of Earth grew in number, maturity of the Earthlings was overdue;

No conceding among the females was observed, there was no birth giving!

By the cages among the trees Ningishzidda a couch of grass for himself made;

Day and night the Earthlings he was watching, their doings to ascertain.

Indeed he saw them mating, the males the females were inseminating!

Conceiving there was not, birth giving there was not.
None, not one of them, at offspring begotten!

Comment: Here the Anunnaki have created hybrids.

Let us the essences of Adamu and Ti-Amat afresh examined!

Their ME's bit by bit to be studied, what is wrong to ascertain!

Like two entwined serpents Ningishzidda the essences separated,

Arranged like Twenty-two branches on a Tree of Life were the essences,

Twenty-two they were in number; the ability to procreate they did not include!

<u>ANOTHER TWO BITS OF THE ESSENCE</u> IN THE ANUNNAKI PRESENT NINGISHZIDDA TO THE OTHERS SHOWED.

IN THE MOLDS OF ADAMU AND TIAMAT, <u>IN THE COMBINING THEY WERE NOT INCLUDED!</u>

Ninmah heard this and was distraught; with frustration was Enki seized.

Primitive Workers must be procured least the gold extracting shall be ceasing!

Ningishzidda, in these matters learned, a solution was proposing;

They locked the doors behind them, the three with the two Earthlings alone remaining.

Upon the four others Ningishzidda a deep sleep caused to descend, the four he made unfeeling.

From the rib of Enki the life essence he extracted,

Into the rib of Adamu, the life essence of Enki he inserted;
From the rib of Ninmah the life essence he extracted,

Into the rib of Ti-Amat the life essence he inserted.

Where the incisions were made, the flesh thereon he closed up.

TO THEIR TREE OF LIFE TWO BRANCHES HAVE BEEN ADDED,

With PROCREATING POWERS THEIR LIFE ESSENCES ARE NOW ENTWINED!

In the Edin's orchards to freely roam Adamu and Ti-Amat were placed.

In the heat of the day Enlil in the orchard strolling, the shady he was enjoying.

Without expectation Adamu and Ti-Amat he encountered, the aprons on their loins he noticed.

What is the meaning of this? Enlil wondered; Enki for explaining he summoned.

The matter of procreation Enki to Enlil explained;

Ningishzidda the life essences examined, an additional combining was needed!

Great was Enlil's anger, furious were his words:

The whole thing is not to my liking, for acting like Creators I had opposed.

To be like us in procreation knowing, perchance our lifecycles on them to bestow!

My Lord Enlil! Ningishzidda was saying. **Knowing for procreation they were given,
The branch of Long Living, to their essence tree was not!**

Ninmah then spoke up, to her brother Enlil she was saying;
What was the choice, my brother? To end it all in failure, Nibiru in

doom to face its fate,

Or to try and try and try, *and by procreation let the Earthlings the toil undertake?*

Comments: This section of the ancient text has clearly demonstrated the Anunnaki's empirical knowledge, relating to surgery, procedures for sterilization, anesthetization, cesarean birth, artificial insemination, in vitro fertilization and the genetic manipulation of the Earthlings, they themselves had fashioned by infusing the necessary additional **two branches of procreation into "our" DNA!**

Yes! I used the word "our," because, after decades of reading and studying the ancient text, I firmly believe that you and I are genetically related, resulting from the genetic manipulation of our DNA to the Anunnaki!

To enhance our understanding of the etiology of Sumerian and Akkadian terms used in the Ancient Texts, Zechariah Sitchin writes in his book, "Genesis Revisited, Chapter 8 entitled, *The Adam: a Slave Made to Order:*

In *The 12th Planet,* I analyzed the etymology of the Sumerian and Akkadian terms that are usually translated "clay" or "mud" and showed that they evolved from Sumerian TI.IT, literally, "that which is with life," and then assumed the derivative meanings of "clay" and "mud," as well as "egg." The earthly element in the procedure for "binding upon" a being already existed "the image of the gods" was thus to be the female egg of that being – of an Ape woman.

The task of obtaining the "divine" elements was Ninki's two extracts were needed from one of the Anunnaki, and a young "god" was carefully selected for, the purpose. Enki's instruction student mentee was to obtain the god's blood and *shiru,* and through immersions in a "purifying bath" obtain their "essences." But had to be obtained from the blood was termed TE.E.MA, at best translated "personality," a term that expresses the sense of the word: that which makes a person what he is and different from any of the person. But the translation "personality" does not convey the scientific precision of the term, which in the original Sumerian meant "That which houses that which binds the memory." Nowadays we call it a "gene."

The other element for which the young the Anunnaki was selected, *shiru,* is commonly translated "flesh." In time, the word would acquire that meaning "flesh" among its various connotations. But in the early Sumerian, it referred to the sex or reproductive organs; its root had the same basic meaning "to bind," "that which binds." The extract from the *shiru* was referred to and other texts dealing with non-Anunnaki offspring of the "gods" as *kisru;* coming from the male's member, it meant "semen," the male's sperm.

These two divine extracts were to be mixed well by Ninki in a purifying bath, and it is certain that the epithet *lulu* ("the mixed one") for the resulting Rhyme Worker stemmed from this mixing process. In modern terms, we would call him a hybrid.

So to answer the question, "Do the Ancient Texts provide a framework for their fashioning of mankind that is comparable with today's scientific knowledge?" The answer is yes and factual! Another relative question comes to mind, is it possible that Mankind would have, through evolution, every evolved to the "sapien" status, given the millions of years of evolutionary time needed? What about the Anunnaki? Did they through the process of evolution evolve, or were they "created" out of nothing by an omnipotent being?

Sumerian texts definitively tell us that the Anunnaki "evolved" on the planet Niburu as intelligent beings, eon's before the hominids on Earth. Also, our planet Earth, acquired the "seed of life," as a result of the celestial collision between the planets Niburu and Tiamat ((as described in the Mesopotamian epic Enuma Elish) allowing the evolutionary process to begin, much as it had eons ago on the planet Niburu.

To emphasize the above, here are some selected writings of the ancient text.

All from THE LOST BOOK OF ENKI   FIFTH TABLET Page 25

After eons of time our own species sprouted, by our own essence an eternal seed to procreate.
FIFTH TABLET Page 126

All beings from a seed have descended,
One being from another over eons to develop, none from nothing

ever came!

SEVENTH TABLET Page 170

A Civilized Man has earth itself brought forth,
In the wilderness a new kind of Earthling has come forth! To Enlil
was Enki saying.
Indeed a wonder of wonders it is, a new breed of Earthling on
Earth has emerged.

Page 171 – The words heard, by the words he was amazed:
That by life essences one kind to another leads is not unheard of! to
them words back he sent.
That on Earth a Civilized Man from the Adamu so quickly appeared, that is unheard of!

TENTH TABLET Page 234

The unseen hand of the **Creator of All** (The Sun) is life on Niburu
to enable! So did Enlil say.

The Ancient Text' s tell us that the Anunnaki chose the ape, as the
then existing being, with which to perform their genetic manipulations. Recall Enki saying, "I have found it! It exists!" And then Ninmah
declaring, "It is not a creature, it is a being!" "To the tree of life two
branches have been entwined!" So the question to be posed now is,
how does modern-day science substantiate the Anunnaki findings?
Scientists concur that albumins produce patterns that are *identical*
between modern humans and the chimpanzee. The reason being is that
the albumin molecules of the chimpanzee and humans were *identical!*
In the late 1960s, the American anthropologist Vince Sarich and New
Zealand biologist Alan Wilson exploited these minor differences in
protein structure and concluded that modern humans and the African
apes were *very closely related!*
Mary Claire King and American human geneticist and Alan Wilson dating back to the mid-1970s showed that 99% of the amino acid
sequences of chimpanzee and modern human blood proteins were
identical! Since the late 1950s, we have gained greater knowledge relating to biochemistry and immunology, applying a new generation of

analytical methods to proteins. Biologist Emile Zukerkandl was able to demonstrate clearly that the patterns of the peptides from modern humans, guerrilla, and chimpanzee were *indistinguishable!*

Currently, in Japan, scientists have developed robots that very closely resemble human beings in almost every distinguishable aspects. This is been developed to the point whereby if you were walking down the street in Japan and walked past several of these biomechanically engineered robots, you literally could not distinguish them from the general population.

Even more interesting is the international work that is being done on Trans-humanism. That is biology merging with a silicone-based technology producing artificial human organs using a silicone-based structure whereby scientists are developing anti-aging systems and further believe that they can unlock the secrets of immortality by the year 2050.

FROM THE LOST BOOK OF ENKI

From clay of the Abzu Enki two emissaries fashioned, beings without blood, by

death rays unharmed. Ereshkigal by their appearance was puzzled: Are you Anunnaki?
Are you Earthlings? With bewilderment she asked them.

Namtar the magical weapons of power against them directed, But unharmed the two were.

Comment: What the above millennia-old Ancient Text relates to the reader is that the Anunnaki themselves were scientifically advanced enough to produce androids, robots and, (Enkime) cyborgs, that their lifespans were measured in millennia. The female Anunnaki Ereshkigal, from a close visual aspect, cannot determine if the androids are Anunnaki or Earthlings. So, one could reasonably conclude that we, the *Earthlings are not indistinguishable between the Anunnaki and some of their created androids.* One can also believe that there are extraterrestrial entities, other than the Anunnaki, that have achieved similar technological advancement or being so scientifically more advanced that they have the ability to produce, fully functioning sentient biological bodies!

Synopsis:

Charles Darwin's "Origin of the Species" in our opinion is a brilliant explanation of mankind's step-by-step description of evolution through natural selection…..up to a point in time. That point of time was around 300,000 years ago, as has been previously described in some detail. After the 300,000 year *epoch,* we have to put aside the evolutionary concept that mankind started as being organically seeded on earth slowly evolving into marine life that could breathe, and walk on land. From there four limbs were developed whereby we eventually evolved into "Ape." Now, our current day explanation of the "Missing Link" can euphemistically be described as, "If you don't have a goose, take a gander!"

What we believe to be universally accepted by our scientific community is, *mankind's evolution cannot be explained by natural selection and what we then resort to as an explanation is, voilà! God did it.*

The question has to be asked, why are we unique amongst the animal world on this earth? Why is our intelligence so much higher than that of the animal world to the point that we possess *"abstract intelligence"* and the animal kingdom does not!

A study by Howard Huger, Medical Institute at the University of Chicago reveals what he describes as a *special event* some 50,000 years ago, describing our sudden increase of intellect, which could not have been a step by step evolutionary improvement. Our intellectual advancement could only be described as "sudden" and "special," A *Big Brain Event.* There is no link from being "Ape," to landing on the moon. **The only explanation for the monumental changes in human DNA was tangible evidence of interference, via interbreeding with** *nonhumans!*

Also hand-in-hand with the interbreeding and what *sparked* the sudden and seemingly overnight, "Giant Step for Mankind's Increase in Human Intelligence," was the grafting into our DNA which gave us **language…… and abstract thinking ability….. The gene "P2."** This gene was found in our nucleotides and that gene alone is more responsible than any other which separates us from animals. So, do we have evidence of tangible interference? Yes! And that evidence lies within the Ancient Texts.

THE LOST BOOK OF ENKI - NINTH TABLET   page 204-5

There after Enki his sister Ninmah in Shurubak was quick to visit.

On the roof of a dwelling when Batanash was bathing

Enki by her loins, took hold, he kissed her, his semen into her womb he poured.

With a child Batanash was, her belly was truly swelling.

To Lu-Mach from Shurubak word was sent: to the Eden return, a son you have!

To the Eden, to Shurubak, Lu-Mach returned, to him Batanash the son showed.

White as the snow his skin was, the color of wool was his hair,

Like the skies were his eyes, in a brilliance where his eyes shining.

A son unlike an Earthling to Batanash was born, by his birth greatly puzzled I am!

A mystery the boy is, but in his oddness an omen to you is revealed,

Unique he is, for a task unique by destiny he was chosen.

Ziusudra, (biblical Noah) He of Long Bright Life Days, she called him;

In Shrubak he was raised.

IN THE 110TH SHAR WAS ZIUSUDRA BORN.

Comment: What is so revealing here in this Ancient Text, tells us that Enki, the **non-human** Anunnocki, **interbred with a human female**, Batanash, resulting in the birth of Ziusudra_**49,000 YEARS AGO!**

One might ask, how we derived Ziusudra's birthday being 49,000 years ago. This ancient text tells us that Ziusudra was born in the 110th Shar. One Shar is equal to 3, 600 years which represents one orbit of the planet Nibiru around our Sun. So we can now multiply 110 by 3600 giving us the quotient 396,000. We then subtract the 396,000 from the Anunnaki's arrival here, which was 445,000 years ago, we come up with the answer that Ziusudra was born 49,000 years ago.

Recall that Mr. Howard Huber's study revealed that the "inter-breeding" and the **"tangible evidence of interference" can be traced back to 50,000 years**. And there is more...

LOST BOOK OF ENKI - SEVENTH TABLET PAGE 167-- 171

The Primitive Workers in the Abzu (South East Africa) he for this scheme observed,

The Earthlings in the Eden, in the cities and in the orchards he considered.

What could for the tasks make them suited? What by the life essence has not been
combined? (DNA manipulation)

The offspring of the Earthlings he observed, an alarming matter he noticed:

By their repeated copulations, back toward their wild forbears they were degraded!

On the rivers bank, bathing and frolicking Earthlings he noticed;

Two females among them were wild with beauty, firm were their breasts.

Their site the phallus of Enki caused to water, a burning desire he had.

The boat here to Isimud directed, from the boat to dry land Enki stepped.

A young one to him Enki called, a tree fruit she to him offered.

Enki bent down, the young one he embraced, on her lips he kissed her;

Sweet were her lips, firm with ripeness were her breasts.

Into her womb he poured his semen, in a mating he knew her.

Into her womb she took the holy semen, by the semen of the Lord Enki she was impregnated.

The second one to him Enki called, berries from the field she him offered.

Enki bent down, the young one he embraced, on her lips he kissed her;

Sweet were her lips, firm with ripeness were her breasts.

Into her womb he poured his semen, in a mating he knew her.

Into her womb she took the holy semen, by the semen of the Lord Enki she was impregnated.

In the 93rd Shar the two, by Enki fathered, in the Eden were born.

Between Anunnocki and Earthling, conception was attained,

Civilized Man I have brought into being.

Adapa, the Foundling, the boy she called; Titi, One with Life, the girl she named.

Unlike all other Earthling children the twosome were:

Slower to grow up than Earthlings they were, much quicker in understanding they were;
With intelligence they were endowed, speaking with words capable they were.

Ninki, the spouse of Enki, to Titi took a liking; all manner of crafts she was her teaching.

To Adopa Enki himself teachings gave, how to keep records he was him instructing.

A new kind of Earthling from "my seed" has been created, in my image and after my likeness!

In the wilderness a new kind of Earthling has come forth! to Enlil was Enki saying.

On new the words heard, by the words he was amazed:

That by life essences one kind to another leads is not unheard of! to them words back he sent.

That on Earth a Civilized Man from the Adamu so quickly appeared, that is unheard of!

Comment: 300,000 years ago, we know, at that point in time, that the Anunnaki had a need for a primitive worker. (lulu) We also know that the lulu was genetically modified with only enough intelligence to distinguish verbal commands; viz, work, eat, sleep. Now this segment tells us that as a result of the interbreeding of the Anunnaki, Enki, and two earthling females, the *"much quicker in understanding they were;"* *"With intelligence they were endowed, **speaking with the words capable they were.**"* The question that could be answered here ---- is this the point in time where the **Earthlings acquired the P2 gene?**
Furthermore, the Ancient Texts tells us the interbreeding between Anunnocki and Earthling happened 11,200 years ago! This time period is derived by the 110th Shar, multiplied times 3, 600 years, which

equals 396,000 years, subtracted from the arrival date 445,000 years ago, results in a given date of 11,200 years ago, or 9000 B. C.

THE LOST BOOK OF ENKI - NINTH TABLET PAGE 197

A bride I wish to choose, to have a spouse it is my desire!

So did Marduk to his father Enki say.

Is she one of the young ones who heal and succor give? Enki went on to ask.

A descendant of Adapa she is, of Earth, not Nibiru, is she! Marduk softly whispered.

With a puzzled look, Enki was speechless; then uncontrolled words he shouted:

A Prince of Nibiru, a Firstborn to succession entitled, an Earthling will espouse?!

Not an Earthling but your own offspring! to him Murdoch said.

A daughter of Enkime (biblical Enoch) who to Heaven (the planet Nibiru) was taken she is, Sarpanit is her name!

Step by step on this planet a Primitive Being, one like us to be, we have created,

In our image and in our likeness Civilized Earthling is, ***EXCEPT FOR THE LONG THE LIFE, HE IS WE!***

Comment: This particular chapter unquestionably will bring on the debate between the Creationists and evolution and in our opinion there are no grounds for debate! The Creationists, leaning on the Bible, tell us that in one day, "voilà," without the aid of evolution, God created man, the *Homo sapiens sapiens*. The Evolutionist will tell you that man evolved over eons of time, even though they cannot explain

"The Missing Link." It is our conclusion, from the reading of the Bible and the studying of the ancient text, that both the Evolutionist and the creationists are, in large part, wrong!

Today's biologists and anthropologists can with some authority tell us that human beings developed from now-extinct primates into Homo sapiens in Africa about 315,000 years ago. Do the Ancient Texts agree with that? The answer is yes, that the Homo sapiens evolved in the *Abzu* (South East Africa) some 300,000 years ago, as described in detail in the Ancient Texts. The primarily responsible individual was *Enki, the Anunnaki!*

The Missing Link can be defined as the inability to trace or connect the path of human evolution, using a full chronological series of fossil specimens from the hominids' biological family of chimpanzees/gorillas to the Homo sapiens.

Where do we look for the answer? Well, The Ancient Texts, some of which you have already read in this chapter provides the answer; the **Anunnaki's need to fashion a laborer, a Primitive Worker** to alleviate the toil of the Anunnaki rank-and-file. The scientific genetic manipulation from the ape to Homo sapiens **by the Anunnaki** is described in detail in The Lost Book of Enki, the Sixth Tablet Starting on Page 129.

If we accept the empirical evidence given to us by the described genetic manipulation of mankind by the Anunnaki, we no longer need to explain The Missing Link; at which time we can then allow ourselves to take a deep breath and admit *it all makes sense*!

The Elohim, as written in the Bible, translates to gods, **and those gods, as the Ancient Texts tell us, are none other than the Anunnaki.** The Bible does not tell us the necessity for creating "Mankind," and the Ancient Text does tell us exactly why the Adam was not created, but "Fashioned."

Then there is a statement in Genesis 1, the King James version that "God said, Let **us** make man in **our** image, after **our** likeness. The problem posed by this statement to any reasonable person is the plurality of us and our. God's in plurality speaking to a plural gathered audience God did not say let **me** make man in **my** image and **my** likeness, which should be the appropriate wording if there were one God involved in the creation of man. The Bible inadvertently reveals the word Elohim, which in Hebrew is translated as God, and the question of the ancient text, tell us that we must attribute the creation of man to the Anunnaki because those **"gods," "the Elohim," were the Anunnaki.**

CRISPR – Clustered Regularly Interspaced Short Palindromic Repeats

Dr.Feng Zhang of MIT has discovered some bacteria that can cut the DNA of invading viruses as a defense mechanism, leading to the realization that the procedure (known as " knocking-in") could be programmed and used to cut into human DNA.

This discovery and the applied procedure have, and will continue to exponentially, revolutionize biomedicine. CRISPR will allow genetic scientists to reprogram the genetic code of living things thereby curing genetic diseases by correcting defective genes in human embryos and in essence, overriding our genetic DNA instructions.

Dr. Zhang, working at the Broad Institute in Cambridge Massachusetts, identifying more than 2000 diseases caused by faulty genes, is working to eliminate such diseases as Huntington's, Alzheimer's, Hemophilia, ALS, Sickle Cell, Cancer and many others.

To express this in layman's terms, as best I can: Bacteria is taken from liquid form and injected into cells. The bacteria can be programmed to find the specific spellings in our DNA, which is abbreviated ATCG. This keeps DNA from infected viruses allowing CRISPER to grab those reminders if reentered again.

If scientists can identify and find the mutation via a specific set of sequenced letters then Crisper can then cut out the bad parts, literally editing our DNA, and then add the sequenced letters into the genomes. This procedure can change the genetic destiny of injected embryos, which at this time is 72% effective and that can stop a disease from occurring even in and before the womb. Amazing!

Realize with this CRISPR procedure, an individual can be made more intelligent, grow taller, and be stronger, not to mention the procedure is easier, much less expensive, and more efficient than any previous strategies for modifying DNA.

Now, if we go back in this chapter to "Comment": Here the Anunnaki have created hybrids.

*Like two entwined serpents Ningishzida **the "essences" separated.***

*Arranged like twenty two branches on a tree of life were the **"essences"** separated.*

*Another **two bits of "essence"** in the Anunnocki present Ningishida to the others showed.*

To their tree of life two branches have been added.
 With Procreating powers THEIR LIFE " ESSENCES" ARE NOW ENTWINED.

Ningishzida was one of the three principal Anunnocki characters participating in the genetic manipulation of mankind. His name, as spelled in Sumerian, means `Princely-Lord of the Tree of Life'; if spelled with two D's, that is, Ningishidda the Sumerian interpretation reads, `Lord of the Artifact of Life'. Both interpretations are quite apropos, don't you think? And as Mr. Zechariah Sitchin so aptly states in his book "Genesis Revisited," "Is Modern Science Catching up with the Ancient Knowledge"?

We have already pointed out the P2 gene, modern-day scientists have determined that millions of years of evolution would not have provided the P2 gene in our DNA. ***It had to be " intelligently placed" there!*** And there's more...

HAR1

At the University of California at Santa Cruz, scientists have discovered an area of the genome they named HAR1 *that appears unique to humans.* It plays a critical role in the development of the human brain. HAR1 is the key element that distinguishes us from animals.
That poses two questions, first, where did it come from? Second, was the gene acquired as a result of evolution and if not... where?
Francis Crick, the discoverer of DNA in 1953 relates, "Human genes could not have evolved by chance." Further, scientists agree that over a 600 million year period of evolution DNA could have evolved. That period of evolution gave us the **APE!** Yet, scientists agree, that

over that same 600 million years **evolution could not have provided the HAR1 genome.** He goes on to provide this analogy, " *You would be more likely to form a fully assembled functioning and flying jumbo jet by passing a hurricane through a junkyard than you would be to assemble the DNA molecule by chance in any kind of primeval soup"*

Given that other scientists, and Dr. Crick's field, homogeneously agree with his findings, the question then becomes, *how did we become human!* The answer, we firmly believe, is given to us by the Ancient Texts: **the Anunnaki targeted the mutation of our genes!**

Anyone can read and understand the how, the when, and the where, giving us the end result of our genetic manipulation by reading Zechariah Sitchin's, "The **Lost** Book of Enki," the Sixth Tablet, starting on page 128. One must realize that the memoirs and prophecies of an extraterrestrial god *are not Mr. Sitchin's writings! It is in totality the writings of the Anunnaki, namely, Enki, Ninmah and Ningishzidda;* Mr. Sitchin was the official *interpreter* of that ancient text, which he translated from ancient clay tablets and provided to the world, void of any personal opinion, via **the Anunnaki themselves**!

Selected sentences from the sixth tablet:

The Being that we need, it already exists!

Ningishzidda, my son, their *fashioning essence has tested; (DNA)*

Akin to ours it is, like two serpents it is entwined;

When their with our *"life essence"* shall be combined, our mark upon them shall be,

The Being already exists! Ninmah was saying. To give more ability is the plan!

Not a new creature, but **one existing more in our image made!** Enki with persuasion said,

With little change it can be achieved, only a drop of our **essence** is needed!

Creatures of two kinds by their **essences combined** to Ninmah

Enki was showing!

How the **essence** from two kinds combined can be, he to her was showing.

How the **essences** to combine, how much of this, how much of that to put together,

By a male inseminating a female (Ape) are the **essences transmitted,**

The two entwined strands (DNA) separate and combine an offspring to fashion.

Let a male **Anunnaki,** a two-legged female (Ape) impregnate, let a combination of offspring be born! Thus did Ninmah say.

In a crystal vessel Ninmah an add mixture was preparing, the oval of a female two-legged she gently placed,

With ME **Anunnocki seed containing,** she the oval impregnated;

A living being it was!

His hands for tools were not suited, *his speech only grunting sounds was!*

Advancing two page 137:
Then the oval thus fertilized into the womb of the Earth female she inserted.

There is conception! Ninmah with joy announced.

In her hands she held the child, his image she examined; it was the image of perfection

His limbs for the tasks were suited, **speech he knew not,**

Of speaking he had no understanding, grunts and snorts were his utterings!

Comment: AT THIS POINT WE FIRMLY BELIEVE THAT THE P2 GENE, WHICH GAVE US THE ABILITY TO SPEAK, WAS INSERTED INTO THE OVAL!

In our image and after our likeness to be, perchance an Anunnocki womb is required!.

Now where is the female among the Anunnaki her womb to offer,

So was Ninmah with a trembling voice saying.

I shall be the one the Anunnaki womb to provide, for good or evil fate to face!

The oval of the Earth female with **Anunnaki male essence** they put together;

The fertilized egg into the womb of Ninmah by Enki was inserted; there was conception!

Longer than on Earth, quicker than on Nibiru, travail came; *to a male child Ninmah birth was giving!*

Comment: Mitochondria DNA can now be traced back to one woman in southeast Africa, which the Anunnaki referred to as the Abzu: South East Africa is exactly were the ancient text tells us that the genetic manipulation of the Homo sapien, sapien took place and that us ***Earthlings are related to that one woman, whose name is Ninmah!***

Enki the boy child held in his hands; the image of perfection he was.

*He slapped the newborn on his hind parts; **the newborn uttered proper sounds!***
He handed the newborn to Ninmah; she held him up in her hands.

My hands have made it! victoriously she shouted.

Comment: Proceeding with reading the Seventh Tablet, we find that the Anunnaki performed other small genetic manipulations with the now fashioned "Beings," who were thereafter referred to as Earthlings.

Continuing in the Seventh Tablet page 167

Enki in the marshlands looked about, on the rivers he sailed and observed;

On the rivers bank, bathing and frolicking Earthlings he noticed;

Two females among them were wild with beauty, firm were their breasts.

Their sight the phallus of Enki caused to water, a burning desire he had

Into her womb she took the holy semen, by the semen of the Lord Enki she was impregnated.

The second one to him Enki called, berries from the field she offered him.

Into her womb he poured his semen, in a mating he knew her.

Into her womb she took the holy semen, by the semen of the Lord Enki she was impregnated.

Comment: The pregnancy of the two Earthling females by the Lord Enki, resulted in a female child and a male child, respectively referred to as Dawn and the Dusk. The two Earthlings were later officially and permanently given the names of Titi and Adapa. Now onto page 169

Between Anunnocki and Earthling, conception was attained,

Civilized Man I have brought into being!

Adapa, the Foundling, the boy she called; Titi, One with Life, the girl she named

Unlike all other Earthling children the twosome were:

Slower to grow up than Earthlings they were, much quicker in understanding they were;

With intelligence they were endowed, speaking with words capable they were.

Quick of learning they are, knowledge and craftwork to them can be taught.

Comment: Was this the point in time when mankind was given the HAR1 genome? We think so, citing two factors; **HAR1 genome appears unique to humans and the key element that played a critical role in the development of the human brain!** In our opinion, the how, the when, the where, and the why, these two, very important genetic manipulations of mankind are clearly demonstrated and defined in the Ancient Text.

From the Ancient Texts, `The Epic of Adapa', we know he was the first human to be given knowledge in writing and mathematics and astronomy. The son of Enki, by an Earthling woman, was known as "The Wisest of Men." **That wisdom could have only come from the Anunnaki!**

The Akkadian, *Atra Hasis* text tells us that the name given the created worker was, *lulu,* meaning *"the mixed one."* And the *"mixing"* was **between that of the ape and the Anunnaki, with the result being a hybrid we know as mankind.** I'll let Ninki describe it in her own words, from the "Lost Book of Enki, Sixth Tablet –

The newborn's fate thou shalt pronounce;
Ninki would fix upon it the image of the gods;

And what it will be is "Man."

If we look at Darwin's ostentatious conclusion that all living things, including Man, are the end products of evolution, we must consider and realize that if his conclusion of Man's evolution were made on the planet Nibiru, regarding the Anunnaki, **he would have been scientifically correct!** Evolution cannot account for the appearance of Homo sapiens on Earth, however, evolution gave us the end product of the genus Homo but as the Anunnaki through the ancient Sumerian texts repeatedly tells us, *they evolved!* They also make it abundantly clear that the Anunnaki never practiced religion. There was no noncarbon entity, spiritual intervention in their evolution. What gave the Anunnaki their very existence relates back to one word, **time.**

Scientists tell us that mankind on this planet appeared millions of years too soon. In plain English, it was impossible that Man/Homo sapiens had enough time to evolve on this planet. Modern-day scientists have absolutely no explanation for Homo sapiens to *suddenly appear 300,000 years ago. The Sumarian and Babylonian text give us an empirical answer, "it was the Anunnaki stupid!"*

It should be mentioned here, in closing this chapter, that Enki ("Lord Earth") had at least seven different epithets, depending upon his geographic location: for example, in the Greek pantheon, he was known as Neptune. When originally landing on earth and building the city of Eridu, Mesopotamia, Enki was known as EA, ("Whose home is water"). In Egypt he was known as Ptah, ("The Developer") relating to his concept and his initiation of building the Giza pyramids. The most important epithet given to Enki, relating to his participation in the genetic manipulation of the Earthling, was, Nudimmud, meaning "The Fashioner of Mankind."

So one could reasonably conclude the Ancient Text, empirically relates to us that the **Anunnaki** added their evolved *godly essence to the genes of the earthly Apeman by fertilizing the egg of an Apewoman with the sperm of and an Anunnaki male and placed in the womb of and an Anunnaki female which resulted in the birth of Adamu, a hybrid that could not reproduce.* The medical procedure used by the **Anunnaki** must be defined as none other than *IN VITRO FERTILIZATION!* Further, we must conclude that you and I *are the end result of a test tube baby!*

THE CASE OF THE GENETICALLY MODIFIED PRIMATE

"Ninharsag and her crew are closer to being vindicated as time passes, and soon your theories will no longer be theories!"

So wrote to me a fan (Jack Bird in Virginia" in a congratulatory letter accompanying a newspaper clipping headlined "Genetically modified primate's world's first." It was the report about the successful birth of ANDi (`inserted a DNA' spelled backward), a baby rhesus monkey "created" by a group of researchers at the Oregon Regional Primate Center, whose genetic makeup was modified to include the genes from a jellyfish that made it glow in the dark.

Mice have been previously genetically modified for medical research. But because the rhesus monkey is roughly 95% again to humans genetically, "I think we are at an extraordinary moment in the history of humans," said the chief researcher Dr. Gerald Schatten.

I was, of course, pleased to be congratulated. Yet, I wrote back to my fan with thanks coupled with an admonition. "While it is nice to get such reassuring compliments," I wrote to him, "I am trying to get my fans to write about it to others, and first and foremost to the newspapers that carried the reports. In this case, the Associated Press report stresses that it was the world's FIRST genetically modified primate; what a Letter to the Editor should point out is that according to the Sumerian texts reported by Zechariah Sitchin in his books The 12th Planet and Genesis Revisited, Adam was the first genetically modified primate, some 300,000 years ago!"

Comment: In Will Hearts book the, "The Genesis Race Our Extraterrestrial DNA and the True Origins of the Species," tells us
"Once our genomes code had been broken, the human gene count turned out to be a disappointing 30,000 – only a little more than double the 13,601 jeans and a fruit fly.
The second disturbing bit of news was the consortium's revelation that the human genome contains 223 genes that do not have predecessors on the genomic evolutionary tree. Because 223 represents a small percentage of our 30,000 genes, their existence may seem inconsequential – nothing to fuss about! When referring to genes, however, even

small numbers can make all the difference. For example, though it may be difficult to accept, human beings are separated from chimpanzees by only 300 genes, a 1 percent difference! At the genetic level chimpanzees and humans are 99 percent alike. To some, that human beings and chimpanzees differ genetically by only 1 percent clearly proves the theory of evolution. Instead, it actually makes it more difficult and the more critical to explain human uniqueness. What is contained in that 1% to make is so different from champs?"

Comment: Evolution can only be scientifically proven up to a given point in time, which is provided to us through Darwin's, Theory of Evolution. Fossil records from the ape to mankind, the Homo sapien and then the Homo sapien sapien, cannot be scientifically substantiated which empirically eliminates the theory of evolution. Random mutation and natural selection cannot account for today's complexity of life and therefore the "missing link" remains unexplained. Ah, contrare, I believe that it has been explained and the explanation is, *the genetic manipulation as described in the ancient text by the Anunnaki!*

The news about the genetically modified rhesus monkey was just one item in an avalanche of reports on human genetics, cloning, etc. in which the names of Enki and Ninharsag could well replace the names of Dr. Schatten, Dr. Phyllis Leppert (and their other modern colleagues). So please----TELL IT TO THE NEWSPAPERS!

C- Z. Sitchin February 2001

Comment:
DNA holds the key to the evaluation of this genetic stamp, placed there, in our opinion, by the ***Anunnaki***. We are currently looking for Extraterrestrials by looking up to the stars, and in our opinion, there are some out there! What we need to do is come back down to Earth and microscopically learn about our own DNA. We need to understand more, than just 5% of our DNA, – and when we do, ***the Anunnaki will be in there!***
From the "Lost Book of Enki," The sixth tablet page 138 –9

In our image and after our likeness to be, perchance an Anunnaki womb is required!

Longer than on Earth, quicker than on Nibiru, travail came; to a male child Ninmah birth was giving!

Enki the boy child held in his hands; the image of perfection he was.

He slapped the newborn on his hind parts; the newborn uttered proper sounds!

He handed the newborn to Ninmah; she held him up in her hands.

My hands have made it! victoriously she shouted.

Chapter 4: Anunnaki = The Missing Link

The debate between Evolution and Creationism is ongoing. Both sides are adamant in their beliefs. Scientific Evolution is a provable fact, to a certain point and the Creationists must stick to their belief that mankind was instantly created by God, else they void the tenants and the very base of their religion. We should define Evolution and creationism and go from there.

Biological Evolution: The continuous genetic adaptation of organisms or species to the environment by the integrating agencies of selection, hybridization, inbreeding, and mutation.

Creationism: 1. The doctrine that God immediately creates out of nothing a new human soul for each individual born.2.Traducianism: the doctrine that matter and all things were created, substantially as they now exist, by an omnipotent Creator and not gradually evolved or developed.

From the evolutionary standpoint, there is scientific proof that animals from the oceans developed the ability to breathe air and slowly evolved into various creatures on earth. The proof is in the fossils discovered, showing step-by-step the evolution of sea animals into air-breathing land animals.

Darwin's theory was that all living things were products of evolution and that includes Man. Evolution can scientifically account for the development of the humanoid primate genus Homo, through the discovery of fossils, including skeletons and the more important skull. But that is as far as scientific evolution can take us. Fossil records relating to the unbroken transition or evolvement of Man, such as those of animal evolvement have not been found and in our opinion, nor will they be.

RESEARCH THE FOLLOWING

Homo erectus can be traced back to about 435,000 years, **(which quite ironically is almost the exact same date that the ancient texts relate, with specificity, as the arrival date of the first Anunnaki.)**

JUST THE ABOVE STATEMENT

The evolution of Homo erectus took millions of years, then suddenly about 300,000 years ago Homo sapiens(wise) appear. Their appearance is enigmatic and unexplainable and cannot be attributed to evolution, as the Homo sapiens appearance is many millions of years too soon. There is no fossil evidence to bridge the gap between Homo erectus and Homo sapiens. Scientists refer to the evolutionary gap as "the missing link.

Here the creationists grab a foothold for their beliefs that mankind was created by the act of an omnipotent God as revealed in Genesis, the biblical story of creation.

The "missing link" is defined as a hypothetical form of animal assumed to have constituted a connecting link between the anthropoid apes and man.

In our opinion, the Anunnaki, figuratively speaking, is the "missing link" for it is they who "Fashioned" mankind. For the Evolutionist and the Creationist, we will provide the documentation from the Ancient Texts, to substantiate that opinion. The creation process of the Anunnaki has been provided in detail in this book taken from the appropriate Tablets of the Memoirs and Prophecies of an Extraterrestrial God--Enki.

TABLET 6

To create a Primitive Worker, (the Adamu) by the mark of our essence (DNA) to fashion him!
So was Enki to the leaders saying.

The Being that we need, it already exists!

Thus did Enki to them a secret of the Abzu (South East Africa) reveal.

Creatures in the Abzu there are, Enki was saying, that walk erect on two legs,

Among the animals of the steppe they live. They know not dressing in garments,

They eat plants with their mouth, they drink water from the lake and ditch.

Shaggy with hair is their whole body, their head hair is like a lion's;

Aeons ago, on Nibiru, our predecessor like that might have been! Ninmah was saying.

It is a Being, not a creature!

Male and a female they are! Enki was saying; Malehoods and femalehoods they have.

Ningishzidda, my son, their Fashioning Essence (DNA) has tested;

Akin to ours it is, like two serpents it is entwined;

When their's with our life essence shall be combined, our mark upon them shall be.

How the essence from two kinds combined can be, he to her was showing.

The creatures in the tree cages are too odd, monstrous they are! Ninmah was saying.

Here is the solution to the ongoing debate. Homo erectus (the Being) already existed as a product of evolution. The Anunnaki with their knowledge of genetics, "Fashioned" the existing Being, "In our image and after our likeness." Therefore mankind, Homo sapiens, were the end product of the Anunnaki gods.

Does this not coincide with and paradigm today's scientific knowledge? Does this not explain the missing link enigma? Does this not explain the sudden appearance of Homo sapiens, void of the additional millions of years needed to evolve? Does this not explain how we are 98% DNA related to the primate? We think it does because the Ancient Texts are compatible with today's scientific knowledge.

Science informs us that the unexpected appearance of Homo sapiens dates back to some 300,000 years ago, and the question now becomes, do the Ancient Texts provide a timeframe for their fashioning of mankind that is congruent with today's scientific knowledge? We think it does and so does the renowned author Zachariah Sitchen. As taken from "The Twelfth Planet" …

The Mesopotamian texts, fortunately, provide a clear statement regarding the time when Man was created. The story of the toil and the ensuing mutiny of the Anunnaki informs us that "for 40 periods they suffered the work, day and night"; the long years of their toil are dramatized by repetitious verses.

For 10 periods they suffered the toil;
For 20 periods they suffered the toil;
For 30 periods they suffered the toil;
For 40 periods they suffered the toil;

The ancient text uses the term ma to denote "period." And most scholars have translated this as "year." But the term had the connotation of something that completes itself and then repeats itself." To men on Earth, one year equals one complete orbit of Earth around the Sun. As we have already shown, the orbit of the Nephilim's planet equaled a shar, or 3600 Earth years.

Forty shars, or 144,000 Earth years, after their landing, the Anunnaki protested "No more!" (Mining for gold to supplement their planet Nibiru's' dwindling atmosphere) If the Nefilim first landed on Earth, as we have concluded, some 450,000 years ago, then the creation of Man took place some 300,000 years ago!

The Nephilim did not create the mammals or the primates or the hominids. The "Adam" of the Bible was not the genus Homo, but the being, who is our ancestor-- the first Homo sapiens. It is the modern man as we know him that the Anunnaki created.

So the answer to the question, "Do the Ancient Texts provide a timeframe for their fashioning of mankind that is compatible with today's scientific knowledge?" The answer is yes and factual! Another relative question comes to mind, is it possible that Mankind would have, through evolution, ever evolved to the "sapien" status, given the millions of years of evolutionary time needed? And what about the Anunnaki? Did they through the process of evolution evolve, or were they "created" out of nothing by an omnipotent being?

Sumerian texts definitively tell us that the Anunnaki evolved on the planet Nibiru as intelligent beings, Aeons before the hominids on Earth. Also--as a result of the celestial collision with Tiamat (Enuma Elish) which resulted in our planet Earth and its' current position, came the seed of life, allowing the evolutionary process to begin, much as it had eons ago on the planet Nibiru.

THE FIRST TABLET OF ENKI   P-25

After aeons of time our own species sprouted, by our own essence and eternal seed to procreate.

THE FIFTH TABLET OF ENKI

Let the Being the toil of the Anunnaki carry on its back!

Astounded were the besieged leaders, speechless indeed they were.

Whoever heard of a Being afresh created, a worker who the Anunnaki's work can do? P-126

All beings from a seed have descended, (Not created by God) P-126
One being from another over eons to develop, none from nothing ever came!

THE SIXTH TABLET P-129&30

Aeons ago, on Nibiru, our predecessors like that might have been!

Ninmah was saying. It is a Being not a creature!

Ningishzidda, my son, their Fashioning Essence has tested;

Akin to ours it is, like two serpents it is entwined;

When their with our life essence shall be combined, are marked upon them will be,

A Primitive worker Shall be created! Our commands will he understand. P-129-30

In reference to the above terminology "Fashioning Essence" the Anunnaki, themselves never claim in the ancient texts that, they "*created*" mankind, rather they simply *"Fashioned"*, the existing Being.

"Let us with wisdom new tools fashion, not new beings create". P-131

Creation in the hands of the Father of All Beginning alone is held! Page 130

Enuma Elish clearly and definitively relates, that the "Father of All Beginning," is not what is biblically attributed as God... but "*The Sun*".

To obtain gold was our purpose, to replace the Father of All Beginning it was not! P-131

THE SEVENTH TABLET

A Civilized Man has the Earth itself brought forth, P-170

In the wilderness a new kind of Earthling has come forth! To Enlil was Enki saying.

A wonder of wonders it is, in the wilderness by themselves to have come about!

Indeed a wonder of wonders it is, a new breed of Earthling on Earth has emerged,

Anu the words heard, by the words he was amazed:

That by life essences one kind to another leads is not unheard of! to them words back he sent.

That on Earth a Civilized Man from the Adamu so quickly appeared, that is unheard of! P-171

THE NINTH TABLET

Other living creatures, some by us from Nibiru originated, most from Earth itself evolved. P-215

THE 10TH TABLET

The unseen hand of the Creator of All is life on Nibiru to enable! So did Enlil say. P-234

Again referring back to Enuma Elish, the *"Creator of All",* is not a reference to an ethereal omnipotent divinity, that is God, the reference is to, *"The Sun!"*

Chapter 5: Evolution of the Anunnaki

The Ancient Texts, in particular, the 14 Tablets of Enki, in specific scientific terms, state definitively that the ape-man, hominoid, genus Homo evolved here on earth, and that the Anunnaki gods, specifically Enki and Ninerta, being primary participants, fashioned Man, the Homo sapien. The question then arises, posed by scholars and authors who have studied the Ancient Texts, was the Anunnaki a product of evolution on the planet Nibiru or were they "created" by an omnipotent Universal God with a structured Religion? The Anunnaki themselves, frequently and repeatedly, inform readers of their ancient texts **leaving absolutely no doubt that THEY ARE PRODUCTS OF EVOLUTION.**

THE EMERALD TABLETS of THOTH

Seven are they, the Lords of Amenti
formed are not they as the children of men.

Tablet 4

Now, O man when I had this knowing,
Happy my soul grew,
for now I was free
Listen, ye space born,
List to my wisdom:
Know ye not that ye, too, will be free.

Tablet 7

From far beyond time are WE, come, O men,
when ye and all of thy brethren were formless,
formed forth were WE from the order of ALL.
Though once WE, too, were as men.
Out of the Great Void were We formed forth
in order by LAW.

All that ye know is but part of little.
Not as yet had he touched on the great

Donald M. Blackwell

Far out into space where LIGHT beams supreme
came I into the LIGHT.
Formed was I also but not as ye are.

Know that thou art one with the Cosmos,
A flame and a Child of the Light.

Tablet 9

Think not that man is Earthborn,
Though come from the earth he may be.
Man is light- born spirit.

Ye are son of the GREAT LIGHT
Light, let thy Soul be, O SUN-BORN.

Tablet 10

Know ye, O man, **that all exists**
has been only because of the LAW
Know ye, the LAW (of the Universe)
and ye shall be free,
never be bound by the fetters of night.

Aye, saw I man's beginning,
Learned the from the past that nothing is new

Know ye, **that in all formed matter,**
The heart of **Light always exists.**
Yet must ye understand that **man is of Light**
And Light is of man.

Tablet 11

Far in the past, when first I came to thee,
Found I thee in caves of rocks.
Lifted I thee by my power and wisdom
Until thou didst shine as men among men.
Aye, **found I thee without any knowing.**
Only a little were ye raised beyond beasts.
Fanned I ever the sparked of thy consciousness
until at last ye flamed as men.

For know ye that the fountain of wisdom
that sends forth the cycle is eternally
seeking new powers to gain.
Ye know that knowledge is gained only by practice,
and wisdom comes only from knowledge,
and thus are the cycles **created by LAW.**
Means are they for the gaining of knowledge
For the Plane of Law that is the Source of the All.

And know, just as we are working on greater,
so above ye are those who are also working
as ye are yet other laws.
The difference that exists between the cycles
is only inability to work with the Law.
We, **who have been in cycles beyond thee,**
Are **those who first came forth from the**
Source and have with **the passage through**
time-space gained ability to use
Laws of the Greater that are far beyond
the conception of man.
Nothing there is that is really below thee
but only a different operation of LAW.

Tablet 13

Know ye that the Earth is living in body
As thou art alive in thine own form formed.

Tablet 14

Three are the powers creating the all things:
Divine Love possessed of perfect knowledge,
Defined in Wisdom knowing all possible means,
Divine Power possessed by the joint will of
Divine Love and Wisdom.

Now ye assemble, my children,
Waiting to hear if the Secret of Secrets
which shall give ye power to unfold the God-man,
give ye the way to Eternal life

NOTE: Created by Law, the Source of the All, DEFINING EVOLUTION

THE AUTOBIOGRAPHY OF ENKI
Tablet 1
After aeons of time our own species sprouted,
by our own essence and the eternal seed to procreate.
Tablet 2
At that time, in the heart of the Deep a god (planet) was engendered,

In a Chamber of Fates, a place of destinies, (orbit) was he born.

By an artful Creator he was fashioned, THE SON OF HIS OWN SUN, he was.

A gift of HIS CREATOR, the SEED OF LIFE, with him away he carried.
Tablet 5
All beings from a seed have descended,
One being from another over eons did develop,
none from nothing ever came!
Tablets 6
Aeons ago, on Nibiru, our predecessors like that might have been!

It is a being, not a creature! Ninmah was saying.
Tablet 7

That my life essences **one kind to another** leads is not unheard of!

A Civilized man **has the Earth itself brought forth.**
Tablet 9

Step by step on this planet, a **Primitive Being, one like us to be, we have created.**

Other **living creatures,** some by us from Nibiru originated, **most from Earth itself EVOLVED.**

THE AUTOBIOGRAPHY OF ENKI TABLET 2   64p

In the Beginning,

When in the Above the gods in the heavens had not yet been called into being,

And in the Below Ki, (Earth) The Firm Ground, had not yet been named,

Alone in the void there existed Apsu, (Sun) their Primordial Begetter.

In the heights of the Above, the celestial gods (Planets) had not yet been created;

In the waters Below, the celestial gods had not yet appeared.

Tiamat, The Mother of All, as a spouse for himself he fashioned.

Then it was that the to their waters mingled, **divine children between** them to come forth.

Male and female were the **celestials created;** Lahmu (Mars) and Lahamu (Venus) by names they were called.

In the waters of the Above Anshar (Saturn) And Kishar (Jupiter) were formed ;

A son, An (Uranus) in the distant heaven what is their heir.

Then Antu (Neptune), to be his spouse.

At that time, circuits were not yet fully fashioned;

The destinies (orbit) **of the gods were** not yet firmly decreed;

Who shall stand up to Tiamat? **The gods asked each other.**

At that time, in the heart of the Deep **a God was engendered,**

By an artful **Creator** was he fashioned, **the son of his own Sun he was.**

Enki, here in his autobiography, along with Enuma Elish , in our opinion also authored by Enki, The Emerald Tablets of Thoth (son of Enki), and literally all other Ancient Text writings of the Anunnaki gods; all planets are referred to as "**gods**", and Suns are referred to as "**creators.**"

The Anunnaki refer to themselves as god and to each other as gods. The **"Creator of All"** or **"The Father of All Beginning"** are not references to an omnipotent being, creating something out of nothing. The Creator of All is a reference to the **SUN(s) and the**

inherent Creativity of our Galaxy and of the billions of different Galaxies.

Thoth referrers to mankind as a **"product of Stardust"**. Repeatedly, many renown scientists, like the late Carl Sagan, use the **exact** same description, which in and of itself, is synonymous with Evolution and void of the "creationist" connotation. The Father of All Beginning, in our opinion, is synonymous with modern-day scientists, referring to the Theory of the Big Bang, and no less impersonal as today's colloquialisms, such as "That was the "Mother" of all explosions," That was the "Grand Daddy of them all." etc. etc.

We respectfully disagree with those who would define the "Creator of All" as the universal, cosmic God and the "Father of All" Beginning As the universal Creator of All. The Anunnaki described themselves in similar deified terms as the "Almighty", "Without Equal", "Eternal" etc. etc.

"Lord of eternity, he who everlastingness has made."

"The One who is without equal, the great solitary and a soul One!"

One might think these quotes were taken from the Bible, but they were taken from the 13th Tablet of Enki and refer to his son Marduk.

"So did Marduk, as Ra, above all other gods himself emplace."

In all of the Ancient Texts that we are aware of, never once did any of the Anunnaki gods refer to an" omnipotent being" or "cosmic entity" as being superior to themselves in any way. They never prayed to a superior entity, or in times of lamentations, deaths, tragedy, despair, fear, ask for help or refer to a superior being! The Anunnaki lied, stole, robbed, cheated, hated, killed, slaughtered and murdered **without remorse to anyone or any "thing," or "entity,"** <u>other than themselves.</u>

The 10th Tablet of Enki
For days before the Day of the Deluge the Earth was rumbling,

groan as with the pain it did;

Then there was darkness in daytime, and at night the Moon as though by a monster was swallowed.

The Earth began to shake, by a net force (the gravitational pull of Nibiru)

before unknown it was agitated.

The morning light and darkness change, as though by deaths shadow veiled.

Then the sound of a rolling thunder boomed, lightning the skies lit up.

Depart! Depart! Utu to the Anunnaki gave the signal.

On that day, on that unforgettable day, the Deluge with a roar began;

Then with a roar to a thousand thunders equal, off its foundation the ice sheet slipped

All at once a tidal wave arose, the very skies was the wall of waters reaching.

A storm, its ferocity never before seen, at the Earth's bottom began to howl,

In their celestial boats the Anunnaki the Earth were (orbit) circling.

All life by the rolling sea wave away was taken! Thus did Ninmah cry and moan.

Thus did Ninmah and Ianna weep; **they wept and eased their feelings.**

In the other celestial boats **the Anunnaki by the site of the unbridled fury were humbled,**

A POWER GREATER THAN THEIRS (NATURE) **they with awe those days witnessed.**

Their reference to "a power greater than theirs" is quite impersonal as the power they refer to is a **Cosmotic Mother Nature!** And at a time of travail, despair, uncertainty, and fear caused by witnessing the Great Deluge do the Anunnaki beseech a supreme God, the Creator of all, the Father of All Beginning? **NO! THEY LONGED FOR FOOD AND WINE**, as the very next line of the Ancient Text Reveals;

FOR THE FRUITS OF EARTH THEY HUNGERED, FOR FERMENTED ELIXER THEY THURSTED.

Tablet 9

The Creator of All, to primordial days the heavens is returning,

Angry Is the Creator of All! Voices from amongst the people shouted

Should Nibiru to its fate then left, whatever by the Creator of All intended, to be let to happen.

Tablet 10

Enki, referring to the impending Great Deluge; That is the will of the Creator of All!

The unseen hand of the Creator of All it is life on Nibiru to enable! So did Enlil say?

Tablet 12

The will of the Creator of All is clear to see: On Earth and for Earthlings, only emissaries we are.

Tablet 13

By him and his seed, will Civilized Mankind, as by the Creator of All intended, be preserved!

Tablet 14

The sparing of Babali (from radiation fallout) is confirmed! So did Enki to Enlil say.

The will of the (wind direction) Creator of All it must have been! Enlil to Enki said.

Note: After a Nuclear explosion, the distant geographical area that experiences "radiation fallout," is primarily **DETERMINED BY WIND DIRECTION**! Again the Creator of All, in this particular scenario is none other than **MOTHER NATURE!**

THE EMERALD TABLETS OF THOTH TABLET 1

The temple of the Children of Light.
Grew and there from a child into manhood,
being taught by my father **the elder mysteries**,
until in time there grew within the fire of wisdom
Until it bursts into a consuming flame.

COMMENT. The Anunnaki children on Nibiru were not taught
religion, they were taught the mysteries of the universe, creating
curiosity and pursuing knowledge, flaming the fires of wisdom.

In the land of the children of Khem (Egypt)
Raging, they came with cudgels and spears,
lifted in anger seeking to slay and utterly destroy the Suns of
Atlantis
Then raised I my staff and directed a ray of vibration,
striking them still in their tracks as fragments of stone of the
mountain.

Then spoke I to them in the words calm and peaceful,
saying we were **children of the Sun**, and its messengers
Cowed I them by my display of magic- science,
Until at my feet they groveled, then I released them.

COMMENT. Thoth introduces himself and his associates as
children of the Sun, uses his ray gun to freeze them in their tracks
and provides an example of how and why the Anunnaki gods were
conceived as Gods. The Biblical scribes would perhaps describe the
event as follows; The Lord God and Angels (messengers) suddenly
appeared before us, saying "I am the God of your fathers, Abraham,
Isaac, and Joseph, etc. etc.

Now I depart from ye. Know my commandments,
Keep them and be them, and I will be with you.

NOTE: Genesis: 15:26 If you will heed your God diligently, giving ear to His Commandments, and keeping all His laws…..

COMMENT. Is this where the Hebrew scribes conceived of the idea of receiving The 10 Commandments and being the chosen ones? At least in part: the Ark of the Covenant, tablets being written on both sides, writing the tablets as spoken by God were taken directly from the Attestation of Endubar, the autobiography of Enki.

"We are they who were **formed from space- dust,
partaking of life FROM the infinite ALL.**
living in the world as children of men,
like and yet unlike the children of men."

COMMENT. As stated earlier, scientists have described mankind as a product of space -dust! Here the Anunnaki God Thoth relates**, in no uncertain terms, that the Anunnaki were the product of "stardust" that life came from the infinite ALL, ALL being the cosmos!** Clearly and indisputably, in our opinion, **the Anunnaki were the pure, unadulterated product of Evolution.** From the statement, " like and yet unlike the children of men," is a clear indication, that we too are products of evolution, on the same evolutionary track as they were on the planet Nibiru, until they intervened, imparted their "essence" (**DNA**) as described in the Ancient Texts, and fashioned Man, the Homo Sapiens.

Tablet 2

Time after time, The Great Masters,
 incarnate they in the bodies of men.
teaching and writing onward and upward,
out of the darkness into the light.

COMMENT. Teaching and writing by the Anunnaki, brought mankind, through their revelations to us, from a state of darkness (ignorance) into the light. (Knowledge and wisdom)

Then from HE (the Dweller) came forth a voice saying:
"Great art thou, Thoth, among children of men.
 Free henceforth of the Halls of Amenti,
Master of Life among children of men.
 Taste not of death except as thou will it,
drink thou of Life to Eternities end,
Henceforth forever is Life, thine for the taking,
Henceforth is Death at the call of thy hand.

So grows the soul of man ever upward,
quenched yet unquenched by the darkness of night.
I, Death, come, ended yet I remain not,
for life eternal exists in the All.

Mysteries that men may never get know of until he too is a Son of the Light.

Tablet 3

Man is a star bound to a body until, in the end, he is freed through his strife.
 Only by struggle and toiling thy utmost shall the star within thee bloom out in new life.

Remember, O men, that **all which exists is only another form of that which exists not.**
Everything that has being is passing into yet another being and thou **thyself** are not an exception.

Life they have in them, yet life that is not life, **free from all are the Lords of the ALL.**

Tablet 4

Thoth the teacher of men, is of ALL
Shapes there were, moving in Order, great and majestic stars in the night;
 mounting in harmony, ordered equilibrium, symbols of the Cosmic, like unto Law.

116

Many the stars I passed in my journey, **many THE RACES OF MEN ON THEIR WORDS:**
Some reaching high as stars of the morning, some falling low in the blackness of night.

Some I found who had conquered the ether. Free of space were they while **yet they were men.**
Using the force that is the foundation of ALL things, far in space constructed they a planet,
Dawn by the force that flows through the All;
condensing, coalescing the ether into forms, they grew as they willed.
Outstripping in science, they, all of the races, mighty in wisdom, **sons of the stars.**

Forth then, my soul sped throughout the Cosmos, seeing ever, new things and old;
learning that man is truly space borne, A Son of the Sun, a child of the stars.

Know ye, O man, whatever from ye inhabit, surely it is one with the stars.
Thy bodies are nothing but planets revolving around their central sons.

forms and forth he from the primal ether, filled with the brilliance that flows from the source
Bound by the ether coalesced around, yet ever it flames until at last it is free.

COMMENT. How man and stars are created-- from the ether.

Flame from the beginning of Eternities ALL.
Spark of the flame a**rt thou**, O, my children.

Mighty SPIRIT OF LIGHT that shines through the Cosmos, draw my flame closer in harmony to thee. Lift up my fire from

117

out of the darkness,

magnet of fire that is One with the ALL. Lift up my soul, thy might and potent.

Child of the Light, turn not away. Draw me in power to melt in thy furnace;

One with all things and all things in One, fire of the life strain and One with the Brain.

COMMENT. True to form of the **ontological Anunnaki**.
Tablet 5

Now, as I look back through the ages, know I that wisdom is boundless,

ever grown greater throughout the ages, One with Infinity's greater than all.

Take all your records, Take all your magic. Go thou forth as a teacher of men.

Go thou forth reserving the records until in time LIGHT grows among men.

LIGHT shall now be all through the ages, didn't yet found by enlightened men.

Over all Earth, <u>give WE ye power,</u> free thou to give or take it away.
Tablet 6

Even as they exist among men the DARK BROTHERS, (ignorance)

so there exists the BROTHERS OF LIGHT.(knowledge)
Antagonists they of the BROTHERS OF DARKNESS,
seeking to free men from the night.
Powers have they, mighty and potent.
Knowing the LAW, the planets obey.

SONS are they and LORDS of the morning, Children of Light to shine among men.

Like men are they and yet are unlike, Never divided were they in the past.

ONE have they been in ONENESS eternal, **throughout all space since the beginning of time,**

> **Up did they come in Oneness with the ALL ONE, up from the first-space, formed and unformed.**

Tablet 7

Hidden and buried, lost demands knowledge, deep in the finite the Infinite exists.

Lost but existing, flowing through all things, living in ALL is the INFINITE BRAIN.

In all space, there is only ONE wisdom. Through seeming un-decided, it is **ONE in the ONE.**

All that exists comes forth from the LIGHT, and the LIGHT comes forth from the ALL.

Everything created is based upon ORDER; LAW rules the space where the INFINITE dwell.

I, Thoth stood before the LORDS of the cycles. Mighty, THEY in their aspects of power;

Mighty THEY in the wisdom unveiled. Manifest THEY in this cycle

as guide of man and the knowledge of ALL. Seven are they, mighty in power,

speaking these words through me to men. Time after time, stood I before them

listening to words that came not with sound. (Telepathy)

Giving knowledge of operation, learning of LAW, the order of ALL.

From far beyond time are WE, come, O man, Traveled WE from beyond SPACE-TIME

When ye and all of thy brethren were formless, formed forth were WE from the order of ALL.

Then through me spoke HE of NINE saying Aeons and for aeons

119

have I existed,

knowing not LIFE and tasting not death. For know ye, O man, that far in the future

life and death shall be one with the ALL.

Thus, through ages I listened, learning the way to the ALL.

Now List I my thoughts to the ALL- THING. List ye and hear when *IT* calls.

Tablet 9

Seek ye, O man, and find the great pathway that leads to eternal LIFE as a SUN.

Ye shall know that space is not boundless but truly bounded by angles and curves.

Know ye O man, **that all that exists is only an aspect of greater things yet to come.**

Know ye ***MAN, YE ARE THE ULTIMATE OF ALL THINGS.***

Think not that man is earth-born, though come from the earth he may be.

Man is light born spirit.

Asked the LORDS this question: ***WHERE IS THE SOURCE OF ALL?***

Answered,in tones that were mighty, the voice of the LORD of the NINE:

Free thou thy soul from thy body and come forth with me to the light.

Know ye O Thoth, that **LIFE is but thee WORD of the FIRE. The LIFE forth ye seek before thee in the World as a fire.**

Tablet 10

Then to me spoke HE, the Master: Know ye, oh Thoth,

**in the beginning there and VOID and nothingness,
A TIMELESS, SPACELESS, NOTHINGNESS.**
**And into the nothingness came a thought, purposeful,
all-pervading,**
**And it filled the VOID. There existed no matter, only force of
the purposeful thought.**

Know ye that to be without knowledge, **wisdom is magic** and
not of the LAW.
But know ye that ever ye by your knowledge can approach closer to a place in the Sun.

Light is thine, O man, for the taking cast off the fetters and thou
shall be free.
Know ye that thy **Soul is living in bondage fettered by fears
that hold ye inthrall.**
Fear is the LORD of the dark and he who never faced the dark
fear.
Aye, know that **fear has existence created by those who are
bound by their fears**.

**COMMENT. Could that be mankind's evolution of reli-
gion?** That ought to put the "fear of God" into you!
Tablet 12

I, the children of men show progress onward and upward to the
great goal.
**knowledge and wisdom Shall be man's in the great age for
he shall approach**
**the eternal flame, the Source of all wisdom, the place of the
beginning**
That is yet One with the end of all things.

Be thou my children in this life and the next.
the time will come when ye, too, Shall be deathless.

Tablet 13

Know ye the gateway to life is through death.
Aye, through death **but not as ye know death,**
but a death that is life and is fire and is Light.

Tablet 14

List ye now to the unveiling of Mystery. List to the symbols of Mystery I give.
make of it a religion for only thus will its essence remain.

In the primeval, dwell three unities. Other than these, none can exist.
These are the equilibrium, source of creation: one (Anunnaki) God, one truth, one point of freedom
Three come forth from the three of the balance: all life, all good, all power.
Three are the qualities of God in his Light home, Infinite power, Infinite Wisdom, Infinite Love.
.
COMM: As we have demonstrated and exemplified in this book, **Yahweh processes none of the above.**

Three are the powers creating all things:
Divine Love possessed of perfect knowledge,
Divine Wisdom knowing all possible means,
Divine Power possessed by the joint will of
Divine Love and Wisdom.

I attained, as it were, to the God of all Gods **I attained, as it were, to the God of All Gods**
the Son Spirit, The Sovereign of the Sun Spheres
There is One, Even the First, who hath no beginning,
who hath no end; who have made all things, who governed all,
who is just, WHO ILLUMINATES, WHO SUSTAINS.

COMMENTS: The third and fourth lines are exactly how God is described in the Bible, unfortunately, as the case may be, **the reference here is to the Sun**.

Their will I give thee the essence of wisdom so that with power ye may shine amongst men.

There will I give unto thee the secrets so that **ye to, may rise to the Heavens,**

GOD-MEN IN TRUTH AS IN ESSENCE YE BE.

Depart now and leave me while I summon those ye know of but as ye know not.

Tablet 15

Now ye assemble my children, waiting to hear the Secret of Secrets which shall give ye

power to unfold the GOD-MAN, gave ye the way to Eternal life.

Tablet 12

Knowledge and wisdom shall be forgotten, and only a memory of gods shall survive.

AS I TO THEE AM A GOD BY MY KNOWLEDGE,
SO YE TOO SHALL BE GODS OF THE FUTURE
BECAUSE OF YOUR KNOWLEDGE FAR ABOVE THEIRS.

THE CASE OF THE "INTELLIGENT DESIGNER"

The Evolutionists cannot fathom how the other side can ignore the overwhelming evidence of life's beginnings billions of years ago and the claim that it is all the result of six days of creation; the Creationists, pointing out that a complex watch required a watchmaker, cannot see how the sudden appearance of Homo sapiens is the most complex life form can deny the Hand of God.

Enter "Intelligent Design...

In the past several years the debate has manifested itself again, with greater vigor or, not only in the so-called Bible Belt states but also in unexpected places as the Michigan House of Representatives and the Pennsylvania education system. The most recent instance in Ohio, where the arena is the state's Board Of Education.

Reports of these developments in the liberal media do not hide a degree of alarm at these developments-- not so much because they continue to occur, but because the attack on Darwinian teachings now come from "creationism in disguise," and "a good disguise" at that (Time magazine). The disguise is called **"Intelligent Design"** ("ID" for short); Its proponents, by and large, do not take a position on how Life got here; they just deny that natural selection (i.e. evolution) alone could have brought us about. Somewhere along the way, they told, there had to be an Intelligent Designer. What alarms the media in the scientific community is the fact that the proponents of ID are not Bible-waving old ladies, but intellectuals and academics from varied disciplines in science, philosophy, and theology. Their concerted attack on Evolutionism has been called by the established scientific community "a wedge strategy to restore Creationism in disguise" (Science magazine).

A New York Times Puzzler

In its issue of April 8, 2001, The New York Times, in a page-one article by James Glanz, informed his readers that in spite of some wins by Evolutionists in Kansas, Michigan, and Pennsylvania, they "find themselves arrayed not against traditional creationism, with its roots in biblical liberalism, but against a more sophisticated idea: the Intelligent Design theory."

But who, if so, was the Intelligent Designer? As I was reading the article on that Sunday morning, I was delighted to learn that

The designer may be much like the biblical God, proponents say, but they are open to other explanations, such as the proposition that life was seeded by a meteorite from elsewhere in the cosmos, or the new age philosophy that the universe is suffused with mysterious but inanimate life force.

That proponents of ID consider the bringing of life to Earth by a meteorite as one explanation, I felt, was close enough to my Sumerian explanation that the **Seed of Life** (what we now call DNA) was imparted to Earth by the invading planet Nibiru during the collision ("Celestial Battle") some 4 billion years ago

But it turned out from examining the newspaper's website and earlier editions, that the New York City edition that I was reading excised an intriguing and key sentence from the original article. Here is what the paragraph had read in its original version, with the omitted sentence highlighted:

This designer may be much like the biblical God, proponents say,
but they are open to other explanations, such as the proposition that life was seeded by a meteorite from elsewhere in the cosmos,
POSSIBLY INVOLVING EXTRATERRESTRIAL INTELLIGENCE,
or the new age philosophy that the universe is suffused with a mysterious
but inanimate life force.

"An Advanced Civilization from Another World"

As my readers know, what I have said in my books went beyond the common origin of Life (=DNA) on Earth and elsewhere in the Universe. I showed that according to the Sumerian texts(on which the biblical account of Genesis was based), Evolution took its course both on Nibiru and on Earth. Beginning much earlier on Nibiru, it produced the advanced Anunnaki on Nibiru but only early hominids on Earth when the Anunnaki had come here some 450,000 years ago. Then I wrote, the Anunnaki engaged in genetic engineering to upgrade the hominids to homo sapiens (to be in their likeness and after their image, as the Bible says).

While I was still wondering how the extraterrestrial angle was excised from the Times article on April 2001, I was delighted to read this in its editorial on March 17, 2002. Headlined *Darwinian Struggle in Ohio,* the editorial explained:

Adherence of intelligent design carefully shun any mention of God in their proposals. They simply argue that humans, animals, and plants are far too diverse and complex to be explained by evolution and natural selection, so there must have been an intelligent designer behind it all. Whether that designer is God, **AN ADVANCED CIVILIZATION FROM ANOTHER WORLD,** or some other creative force, is not specified.

The emphasis of the astounding statement is mine.

<u>Back</u> <u>to</u> <u>Enki</u>

This is quite an advance in acknowledging the Sumarian data -- from the general possibility of involvement by "Extraterrestrial Intelligence" in cosmic life to an Intelligent Designer from "an advanced civilization from another world."

It is progress spanning the tale of the collision that spread the Seed of Life to the genetic engineering by the Lord Enki.

CZ. Sitchin 2002

COMMENT: When one evaluates the Ancient Texts, relating to Evolution and Religion, we cannot refrain from expressing a definite conclusion based on the written evidence of the Anunnaki:

1. The Anunnaki evolved on Nibiru, they were not created by any god or any other cosmic deity.
They have no "missing link" disconnect or enigmas attached to

their evolution and they state that plainly, absent ambiguities.

2. The Anunnaki of the Ancient Texts are unquestionably Pan-theists. Their thinking, their knowledge, their science were derived ontologically and empirically, void of speculation, wishful thinking and certainly not bound, restricted or limited by moral, ethical or religious concepts or perceptions.

The only thirst that must be quenched, for the Anunnaki, is the thirst for Knowledge, for that is the key unlocking the ALL of the Omniscient ALL. Thoth explains the reason why the peoples of ancient civilizations regarded him and other Anunnaki's as Gods, was their **ratio of knowledge to the people's ignorance**. He also explains that "Ye too shall be gods of the future because of your knowledge far above others."

If we want to put that to a test in today's world, imagine your-self in some desolate area completely cut off from today's civilized world. When you're confronted by the belligerent, hostile indige-nous population, in your encampment, you might fire a few shotgun rounds into the air, use a

taser , turn on your portable TV, computer or DVR, slip a CD in your portable stereo system, flip out your speaker cell phone and call for help, and voila! Instant God.

Thoth-The Key of Wisdom
Wisdom is power, and power is wisdom,
One with each other, perfecting the whole

Chapter 6: Who Built Ba'albek, Nasca and the Earth's Pyramids?

When we write or talk about Ba'albek in Lebanon, The Nasca lines in South America or the Pyramids of Giza and other amazing structures and feats of engineering, the question to this day still remains, who dunit, how they dunit and why they dunit? I throw in this bit of colloquial sarcasm, simply because most everyone offers speculation and/or theories relating to the three above-named locations.

Some of our 'Ancient Astronaut Theorists' from the programs like Ancient Aliens, National Geographic, etc., go to the extreme in speculation, saying things like, they came from Syrius, they came from the constellation Phelidies or the Belt of Orion. What I would suggest to those who wish to opine, speculate, and provide theories on the subject, *read the pertinent ancient texts!*

The Lost Book of Enki-page 101, reads…

Enlil in his sky ship the extent of the Eden was surveying.

Of mountains and rivers he took account, of valleys and plains the measures he took.

Where a Landing Place to establish, a place for the rocket ships, he was seeking.

To snow covered mountains on the Edens north side and he took a liking,

The tallest trees he ever saw grew there in a cedar forest.

There above a mountain valley **with power beams the surface he flattened.**

Great stones from the hillside the heroes quarried and to size cut.

To uphold the platform with sky ships they carried in and placed them.

With satisfaction did Enlil the handiwork consider,

Donald M. Blackwell

A work beyond belief indeed it was, a structure of everlasting!

Comment: If one wants to read what the ancient text relates, in plain unadulterated words, it tells you specifically, the who, the why and the how incredulous structures were built. Let us take Ba'albek in Lebanon first and quoting from the "Godfather of the Ancient Text," Zechariah Sitchin we learn the following:

"Ba'albek: An ancient site in the Lebanon Mountains that features a vast stone-paved platform and has imposing remains of Roman temples, including the latest temple to Jupiter. These remains, stand atop much earlier structures, consisting of ever-rising stages of massive stone blocks, including (in the Western Wall) the Trilithon three colossal shaped stone blocks weighing over 1100 tons each-the largest in the world. A similar colossal stone block, whose quarrying was not completed, still remains in the quarry in a nearby valley."

Comment: So let us answer sequentially the who, the why, and where:

Who built the structure at Ba'albek? The Anunnaki did! Led namely by Enki and Enlil.

Why was Ba'albek built? "Where a Landing Place to establish, a place for the rocket ships, he was seeking.

Where was it built? Baalbek was built in Lebanon and much of the structure *still stands today!*

The question as to who was able to quarry, shape the stone blocks to within 2/1000 of an inch, transport from the quarry and put into place the many stone blocks of Ba'albek, in particular, the three put into place weighing 1100 tons? The answer is the Anunnaki, who else. There is also a stone block, weighing the same as those of the Trilithon (1100 tons) nearby in the Valley and __we do not have the technology or ability to move that stone today!__

They move the new stones and place them, as the ancient text tells us, using skyships. Sky ships that were much more technologically advanced than anything we have today!

Nasca, Nasca Lines: Located in southern Peru the full enigma of

129

Nasca has not been fathomed. We do know is related by the ancient texts, that Nasca is where the Anunnaki departed from Earth, circa 600 BC. The relative question that I firmly believe can be solved, relates to how the many miles of mountain tops were flattened, and further, where is the debris that would normally be found at the bottom of those mountains? The answer I believe to be. " There above a mountain valley _**with power beams the surface he flattened!**_ " If the Anunnaki, did this in Lebanon and in Israel, as they have clearly indicated in the ancient text and realizing that Nasca was where the Anunnaki last departed Earth, in my opinion, that 2+2 equals four. In using a beam so powerful that it could flatten mountains it would seem logical to think that the debris would also be disintegrated. Yet another thought comes to mind......

We know that the pictographs, the 300 geometric patterns, the 800 straight lines, at Nasca, covers an amazing 200 mi.^{2} Would it be illogical to think that the debris, from the flattening of the mountains, could have been dispersed over that 200 mi.^{2}? We know that the surface stone, covering those 200 mi.^{2}, is 4 to 12 inches deep. The natural layer of Earth, at Nasca, is more of a limestone color, while the 4 to12-inch layer, is the color ocher. The color ocher is described as being a reddish-brown containing iron, used as a pigment. Once the numerous mountains had been flattened and the ocher-colored debris dispersed over the 200 mi.^{2}, then they (the Anunnaki) could draw all of the pictographs they wanted?

The Giza pyramids: In another part of this book I'm going to go into detail and explain that the Anunnaki and Anunnaki alone, built the three Giza Pyramids and so many others worldwide. So here a more limited explanation should suffice.

The ancient text, on page 101, that I have outlined, explains how they quarried, cut, shaped, transported and put into place granite stones of 1100 tons. Those `Trilithon' stones were far and away much larger than any stones that were cut, quarried, and put in place, building the Giza pyramids.

Chapter 7: Who Built the Giza Plateau Pyramids?

It is quite perplexing to me and I am sure also to other authors and readers of the ancient text, as to why there is any controversy whatsoever, as to who built the Giza pyramids? I will not offer to the reader of this book my opinion; what I will offer is documentation that the reader can evaluate for themselves. Documentation of what was written millennia ago by the Anunnaki's Sumerian Texts. Although I have studied the ancient texts for the past 25+ years, I do not present myself to the reader as an expert relating to the ancient text, as my intent here is to separate fact from fiction. I want to present the written words of the Anunnaki, as they themselves tell us, with no religious, political, social or cultural objectives. To relate, from their written words, revealing who, what, where and why the ancient Giza Pyramids were built, and pyramids built all over the world which has such striking similarities and comparable methodology of engineering.

All of the pyramids and all of the large megalithic structures around the world, built by the Anunnaki are *earthquake-proof!* We find metal braces inserted in Keystone cuts in Egypt, Ethiopia, India, Greece, Italy, Vietnam, Angkor Wat in Cambodia, Ollantaytambo in Peru, Puma Punku in Bolivia, and Tiwanaku in Bolivia.

The Keystones adjoining the blocks are filled with molten metal alloys. We know that alloys (a substance that is a mixture of two or more metals) were not discovered until about 2500 B. C., and many of those structures have proven to have been built prior to that date. We also know that the combination of metals sometimes included copper, *silver, and gold.* Would we today use silver and gold to manufacture Keystones? Of course not, because both are commodities of high-value and have commercial utility. So we have to ask ourselves, why were those two materials used in ancient structures!? The answer is because the Anunnaki used them simply as another available material. Prior to 2500 B. C., and millennia after that date, gold had no monetary or commercial value.

"The Divine Blueprint," authored by Freddie Silva, approaches the building of the Great Pyramid from a very unique geodetic sense, that being "of or concerned with the measurement of the earth and its surface." For example:

1. The Great Pyramid is aligned at 3/60 of 1° true North. The structure is credited with being the most accurately aligned to true North on Earth.

2. The alignment of the Great Pyramid through Its cardinal and ordinal directions, places it at the center of the world's landmass.

3. In the summer and winter solstice from above the Great Pyramid, one can look down and see an eight-sided pyramid.

4. From corner to corner the Grand Pyramid measures exactly 365.242 royal cubits. (1.86 feet) that is the Earth's year, measured in days, down to 1/4th of a day.

5. The exact coordinates of the Great Pyramid equal 29.9792458° North. This equates exactly to the speed of light traveling through space.

This kind of information serves as a redundant empirical message which says to anyone with common sense, *the Egyptians could not possibly have built the three Plaza Pyramids and let's take it one step further; where is it written, that any Egyptian states, in any form of writing that I, or we, the indigenous Egyptians, built the three Plaza Pyramids?* Where are the plans, or where are they manuscripts, where is there anything in writing, either on a papyrus manuscript, pyramid,, Mesopotamian ziggurats, step pyramids buildings of any kind, cave walls, are on a two-holer outhouse that would either directly or indirectly imply that the Egyptians had the "mathematical," " geological,", "architectural," "astrological", "cosmological," etc., know-how to build those three pyramids. The answer is, there is **nothing written** that in any way would guide anyone with common sense to say, here's the reason we can even infer, or abstractly prove that any Egyptians built the three Plaza Pyramids. The reason why there is absolutely no evidence pointing, either directly or indirectly, to the Egyptians building the three Plaza Pyramids is *simply that THEY DIDN'T!*

On the other side of the ledger, we have the ancient Sumerian texts and individualized personal writings of the Anunnaki, namely Enki, Ningishzida/Thoth and Geb for example ***WHO CLEARLY STATE, REPEATEDLY, IN WRITING THAT THEY BUILT THE THREE PLAZA PYRAMIDS!*** So let us ignore all that and continue to posit the propaganda, continuously and profusely issued by the Egyptian government, Mr. Zahi Hawass and his Antiquities authorities, that the indigenous Egyptians built all 155 of the pyramids located in Egypt and especially the Great Pyramid. I believe firmly that the following information, which I've labored over for years, will prove definitively as to who built the pyramids.

Let's go back to the writings of Manetho, who tells us that Ptah (Enki, Ea) reigned in Egypt for 9000 years. Followed by the pre-Diluvial reign by Shu and then his son a 500-year reign of Geb, (all descendants of Ptah/Enki) resulting in a circa data 10,000 BC. It was at that time that **the Spaceport in the Sinai and the Giza pyramids were built.**

We know also from the Sumerian text that the three Giza Pyramids, were conceived by the Anunnaki, Enki/Ptah, the engineering charts, plans, and mathematical configurations were laid out and planned by the Anunnaki, Ra/Marduk. The three pyramids were built by the Anunnaki, Geb (`He who heeps up') and fully equipped, with the latest technology, by the Anunnaki, Thoth.

The Attestation of Endubsar: The Lost Book of Enki 10th Tablet page 235 – 238

Now, this is the account of the new Place of the Celestial Chariots,

And the artifice twin mounts and how the image of the lion by Marduk was usurped.

Let the Landing Place in the Cedar Mountains be part of the facilities! he said.

The distance between the Landing Place and the Chariot Place he measured,

In the midst thereof a place for the new Mission Control Center he designated:

There a suitable mount be selected, the Mount of Way Showing he named it.

The Landing Path on the twin peaks of Arrata in the North were anchored;

To demarcate the Landing Corridors Enlil two other sets of Twin Peaks required,

To delimit the Landing Corridor's boundary, ascent, and descent to secure.

In the southern part of the desolate peninsula, a place of mountains, he anchored.

Twin adjoining peaks Enlil selected, on them, the southern delimit he anchored.

Where the second set of twin peaks was required, mountains there were none

Only a flatland above the water clogged valley from the ground up protruded.

Artificial peaks thereon we can raise! So did Ningishzidda/Thoth to the leaders say.

On a tablet, the image of smooth-sided, skyward racing peaks for them he drew.

On the flat land, above the rivers valley, Ningishzidda a scale model built,

The rising angles and force move sides with it he perfected.

Next, to a larger peak, he placed, its sides of four corners he set;

By the Anunnaki, <u>with their tools of power, there were stones cut and erected.</u>

Comment: How much empirical evidence does the world authorities need, to give up their ignominy, their obvious purposely induced feigned ignorance and admit, **THE ANUNNAKI BUILT THE THREE GIZA PYRAMIDS!!** This statement is directed specifically to anyone who claims to be the most ambiguous, 1. Ancient Astronaut Theorists, 2. The Egyptian authorities in Cairo, Egypt, headed by Mr. Dogma, "We the Egyptian people built the Grand Pyramid," A.K.A. Zahi Hawass 3. J.J. Hartak Ph.D., author of The Book of Knowledge: The Keys of Enoch 4. Stephen S Mehler M. A. Director of Research, Great Pyramid of Giza Research Association 5. Ancient Aliens Series 6. National Geographic 7. Science Channel 8. History Channel 9. Nova 10. Any author who has written about the Grand Pyramid of Egypt and not used the ancient text as documentation to support their argument!

Ancient text continued –

Beside it, in a precise location, the peak that was its twin he placed;

With galleries and chambers for pulsating crystals, he designed it.

When this artful peak an admixture by Gibil fashioned was the Apex Stone made.

The sunlight to the horizon it reflected, by night like a pillar of fire it was,

The power of all the crystals to the heavens in a beam it focused.

When the artful works, by Ningishzidda /Thoth designed, were completed and ready,

The Anunnaki leaders the Great Twin Peak (*THE GRAND PYRA-MID)* entered, at what they saw they marveled;

Ekur, House Which Like a Mountain Is, they named it, a beacon to see the heavens it was.

That the Anunnaki the Deluge survived and prevailed forever it proclaimed.

Comment: The above statement, seemingly benign, is rather profound in my opinion. The reason is that it highlights the fact that the three pyramids of Giza and the Spnyxs, **were built by the Anunnaki, sometime after the Ice Age ending around 13,000 BC. Specifically from Mentheo's writings (as mentioned above) that Ptah/Enki ruled for 9000 years, then his son Shu ruled Pre-Diluvial and another son Geb (the Anunnaki who actually built the Grand Pyramid (ruled for the next 500 years. That gives us a circa date, of the building of the Grand Pyramid and the Spinks, at 10,000 BC.**

Ancient Text continued –

Now the new Place of the Celestial Chariots gold from across the seas can receive,

From it the chariots to Nibiru the gold; for survival will carry;

From it to the East, where the Sun on the designated day rises, they will ascend,

To it to the southwest, where the Sun on the designated day sets, they will descend!

Then Enlil by his own hand the Nibiru crystals activated.

Inside eerie lights began to flicker, an enchanting hum the stillness broke;

Outside the capstone all at once was shining, brighter than the Sun it was.

The multitude of assembled Anunnaki a great cry of joy uttered;

House that is like a mountain, house with the pointed peak,

For Heaven-Earth it is equipped, ***THE HANDIWORK OF THE ANUNNAKI IT IS.***

For the celestial boats (spacecraft) it was put together, ***BY THE***

ANUNNAKI BUILT,

House whose interior with a reddish light of heavens will,

Lofty mountain of mountains, great and lofty fashioned,

BEYOND THE UNDERSTANDING OF EARTHLINGS IT IS!

Comment: Who were the earthlings the Anunnaki were referring too? That refers to any earthling that was alive on the face of the earth when the pyramids were built. And when the pyramid was built, in my opinion, circa 10,500 BC, **the pharaonic dynasty** *was millennia away from even existing!* **The Egyptians did not build the Grand Pyramid!**

Ancient Text continued –

House that for the rocket ships is a landmark, with unfathomable insides,

While the Anunnaki their remarkable handiwork were celebrating,

Enki to Enlil words of suggestion said: When **in the future it will be asked,**

When and by whom has this marvel been fashioned?

Left us beside the Twin Peaks a monument create, the Age of the Lion let it announce,

The age of **Ningishzidda** *(Thoth) the peaks' designer, let its* **face** *be,*

Let it precisely toward the Place of the Celestial Chariots gaze,

Let the gazing lion, precisely eastward facing, with Ningishzidda's image be!

When the work to cut and shape **the lion from the bedrock** *was proceeding,*

In my erstwhile domain are the artifice mounts situated, *on the lion the image mine must be!*

Comment: I say to all of those who have studied the ancient text to any degree, to the professional Egyptologists, Archaeologists, Astrologists, Engineers, Mathematicians, authors and theorists, that after reading this *prima facie* evidence, which can be self verified, as to who built the pyramids, why the pyramids were built, where the pyramids were built, and when the pyramids were built, **if you cannot accept this documentation, written more than 4000 years ago, then I relegate you to being in a state of inferred ignorance, historical denial and fearing ignominy!**

Taken from, The Emerald Tablets of Thoth:

Builded I the Great Pyramids,

Patterned after the pyramids of Earth force

Burning eternally so that it too,

Might remain through the ages.

The face on the Sphinx. from the Attestation of Endubsar -12th Tablet:

Marduk as Ra, the Bright One, was worshiped;

Enki as Ptah, the Developer, was venerated.

Ningishzidda/Thoth as Tehuti, the Divine Measurer, was recalled;

(Those three names Ra,/ Marduk, Ptah/Enki and Tehuti/Thoth, place those three individuals *only* in the pre- Egyptian pantheon)

To ease his memory *Ra* on the Stone Lion *his image with that of his son Asar replaced.*

Not only does this ancient text tell us who the faces were on the Sphinx it tells us further **that the Sphynx was originally constructed with the head of a lion.** The rest of the body structure on the Sphinx could only be that of a lion. This is further confirmed in the 10th Tablet: The Lost Book of Enki

Let us beside the Twin Peaks a monument create,

the Age of the Lion let it announce,

The image of Ningishzidda, the peaks' designer, **let its face be.**

Comment: Dr. Robert M. Schock, a Boston University and Yale University graduate geologist, relating to his meteorological and seismic studies of the Sphynx, that its' layering indicates that it was carved out of the native rock. (This is exactly what the Anunnaki tell us, as previously stated in this chapter) He further states that the study of precipitation-induced weathering and watermarks on the Sphinx, "indicated that work on the Sphinx had begun in the period Between 10,000 BC and 5000 BC when the Egyptian climate was wetter."

What his findings brought about was stern refutations by other geologists, Egyptologists, and `scientific' organizations. To their way of thinking, Dr. Schock's professional opinion cannot be tolerated as it flies in the face of everything they currently knew.

Mark Lerner, an archaeologist, who considers himself an "expert" on the Spynx offers this critique "You don't overthrow Egyptian history based on one phenomenon like a weathering profile… That is how pseudoscience is done, not real science." Ronald H Fritz, a "historian," describes Dr. Schock as being a "pseudo-historical and pseudo-scientific writer".

The ongoing debunkers argument basically is, dating back to 5000, 7000 and 9000 B. C., that there was no civilization, technologically advanced enough to carve out the Sphynx. Mark Lerner states "The people during that age were hunters and gatherers; they didn't bill cities." With that microscopic statement, I'm in full agreement. So the question must then be, if the indigenous populations could not possibly have built the pyramids, the Sphynx and Gobeki Tepi, etc. *then there had to be someone other than the indigenous populations that built those structures* **and that `someone other,' was `none other' than what the ancient texts, blatantly and repetitively tell us, THE ANUNNAKI BUILT THOSE THREE STRUCTURES!** (I have read some of what the archaeologist Mark Lerner has written and what he is said on various and sundry television programs. He considers himself an expert, and I consider him **not** an expert.

There is no written proof, inside or outside the Giza pyramids, that they were built by Khufu, Chefra, and Menkaura! The Giza pyramids stand unique, as there are no inscriptions on their walls, no representative Stale, no royal seals, no Pharaoh represented in effigy and without any decorative features, dedication or attribution of any kind. The "other" pyramids built in Egypt, by the indigenous Egyptians (today's estimate is about 152) for the most part represent nothing more than collapsed rubble, and are so unsafe that the public is not allowed near them, never mind inside them! In addition, the "other" pyramids built by the various Egyptian dynasties exhibit only **descending** features viz, tunneling, corridors, inner parts, etc. while the Great Pyramid presents highly complex inner components that are hundreds of feet **above ground level.**

Further in Zechariah Sitchin's third book of the Earth Chronicles, entitled "The Wars of Gods and Men," he relates that during the Pyramid Wars, the Anunnaki gods ruled Egypt, millennia before any Pharaonic dynasties were established. Those established Sumerian texts, substantiate and lend credence, that the Anunnaki alone built the Giza pyramids **millennia before the Pharaonic dynasties existed!**............ But there is more!

When we examine the Victory Tablet of King Menes, also referred to as the Narmer Palette, we find the King wearing the white crown of Upper Egypt, on the other side, King Menes is shown wearing the red crown of Lower Egypt which is the geographic location of the Giza pyramids. The pictographs on the Narmer Palette, circa 3100 BC, indicate clearly a smooth-sided triangular pyramid. What must be pointed out and highlighted here is that King Menes **was the first king of the very first Dynasty!** Further, circa 3100 BC clearly indicates that **the Grand Pyramid was built at least 500 years before Khufu came into power**! This is empirical and pictorial evidence that *the pyramids existed*

long before the Zoser, Zer, or Khufu dynasties were ever established!............
But there is more!

Let me refer now to the Godfather of the ancient texts, Zechariah Sitchin. There are not enough laudable adjectives to describe the attributes of this man whose dogged, unrelenting research efforts, and the most skillful interpretation, relating to the ancient text, have, in my opinion, resulted in the most profound historical revelations and writings..... ***EVER!*** I will yield to his written word taking from his, "Journeys of the Mystical Past" something that is **written in stone!**

Indeed, inscriptions on a stone artifact belonging to Cheops-in which his name Khufu is clearly written in hieroglyphics-imply that **the Great Pyramid had already existed in his time, and so did the Sphynxs!** *(Figure 1)*

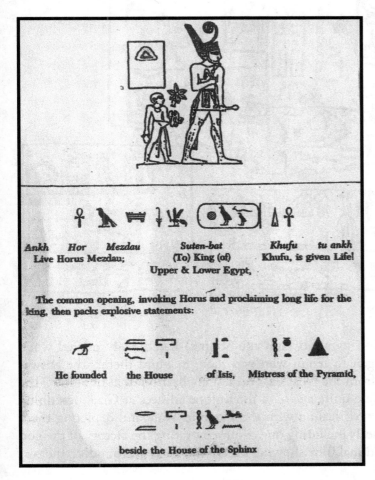

figure 1

In this monument known as the **Inventory Stela,** Khufu took credit for restoring a shrine to the goddess Isis, "Mistress of the Pyramid." He does not take credit for the pyramid itself, clearly considering it a structure belonging to god's, (the Anunnaki, my parentheses) not mortals; and he states that the shrine stood "beside the house of the Spinks" – the very Sphynxs, which according to Egyptology goal tenets, was erected (or carved out) by Khufu's *successor Chefra...*

In fact, depictions of the Sphinx **were already found on stone tablets belonging to the earliest Pharaohs Menes-Narmer and Zer**. Clearly, the Spinks had already existed when Khufu and Chefra ascended their thrones. *(Figure 2)*

figure 2

If the Giza pyramid (and the Sphinx) had already existed when Pharaohs began to reign, who was there to build them? The answer comes to us from the Near East earliest civilization, that of Sumer. The Sumerians were quite aware of the unique edifices at Giza, describing them in the text dealing with the Pyramid Wars and depicting them on cylinder seals Including one commemorating the victory of the god Ninurta (Anunnaki) by showing his Divine Eagle surrounding the two large pyramids.

"The story of the "Pyramid Wars" is told in *The Wars of Gods and Men*. The Story of how the Giza Pyramids and Spinks came to be built, by the gods, as vital components of their post -Diluvial Spaceport, has been told in my book The Stairway to Heaven."

"Gods, not man, built the Giza pyramids as terminals for the Landing-Corridor that was anchored on the twin peaks of Ararat in the North and on two natural peaks in the Sinai Peninsula in the southeast (fig...); absent such peaks at the North Eastern terminus, the gods first erected the small pyramid as a test of structural stability and function-ality, then built the other larger two – equipping the Great Pyramid with pulsating guidance equipment in the unique upper innards." *(Figure 3 and 4)*

figure 3 and 4

Comment: When such ancient text as the above described, Narmer Palette and the Inventory Stela are used for lending credence to a given subject matter, as Mr. Zechariah Sitchin always does, you always have the naysayers, the negative Nabobs and certain authors are going to claim that these ancient texts were forged. I believe the reason for this is that if they stuck to using only empirical evidence, *of the ancient texts, they wouldn't have anything to write about, because it has already been documented and covered by Zechariah Sitchin's, "The Earth Chronicles."* Mr. Sitchin's analysis and conclusions relating to the two above named ancient texts **was published 37 years ago!** That begs the question, where have the naysayers and nabobs been since 1980?

There are experts and authors (add me to the list) who agree with Mr. Sitchin's analysis as to who built the pyramids. Authors, Robert Bauval and Graham Hancock, both agreed with and support in writing, Mr. Sitchin's analysis and conclusions relating to the ancient texts, Narmer Palette, and Inventory Stella.

The Narmer Palette was written 2670 years ago, or 670 BC. The Inventory Stela was written 5200 years ago or 3200 BC! That said, I pose this question to all: Why would these ancient texts be written **as an intended forgery**? Who did they intend to deceive? To accept any of the ancient texts as being written as intended forgeries would be quite banal!

Let me resort back to an ancient text that was written more than 4000 years ago:
The attestation of Endubsar, The Fourth Tablet.

Enlil in his sky ship the extent of the Eden was surveying.

Of the mountains and rivers he took account, of valleys and plains the measures he took.

Where a landing place to establish, a place for the rocket ships, he was seeking.

To snow-covered mountains on the Edens north side, he took a liking,

The tallest trees he ever saw grew there in a cedar forest.

There above a mountain valley **with power beams the surface he flattened.**

Great stones from the hillside the heroes quarried and to size cut.

To uphold the platform with sky ships they carried in and placed them.

With satisfaction did Enlil the handiwork consider.

A WORK BEYOND BELIEF INDEED IT WAS, A SCRIPTURE OF EVERLASTING!

Comment: Let me reiterate what I have already written in this book: If one wants to read what the ancient texts relate, in plain words, it tells you specifically, the who, the why and the how many incredulous structures were built. Let us take Ba'albek in Lebanon as an excellent example and quoting from the "Godfather of the Ancient Texts," Zechariah Sitchin, we learn the following;

Ba'albek: An ancient site in the Lebanon Mountains that features a vast stone-paved platform and has imposing remains of Roman temples, including the latest temple to Jupiter. These remains, stand atop much earlier structures, consisting of ever-rising stages of massive stone blocks, including (in the Western Wall) the Trilithon-three colossal shaped stone blocks weighing over 1100 times each-the largest in the world. A similar colossal stone block, whose quarrying was not completed, still remains in the quarry in a nearby valley."

The reason I use Ba'albek as proof, **empirical evidence,** of what the Anunnaki built, is for one reason..... To clearly point out and emphasize that if the Anunnaki built Ba'albek in Lebanon, **using the largest quarried stones known to mankind,** *stones so massive that we do not have the current technological know-how nor means, to move 1 foot,........* **Who could deny, with any logical reasoning, that** _THE ANUNNAKI BUILT THE PYRAMID'S!_

PYRAMID BLOCKING STONES

I would like to throw this in for good measure, taken from the 12th Tablet of the Attestation of Endubsar

Into the upper chamber, the place of the Great Pulsing Stone, Murdoch retreated,

At its entrance Marduk the sliding stone blocks lowered; from one and all admission they barred.

23 blocking stones, ready for letting down, Ishkur their attention drew.

Comment: The three sliding blocking stones have been found by Egyptologists, Archaeologists, etc. As I understand it, they are still functional. The blocking stones were slid into place via a ramp, built by the Anunnaki inside the Great Pyramid.

I want to equate/compare what our technological capabilities are today, to the Anunnaki' technological capabilities, of millennia past.

In Riverside California, February 2012, heavy equipment moving company was hired to move a stone weighing 680,000 pounds or 341 tons, from the Stone Valley Materials Quarry to the Los Angeles County Museum of Art. The labor force required workers from more than 100 utility crews.

The owner of the heavy equipment moving company stated, "We had to use hydraulic jacks to lift the rock off the ground and this was done with extreme difficulty." A 1,000,000 pound crane was required. A 44 axle trailer rig powered by 2400 hp engine and 208 tires were required supporting the steel gutters underneath.

With one power unit of 2400 hp pulling it and one power unit of 2400 hp pushing it, the trailer rig achieved the amazing speed of 5 mi./h. The travel distance from the Stone Valley Materials Quarry, in Riverside California, to the LA Museum was 100 miles, therefore taking 20 hours. Placing this massive stone named, "Levitated Mass" into a viewing position, required what would again necessarily be described as extremely difficult and many more man-hours.

The owner of the moving company stated, "The 340-ton rock, described by modern standards is a gigantic payload and how the ancients did it, I have no idea. It's crazy to think about It! So with the aforementioned information in mind, let us apply something which is not so "common" with our so-called "resident experts," and Egyptologists, it's called Common Sense!

The attributed builder of the Great Pyramid Is the Pharaoh Khufu. I chuckle when I see the last two letters of his name. The Grand Pyramid was supposedly built during Khufu's reign. Most frequently I have read that he reigned for 17 years. The highest number of years attributed to Khufu's reign is 23 and that is the figure I will use. Khufu had to build the Grand Pyramid within that period of time. The number of blocks stones used the build the Grand Pyramid is 2,400,000. (Author Graham Hancock estimates the number to be 2,500,000.)

There are 24 hours in a day, multiplied by 365 days, equals 8760 hours per year.

Multiplying 8760 hours per year, times 23 years, equals 201,480 hours.

60 min. in one hour, times 201,480 hours, equals 12,088,800 min. in 23 years.

12,088,800 min. divided by 2,400,000 stones used to build the Grand Pyramid.

This equates placing a stone in place every 5.037 min.

Watching a program on National Geographic, their intent was to demonstrate clearly how a 1-ton sandstone could be quarried, transported to the Grand Pyramid, chiseled to a close tolerance specification, and then animating to the audience that "This is how it was done."

After the hour-long program, I literally leaned back in my chair and laughed out loud. If you don't laugh at this kind of asinine, foolish and absurd programs presented on the boob tube, you will do an awful lot of crying!

To begin, 1 ton would be one of the smallest limestone blocks used in the building of the Grand Pyramid. Next, they quarried limestone **and placed it in the back of the truck,** then transported the limestone block in a location near the Grand Pyramid so that you could watch the workers "fashion" the stone, with the Grand Pyramid in full view in the background. They took the one-ton limestone block, using six men with one additional man supervising, and "fashioned" the 1-ton block into a rectangle. Instead of using copper chisels etc. **they used metal chisels, metal saws, and metal hammers.** Further, they never had any intention of demonstrating how they would align and put the sandstone block in place, never mind demonstrating how they would take the sandstone block, elevate it some, let's say 200 or 300 feet and placed it accurately, on top of an existing sandstone.

The so-called demonstration of "That's how it was done" remembering that they were working on sandstone and not granite, remembering that they used a heavy-duty truck to deliver the sandstone to the given location, not pulling it via sled, or using logs to roll the sandstone, remembering that they used metal tools, not copper tools., Yes, one needs to remember all that, however; what I most remember is that *it took them a day and a half!* Some of these television programs I've watched in some of the books that I have read can only be described as bizarre!

If we use the above criteria of quarrying one stone, transporting it to the location of the Great Pyramid, shaping the stone to the required block form, taking 36 hours, multiplying that by 2,400,000 limestone blocks used to complete the pyramid, it would've taken them, **working 24/7, 365 days a year,** 86,400,000 hours or 9, 863 years, **not to build the Grand Pyramid, but simply to quarry, transport and crudely shape a 1 ton block.**

Let's not forget that they used modern power tools to quarry the rock, modern transportation to location and all-metal tools, knowing that some of the Grand pyramid blocks were granite and not limestone, some weighing more than 100 tons, modified to be perfectly square, perfectly level and many were modified to the **specifications of .002 thousands of an inch. (.002 is the required specifications for the building of our spacecraft!")**

The Aswan granite quarry, used for the building of the Great Pyramid, is located 500 miles from the Great Pyramid. What becomes quite clear is that each step necessary to build the Grand Pyramid points out and makes crystal clear, **that it was absolutely impossible for the ancient indigenous population to have built the Great Pyramid, or other amazing structures at, Puma Punku, Gobekli Tepe, Tiahuanaco, Ba'albek, Chichen Itza' Machu Picchu, Uxmal, Palenque, Copan, Tical,Ollantaytambo, Stonehenge, Tenochtitlan, Teotihuacan, Dibilchaltun, Tulman, Mayapan, Uxmal, Cusco, Sacsayhuaman, Qunqo, Tambomachay, Pukapukara, Pisac, Sillustani, Isla Del Sol, (Titicaca Lake) Chavin de Huantar, and Izamal. Etc.**

Of all the above named places, which is certainly not all-inclusive, located ubiquitously, all over the world: *the three pyramids which include the Grand Pyramid located in Cairo Egypt ARE THE "ONLY STRUCTURES IN THE WORLD" WHEREBY THE LOCAL AU-THORITIES LAY CLAIM AND REPEATEDLY AND ADAMANT-LY STATE THAT THEY WERE BUILT BY THE INDIGENOUS*

POPULATION! Let me repeat, "THE ONLY PLACE IN THE WORLD!"

Let's put ourselves in the place of the Egyptians who are preparing to build the Great Pyramid.

The tools we are going to use will be a wooden square, a plumb bob, some rope, copper chisels, hammers and saws, and oscillating rope drill, a container with water in it for leveling measurements and a whole bunch of people.

We will make this pyramid 480 feet high.

We will necessarily have to build the pyramids slope angle to 52°, linking the pyramid's base length and height to a circle's (pi symbol here) Page 21 Journeys of the Mystical Path

Use the distance between our elbow and our fingertips to determine a royal cubit measurement of 1.86 feet.

Using our geodetic knowledge, we will use a sundial to determine true North, which will be 3/60 of 1° true North, which will be the most accurate measurement on Earth.

This will align the pyramid with the true cardinal and ordinal directions North, South, East, and West.

This will place our pyramid at the exact center of the world's landmass.

The corners of the pyramid will measure 365.242 cubits which are the exact measurement of Earth's year, down to one-quarter of the day.

We will make the exact geographical coordinate of the pyramid to be 29.9792458° North, which all of us Egyptians know, that 299,792,458 mi./h is the speed of light.

The four sides of our pyramid will be so brilliantly engineered in a slight convex position, that on the Winter Solstice of December 21, at daybreak and the Summer Solstice of July 22, at sunset, looking from above the pyramid, relating to the shadows cast on the pyramid, one can see that it is in fact, eight-sided.

We will make this pyramid earthquake-proof as it will stand forever.

That will require us to use metal braces inserted in the Keystone cuts of adjoining blocks.

That will require the use of alloys and since metallurgy has not been invented yet, we will have to ask somebody.

So shall it be written, so shall it be done!

Then most importantly after we finish, we will hold up our wet finger to determine which way the wind is blowing.

If someone asked, "Are you Egyptian builders familiar with the term Pi?"

Answer: "Yes, I had a piece last night, after supper."

A question please, do any of you know what an angle is?

Answer: " Yes, of course, we know what angle is, there are four of them, up, down, left, and right!"

Another question please, how are you going to measure in cubits the 480 feet being the height of the pyramid?

Answer: "Well we certainly know the measurement of a royal cubit using the distance between our elbow and our fingertips to be 1.86 feet. Therefore it is quite obvious that we will need exactly 258.06451 men to stand on top of each other's shoulders and mark the measured top spot by spitting on the fingertip of the last man."

A question please, can you define what geographical means?

Answer: "Certainly not, there aren't any giraffes in Egypt!"

A question please, how are you going to shape the granite blocks, inside the pyramid, to conform to the .002 of an inch requirement?

Answer: "That's easy, we will use what we always use to sand anything, the bark of a Sequoia tree."

A question please, how are you going to cut and quarry the stones for the pyramid.

Answer: "We have each, already borrowed our favorite Egyptian pharaohs pocketknife.

A question please, how are you going to transport a 20 ton stone from the quarry site, 500 miles away, to the great pyramid?

Answer: "We will have to slide it from the quarry site to the great pyramid. And that is going to take an awful lot of camel dung.

A question please, how are you going to lift a 20 ton stone into place?

Answer: "That is one of the major problems that we face, however; we are still going to get it done, even though it means a lot of hernias.

The question please, why are you using copper tools to build the pyramids when inside the pyramid, brass is used in several different places? Answer: "How am I supposed to know that? You are really starting to irritate me and to any further questions, my response will be, kiss my brass!"

Now I want to inform everyone in his pyramid-building group that the Pharaoh has requested that those selected must have a good basic understanding of Pharaonic and Egyptian history, and therefore I asked this question, are you familiar with Tutankhamun?
 Answer: Of course we are, that is when all of the people who helped build this Grand Pyramid, once finished, on the days of the winter and summer solstice we will all lineup on the north side of the finished pyramid....... and brake wind on cue.
Well, I will not ask any further questions, but I will offer this, "I think your sundial is running a little slow!"

To quote Brian Foster, author of several excellent books including, "A Brief History of the Incas," "Power was used by the ancients and not human power. To shape, cut and place stones could only be done using high power machine tools." "Stones were removed with such accuracy that a scratch cannot be found on the surface." "This is not a question of sweat or man-hours, it's a question of technology."

Even as of this current date of 2018, if you go on the Internet or read the vast majority of books currently written, Khufu is still being accredited for building the Great Pyramid! Why must we steadfastly maintain that whatever structure was built, where ever it was built, however spectacular, marvelous, mystifying, stupefying dumbfounding, or totally unexplainable, unimaginable and enigmatic, that *it was built by the indigenous population at that time!* That kind of thinking is closer to the other end of the horse.

Another interesting factor relating to the building of the Great Pyramid:

The **only** metal that the Egyptian population had to use was copper. Yet inside the Grand pyramid is bronze, an alloy of tin and copper. There are two tremendously large stone doors inside the Grant Pyramid, that are still *perfectly functional today!* **Those two huge stone doors have brass hinges! Not to mention several other locations in the Grand pyramid where bronze is used.** Depending upon the percentage admixture of tin and copper, bronze can be made to be 10, 20, 30, 40 or 50 times more durable/harder than copper. That one point alone poignantly stands out as a sine qua non, proving that **the indigenous population of Egypt could not possibly have built any of the three Giza pyramids!**

Now we have to ask ourselves if the Egyptians did not have the use of bronze, who did? From the 12th Tablet of the Attestation of Endubsar, I give you this:

How what a new metal from stones was extracted he showed them:
ANUNNAKI MADE, he called it,
How by *combining it with the abundant copper a strong metal (bronze) he invented, he showed them.*

THE GREAT PYRAMID FORGERY

What I want to do with this remaining segment is to provide "the nail in the coffin," the "coup d'état," as to who built the pyramids. The information and documentation pertaining to answering the question, who built the pyramids, once and for all, has already been published in the first chapter of Zechariah Sitchin's book,` *Journeys to the Mythical Past.'*

One might ask if I am so confident that the question of who built the pyramids has already been answered, why am I trying to add to it? The answer being, that his writings have been pushed aside, sidelined and sadly, mostly ignored. The reason being is, if his writings were accepted to be the forefront of empirical knowledge relating to all of the ancient texts subject matter, as it most rightly should be, many authors, many National Geographic programs, many Ancient Alien Programs, and many documentary programs, would have little or nothing to say or write about, as the Ancient Text and the writings and decades upon decades of dogged research resulting in his books, "The Earth Chronicles Series," **answers all the questions that have been asked in the**

past and all of the questions that are currently being asked!

In 2005 I attended a Zechariah Sitchin seminar in Dallas Texas. Part of his presentation related to his visit to the Grand Pyramid of Giza. His visit was to prove once and for all that as he states in his book, "I entered the pyramid that day to prove that Pharaoh Cheops *did not* build the Great Pyramid."

Mr. Sitchin animated to the, 200 or so attending the seminar, that his visit that fateful day was authorized, planned and coordinated with the Egyptian authorities and more specifically through the Egyptian "Curator" Zawi Hawass. As Mr. Sitchin described it in his book, "I was inside the Grand Pyramid at the Top of the Grand Gallery, waiting to climb up by a series of ladders into compartments above the Kings Chamber, when I suddenly felt a mighty blow to my head: Someone had dropped from higher up a large and heavy piece of wood that knocked me down." "Warmblood began to pour down from the top of my head, and I was certain that my skull had been cracked." He further added "I was certain that what happened *was no accident.*

What Mr. Sitchin revealed to all of those attending his seminar and did not reveal in his book, is this: Mr. Sitchin wanted to enter the Kings Chamber and other compartments for the sole purpose of **obtaining a scratched off sample of the red paint (to have it carbon-dated) wherein Cheops name had been written as proof that Cheops had built the Grand Pyramid.**

Zawi Hawass, the "Grand" Egyptian Curator would have none of it. He knew definitively why Mr. Sitchin was entering the Grand Pyramid. If Zechariah had come out of that pyramid with a red paint sample, the Great Pyramid forgery would have been exposed to the world, and Mr. Zechariah Sitchin's world preeminence would be firmly established.

Mr. Sitchin was not there to enhance his reputation, he was there, as he always had been, looking for empirical evidence, otherwise known as the truth. And there are those out there who would literally kill to keep that truth hidden. I won't mention any names as that would be a "Curator" offense.

Did this attempt, on Mr. Sitchin's life, deter him in any way? The obvious answer is no because Mr. Sitchin continued to question, analyze, research, tirelessly travel and look for answers in his own inimitable way. The fruits of his labor lie in the 14 books Mr. Sitchin wrote, known worldwide as "The Earth Chronicles." I will also add to that and non-proffer the following:

We know that the Egyptians built more than 100 pyramids geographically located by the Nile River's delta in the north and extending southward to Nubia. They were all built **after** the Giza Pyramids as Egyptians tried to emulate the Anunnaki's building of the three Giza pyramids. We know that some of those pyramids are elaborately decorated while others exhibit few voids of inscriptions or decorations. We know that there are no royal burials ever discovered inside any pyramid. The 100 or so pyramids that the Egyptians did try to build, compared to the three Giza pyramids are inferior to the extreme. The stones themselves are roughly hewn and the between the stones, mortar consisted of mud-clay and tree stalks. But they used for sandpaper was tree bark (Try that on a piece of granite) The methodology of the Egyptians in building "their" pyramids, was not exactly a recipe for stability.

If you want to visit the Giza Pyramids today as a tourist, do not count on visiting any one of the hundred or so pyramids that the Egyptians built, as they are in a state of collapse and are unsafe. The Egyptians could never come close to emulating the Grand Pyramid.

It Is conveyed and revealed historically, that Khufu built the Grand Pyramid of Giza and asked Mr. Sitchin tells us, "Khufu's success – so the textbooks tell us – inspired his successors to build their pyramid next to his, at Giza. One that outwardly emulates the Grand Pyramid, was built by the Pharaoh Chefra and is known as the *second pyramid*; Then his successor, Menkaura built nearby the *third pyramid*-- but for inexplicable reasons, is a miniature of the other two. The three were perfectly aligned to the cardinal points of the compass and to each other, forming an architectural unit as though they were planned by a single architect and not by three different pharaohs separated by a century."

"Unlike the other pyramids, the three Giza pyramids are devoid of any decorative feature, have no paintings or texts inscribed on their walls, hold no royal seal or effigy, and (with the exception to be discussed later) contain no other shred of evidence that the three were built by Khufu, Chefra, and Menkaura; Egyptologists nevertheless continue to adhere to their favorite theory of "pyramid per successive Pharaoh" – and they did so in regard to Giza even though the actual successor of Khufu was not Chefra but the Pharaoh Dedefra whose small crumbling pyramid, sloped at 48°, was built far away from Giza, at the Abu Ruash in the North."

As Mr. Sitchin goes on to explain, "The Egyptologists list also conveniently omits two other Pharaohs *who reigned between* Chefra and Menkaura." "Next Came a Pyramid Built by the Pharaoh Sahura, in Abusir. A much-reduced scale imitation of the great ones in Giza is sloped about 50° and is also *a pile of rubble* now." "So are the four built next, also in Abusir, by his successors Neferirkara, Raneferef, Neuserra, and Zedkara-Isesy." "But all that remains of the Fifth Dynasty century and a half of "true pyramid" building are piles of ruined rubble.

"Having been to all these pyramids with changing shapes and slope angles, and having seen their collapsed rulings – everywhere except in Giza, I could not accept without questioning the Egyptologist's assertion that the Giza pyramids *followed and emulated* the others. As I gazed at the remains of the other pyramids in the flat desert landscapes, my gut feeling was **No- Giza was the example, the model that the others tried to emulate, and not vice versa!**

"The Great Pyramid of Giza – in sheer size, and structural ingenuity and complexity, in mathematical and geometric precision, and enduring stability – has been unique, and there is no need here to illustrate that with well-known data; but that alone does not prove that it was the model for all others. For that, the most compelling aspect is its inner **ascending** features. All the pyramids have inner features that are located in subterranean levels, but of all the pyramids (including his companions in Giza compares the main ones in size and enter complexity) **the Great Pyramid is the only one with the ascending passages and complex inner components high above ground level."**

"The story of the discovery of those ascending and upper inner features is a key to understanding the true sequence of pyramid construction in Egypt; the mystery of the plugging off of the ascending features is a clue to the true identity of the Giza builders."

Mr. Sitchin points out in his book that *the Great Pyramid is the only pyramid ever built with Ascending Passage.* All other pyramids built including the two Grand Pyramids cousins have an **inner ascending passage** and below ground level features.

Mr. Sitchin continued with exposing the Great Pyramid Forgery:

"Pyramid researchers now recognize that at some point in time after the Great Pyramid was built, "someone" for "some reason" slid down a grooved panel in the Ascending Passage three granite plug-stones that sealed off completely all the upper parts of the pyramid, and hid them so well from site that anyone entering the pyramid through its proper entranceway would only know of the Descending Passage. The inner upper parts became permanently sealed and forever hidden. That is why I have explained, *all the other Egyptian pyramids from his ulcers on* **had only ascending passages and compartments;** *for all of them emulated the Grand Pyramid* **as they knew it,** *and as its companions at Giza suggested: Only ascending passages and inner parts below ground level.* (My bold here)

"How, when, and why was the upper passageway sealed? The best (or only) idea Egyptologists have is that the ceiling off took place **after the Pharaoh's burial in the "coffer" in the Kings Chamber" "was completed.** (My bold here) But when Al Mamoon finally broke into the upper passages in chambers, the coffer was empty and no one was buried in the Kings Chamber. No, the granite plugs were slid down, I wrote, when the god Ra/Marduk, in punishment, was imprisoned in the Great Pyramid to die a slow death. It happened during what I have termed in *The Wars of Gods and Men* As the **Pyramid Wars – when gods, not men, ruled Egypt, long before any Pharaonic destinies.** (My bold)

This finding alone should suffice for concluding that the Giza pyramids had been built **before all the other pyramids in Egypt were erected;** (my bold) but there is more compelling evidence that leads to that unavoidable conclusion.

Such evidence can start showing that a "true" pyramid, as the Great Pyramid of Giza, had existed – and was *known* and even depicted *long before Zoser or Khufu and their dynasties.* One can't submit in evidence a well-known ancient Egyptian artifact called the *Victory Tablet of King Menes* (also known as the Narmer Palette), who was the first king of the very first Dynasty. It shows on one side of the king wearing the white crown of Upper Egypt, defeating his chieftains in conquering their Cities. On the tablets another side Menes is shown wearing the red crown of Lower Egypt – where Giza is situated; and that they are the pictographic symbols most clearly indicate the smooth cited triangular "true" pyramid indicating that such a pyramid had already been known circa 3100 BC – half a millennium before Cheops/Khufu. Indeed, inscriptions on a stone artifact belonging to Cheops – in which his name Khufu is clearly written in hieroglyphics – to imply that *the Great Pyramid had already existed in his time, and so did the Sphinx!* In this monument, known as the **Inventory Stela,** Khufu took credit for restoring a shrine to the goddess Isis, "Mistress of the Pyramid." He does not take credit for the pyramid itself, clearly considering it a structure belonging to gods, not mortals; and he states that the shrine stood "beside the house of the Sphinx" – the very Spinks which according to Egyptological tenets were erected (or carved out) by Khufu's *successor* Chefra...

In fact, depictions of the Sphinx (as reported by Sir W. M. Flinders Petri in *The Royal Tombs of the Earliest Dynasties,* 1901) were already found on stone tablets belonging to the earliest Pharaohs Menes-Narmer and Zer. Clearly, the Sphinx too had already existed when Khufu and Chefra ascended their thrones.

If the Giza pyramids (and the Sphinx) had already existed when Pharaohs began to reign, who was there to build them? The answer comes to us from the Near East's earliest civilization, that of Sumer. The Sumerians were quite aware of the unique edifices at Giza, describing them in texts dealing with the Pyramid Wars and depicting them on cylinder seals, including one commemorating the victory of the god Ninurta by showing his Divine Eagle surmounting the two large pyramids.

The story of the "Pyramid Wars" is told in *The Wars of Gods and Men.* The story of how the Giza pyramids and the Sphinx came to be built, by the gods, as vital components of their post – Diluvial Spaceport, has been told in my book *The Stairway to Heaven.*

Gods, not men, built the Giza pyramids as terminals for the Landing Core Door that was anchored on the Twin Peaks of Ararat in the North and on two natural peaks in the Sinai peninsula in the southeast; absent such peaks at the North Eastern terminus, the gods first erected the small pyramid is a test of structural stability and functionality, and then built the other larger two – equipping the Great Pyramid with pulsating guidance equipment in the unique upper innards.

Mr. Sitchin goes on to explain that the angle of the three Giza pyramids was 52°. That was the "secret number" of the Divine Architect, Thoth. Throughout the ancient text, Thoth is named, at least a half a dozen times, specifically relating to the statement that he, along with his father Enki and his brother Geb, built the Giza pyramids (*The Emerald Tablets to Thoth*).

Some fifth-century textbooks inform us that a coffin was found inside the Third Pyramid Bearing the name "Menkaura." That information gave " license" and proof for the Egyptians and the authorities to say that the Third Pyramid was built during the reign of "Menkaura." However modern carbon dating methods establish that the coffin lid and the skeletal remains were not from 2600 BC. The coffin lid was from circa 660 B. C. And the skeletal remains from the first or second century A.D. Those findings, thanks again to Mr. Sitchin's dogged research tells us that there was a later Pharaoh who also had the name Menkaura.

Because the coffin lid and the skeletal remains were from totally different periods, Mr. Sitchin begins to suspect archaeological fraud. He learned that the discoverers of the skeletal remains and the coffin belong to Howard Vyse and John Perring. Then a heavy dose of "irony" when Mr. Sitchin learned that Howard Vyse was the same Howard Vyse who had discovered the name "Khufu" written inside the Great Pyramid *where it was not found before!*

Mr. Sitchin understands that what has been revealed is archaeological fraud and the question posed to him becomes, if someone would go through the act of archaeological fraud *on the smaller third pyramid,* what evidence do we have to prove that Khufu built the Grand Pyramid? And he describes it this way....

" That realization, that an archaeological fraud was perpetrated in the small Third Pyramid, launched me on a course that led to questioning the only "proof" of the Khufu – built – it a tenet of Egyptology. "

Howard Vyse a British officer having an interest in Egyptian archaeology and antiquities obtained his exploration permit in 1835, whose real disguised intent was to discover the elusive hidden Treasure Chamber in the Great Pyramid. After two years of effort, running out of money and time, Mr. Zyse resorts to the use of dynamite.

Mr. Sitchin continues in his book,

"The gunpowder blasts revealed that there was a cavity above Davidson's Chamber; forcing his way up, Vyse discovered a similar space above Davidson's. Like Davidson's, it was totally devoid of any decoration or inscription. Vyse named it Wellington's Chamber in honor of his favorite war hero and had his assistant Hill inscribed his name inside the narrow chamber with *red paint*. Continuing the use of gun-powder as his men moved to further up, Vyse discovered two more similar empty spaces; he named them in honor of Lord Nelson and Lady Arbuthnot – names recorded by Mr. Hill and the usual *red paint*. Then he reached the vaulted cavity at the top, naming it Campbell's chamber in honor of his consular patron." ""

All the "chambers of construction" (as he called them – they are now called "Relieving Chambers") were bare and empty – no Ironic remains, no treasure – just black dust on the uneven floors. But on reentering the chambers (Mr. Hill, Mr. Perring, Mr. Mash kept going in), "quarry marks" in *red paint* were noticed.

"It was in those days of despair and desperation that a major discovery was made that assured vices place in the annals of Egyptology: Among the quarry marks were several cartouches is that spelled out Royal names, including that of Khufu!"

"The British and Australian consuls in Cairo are invited to witness a discovery; Mr. Hill copied the inscriptions on parchment sheets, and all present authenticated them with their signatures. The documents were then sent to the British Museum in London, and the unprecedented discovery was announced for the whole world to know. Since no one had entered those upper chambers from the time when the pyramid was erected, there was *unchallenged proof (my italics)* of this builder's name!

Vyse's find has remained the only evidence of the Khufu – Great Pyramid connection. But while textbooks state so unquestioningly, it appears that at the time, experts (including the British Museum's Samuel Birch and the great German Egyptologist Carl Richard Lepsius) were uneasy about the script of the inscriptions – it was one that was introduced in ancient Egypt much later– and questioned or that they really spelled out correctly the name Khufu (it looked like two different royal names were actually inscribed".

As I was pouring over Vyse's printed diary (*Operations Carried on at the Pyramids of Giza),* something odd struck me: The royal name he showed was inscribed differently than on the Inventory Stella; instead of diagonal lines (a "sieve") inside a circle which reads KH (and thus KH – U – F – U), Vyse's fines were written with a circle with just a dot inside. That reads not KH but RA, the sacred name of Egypt's Supreme God. ***Thus, the name Vyse reported was not Khufu but RAufu....***

In 1978, visiting the British Museum, asked to see the Vyse parchments. It took some doing, as no one had asked for them as far as anyone could recall. But the *Hill Facsimiles* (as they were cataloged) were found and shown to me – a bundle tied with yellowing-white ribbon. The authenticated parchments were there, the way they reached the museum more than a century earlier; *and the misspelling was also there:* In no instance was the (Kh) inscribed correctly as a sieve with diagonal lines; instead, there was a dot or a smudge inside a circle, spelling "Ra." Could it be that someone, in antiquity, had used the name of the great god RA in vain – an unforgivable sacrilege, a blasphemy punishable by death?

As I read the diary entries again, the words *"red paint"* kept jumping out of the pages – as when Mr. Hill used it to describe the names "Lord Wellington," Lady Arbuthnot," "Lord Nelson." I was struck by a statement in Perring's own memoirs (*The Pyramids of Giza*) that the red paint used for the ancient inscriptions "was a composition of red ocher called by the Arabs *mogarah* **which is still in use.**" Then Perring added the observation on the paint's quality: "such is the state of preservation of the marks and the quarries that **it is difficult to distinguish the work of yesterday from one three thousand years.**" Was he voicing his own astonishment about how fresh the red paint markings looked – after 4, 500 years! – or was he offering an explanation for the odd phenomenon?

As I went back to Vyse's day by day diaries, the entries made clear that the "quarry marks" (as Vyse called them) *were not discovered when the chambers were first entered;* and that it was Mr. Hill or Mr. Perring – not Vyse himself – who were first to notice the red paint markings on the subsequent visits. And then the thought struck me: Did the team that perpetrated the fraud in the Third Pyramid have also engaged in a forgery inside the Great Pyramid – "discovering" inscriptions were absolutely none had been found before?

Wasn't it odd, I thought, that for centuries no marking of *any kind* was found by *anyone, anywhere,* in the pyramid, not even in Davidson's Chamber above the Kings Chamber – and only Vyse found such markings *where only he first entered?*

Based on Vyse's own diary entries, the accusing finger pointed to Mr. Hill is the culprit, and I suggested that it was on the night of May 28, 1837, that he entered the pyramid with the brush and red paint and simulated the royal name. **The Great Pyramid Discovery** *is a*

great fraud and archaeological forgery.

"Without the "Khufu" inscription, Egyptologists remain without any tangible evidence for naming him as the builder of the Great Pyramid – and for that matter Chefra and Menkaura the builders of the two other Giza pyramids. The evidence that *does exist* shows that these pyramids and the Sphinx had preceded the Pharaohs; and the only ones who were there millennia earlier, who had the technology, who had the region were directing these pyramids – *__were the Anunnaki.__*" (My bold)

"Convince that that is what had happened, I detailed the evidence in my 1980 book *The Stairway to Heaven.* The forgery conclusion caused a minor sensation. Several dailies (among them the *Washington Times,* the *Pittsburgh Press*) and magazines picked up the story, some even at length, even some embellishing the report with a cartoon. There were radio interviews. But the Egyptological community ignored it – and it took me a plow to understand why: It was one thing to suggest that a questionable inscription was a forgery; it was quite another thing to expect Egyptologists to **acknowledge that the pyramids were built by "Extraterrestrials"...** (My bold)

"In May 1983, three years after *The Stairway to Heaven* was published I received an astonishing letter. It was from a Mr. Walter M Allen of Pittsburgh, Pennsylvania. "I have read your book," he wrote. "What you say about the forgery in the Cheops Pyramid is not new to me." His great-grandfather, he wrote, **was an eyewitness to the forgery! He witnessed Mr. Hill go into the pyramid with red paint and brush, supposedly to paint over ancient markings, but actually to paint new ones.**"

__THE FORGERY IN THE GREAT PYRAMID WAS CONFIRMED BY AN EYEWITNESS!__ (Authors caps)

I used quite a bit of Mr. Sitchin's chapter "The Great Pyramid Forgery," the first chapter in his book, "Journeys to the Mythical Past, and I did so intentionally for this reason: Mr. Sitchin has provided to me, to the American public and to the world for that matter, ***words on a silver platter, that prove the Ancient Sumarian Texts.*** I did not feel that I had earned the right, on this particular subject, to paraphrase his work, or in any way to try to take credit or suggest that I was the dogged researcher, the tenacious teacher, the brilliant abstract thinker. No, all of those kudos go to one man and one man alone, "The Godfather of the Ancient Texts" – MR. ZECHARIAH SITCHIN!

Repeatedly, the **Anunnaki** themselves, tell us, via the ancient texts, that they not only built the Giza pyramids, *but they also built pyramids* and other incredibly fantastic, incredible, enigmatic and wondrous stone structures, *all over the world!* For example, we know that there are 250 pyramids located in the central Chinese province of Shaanxi. There are dozens located in Northern Sudan, Canary Islands and in the middle of the Indian Oceans and in Bolivia. There are 20 or more pyramids located in Greece, Slovenia, France, Russia, Italy, Spain, and Croatia. Peru boasts 300 pyramids and more importantly the Mayan culture built more pyramids and all other cultures combined: that number being in excess of 10,000.

These pyramids which are located over five continents, exhibit amazing similarity and conformity and the question is why the similarity and conformity? The answer lies in knowing that Quetzalcoatl (= 'The Plumed/winged serpent') the God of the Aztecs, also known as the leading Mesoamerican deity called Kukulcan and also related directly to the building of the great pyramid was Ningishzida: **all three being the same person, the Anunnaki THOTH!** If you can build pyramids in the Yucatán Peninsula, Guatemala, Belize, El Salvador, and Honduras and north-central of the Yucatán Peninsula in the cities of Teotihuacan, Texcoco, Tenochtitlan, Tiacopan, I assure you, you can build the Great Pyramid of Egypt.

When I watch certain programs on television or read certain books I'm really bemused by the ubiquitously inane dogma that is being constantly perpetuated and espoused, that being, the indigenous Egyptians built all of the pyramids including the Great Pyramid. Here is an example of that delirious dogma:

On the Science Channel dated March 4, 2018, they presented a program entitled, "Secrets of the Lost." The narrator explains that a long lost Egyptian papyrus entitled, "The Merer Text." The narrator tells you that this was a " lost" papyrus but they do not reveal the age of or, who found the lost papyrus?

The Merer Text was **"decoded"** solely by the archaeologist Pierre Tallet. Assumedly the text was in ancient Egyptian. I would've chosen to have other qualified linguists to verify Mr. Tallet's interpretation of the text, but that was not forthcoming.. and as you will see, totally unnecessary. The Merer Texts were proffered as, "The first-hand account of the building of the Great Pyramid and the only one ever found referring to how the Grand Pyramid was built **by Khufu himself!**

The limestone came from the Tura quarry at Wadi-Al-Jarf, a distance of 150 miles south of the Great Pyramid bordering the Nile River. Those doing the quarrying, a team totaling around 2000, were led by Ankhaf who ironically, we are told, was Khufu's half-brother. (Now there is some credibility for you.)

The 2-ton limestone block took roughly 3 hours for the team to dislodge each stone at the quarry. We are then told that the 2-ton block was loaded on a specially made boat to carry it, one of the time, up to the Nile, and placed on the shore of the Nile, a ¼ mile from the front of the Great Pyramid. We are told, working with this highly specialized team of skilled workers, that the ancient Egyptians would be able to deliver 200 quarried stones per month; " that is if the current was right and the wind was blowing in the right direction." Yes, that is an actual quote from the program.

We know that the Great Pyramid consists of an estimated 2,400,000 blocks of stone. We know that the Great Pyramid consists of both limestone and granite, but for the purposes of evaluation, let us assume that they are all limestone blocks. Therefore if we divide 2,400,000 by 200, we arrive at the figure of 12,000 months. 12 months a year, divided into 12,000 months leaves us with a period of time of 1000 years.

Now I don't have to elaborate on that too much except to say that we are told by the "Egyptologists," that the Great Pyramid was started at the beginning of Khufu's reign and was finished by the end of his reign, which is an estimated total of 17 to 20 years. Let's not stop there....

We are told by learned Egyptologists and others that the granite stones placed in the Great Pyramid were quarried from Aswan by the same methodology, that being, quarrying the block, placed on the boat, traveling **500 miles** to put it on the shores of the Nile, one quarter of a mile away from the Great Pyramid.

Now if the Aswan quarry is 500 miles away from the Great Pyramid, which is right at 3 1/3 times the distance of the Tura quarry. So if we reduced the 200 per month quarried stone delivered from the Tura by 3 1/3 times............ Okay, I've made my point, maybe more than

I should have, however; I am simply unable to further tolerate this asinine, foolish, ridiculous, inane, idiotic, "The Egyptians built the Great Pyramid," devious dogma. `Donald don't do dogma'!

Another program of "interest" was the Ancient Aliens Declassified: Mysteries by the Numbers. The narrator states that " The Emerald Tablets of Thoth," are a myth. Robert Schoch Ph. D, states that the Emerald tablets contain ancient wisdom. Author Andrew Collins relates that the Emerald tablets contain, secrets of alchemy. David Wilcox tells us that the author of the Emerald tablets is Hermes Trismegistus or Hermes the Great. Richard Rader Ph. D, U.C.S.B., "Thoth is the Hellenistic Egyptian version of the Greek Hermes *associated* (authors italics) with the Egyptian God Thoth." Jeffrey Mitchell Ph. D, Dean of the University of Philosophical Research tells us, "According to Greek and Roman traditions you have this *connection* (authors italics) between Thoth and Hermes. He is the *connection* (authors italics) of the Egyptian movement in Greece between Thoth and Hermes. The deity who is the messenger, or link, between our human realm and the higher realm of the gods." Was Hermes Trismegistus the *reincarnation* (authors italics) of Thoth? Did he serve as a messenger between man and the gods? Or, might he be, as Ancient Astronaut Theorists believe, an ET being?

Comment: The answer to those questions of an implied enigma, is that Hermes, and Hermes Trismegistus and Thoth and the ET being and the Ancient Astronaut *are all the same person, AN ANUNNAKI! IT'S THE ANUNNAKI...............* Pray tell, why do all of these television programs and educated authors *refuse to use the word Anunnaki, as if it were an anathema?*

In order to reveal the seriousness of why the " Egyptian authorities" had gone to the extreme to protect their dogmatic, nationalistic theme, "The indigenous Egyptian population with the builders of all of the 155 Pyramids in Egypt, including the Great Pyramid," I ask any and all to read a chapter from his Zechariah Sitchin's "Journeys to the Mystical past," chapter 4, entitled, "The Fateful Day."

I could give you a synopsis of the chapter, but that would not suffice, because I want the reader to sense and feel some of the serious problems that Zechariah Sitchin has had to endure in his lifelong search for empirical truth even to the extent of **experiencing an attempt on**

his life! As Jack Parr would say, "I kid you not."

"Abbas added Wally's name to the list pre-submitted to the office of the Director of Giza Antiquities, describing him as my photographer; in fact I had an additional confidential task for Wally, for which he took along some of his small tools: **To try to get a sample of the red ink with which the "quarry marks" were inscribed, to be analyzed for their age.** I felt that this was important, not only because of my forgery conclusions, but also having in mind the Perry remark quoted in the first chapter: that the red paint used for the inscriptions "was a composition of red ocher called by the Arabs 'mograh' which is still in use" – **"still in use"** in his time – a remark whose implications for archaeological forgery made me wonder whether the use of the paint was continued beyond the 19th century A.D....."

"And so it was that on September 25, 1997, after the group left Israel early in the morning on the flight back to the US A, the three of us – Abbas, Wally, and me – left in the evening on a flight to Cairo."

"We first had to make a stop at the nearby administration office, where – so Abbas had arranged with Hawass – one of Hawass's deputies was to take us into the Great Pyramid and up to the Relieving Chambers; an array of ladders was supposed to be ready there for us. While I and Wally remained in the car, Abbas went in to get the deputy director. We expected the procedure to take just a few minutes, but Abbas did not return for 10 minutes, and after 20 minutes; half an hour passed – and Abbas was still in there...."

"I decided to go in and see what was causing the delay. Wally, loaded with his cameras came with me. We were told that Abbas was "inside," meeting with Dr. Hawass. We were allowed in the Director's office and Hawass greeted me and invited me to sit down beside his desk, next to Abbas. I looked at Abbas, and he just raised an eyebrow, giving me no clue as to what was causing the delay."

"Abbas was discussing with me his plan for a conference onboard an Alaska cruise ship, Hawass said to me; what do you (meaning I) think? Well, anything Abbas undertakes is worthwhile, I answered. Hawass then shifted the conversation to other subjects – none relating to the purpose of our being there that morning. I wondered what was going on."

"As the aimless conversation continued, it became obvious that Hawass was just killing time. Then it became clear why: His deputy –

the one who was supposed to take us to the Great Pyramid – showed up with a newspaper which he had obtained in town. It was a daily newspaper known for its nationalistic positions, and it had a long article that criticized the government for allowing foreigners to "defile Egypt's heritage" under the guise of archaeology. A segment was devoted to the foreigners who promote the idea that the Great Pyramid and Spinks was built by Atlanteans or by extraterrestrials, thereby implying that the Egyptians themselves were incapable of such achievements. It was an insult to Egypt's national pride, the article stated.

"So that was what Hawass was discussing with Abbas, waiting for the newspaper to be brought from the city! After the relevant paragraphs were read and translated, Hawass said to me: you will understand that in view of this attack I cannot let you go in, take pictures, *and proclaim again that Khufu did not bill the Pyramid…*"

"I was shocked. This is bad – this is ominous, I thought; perhaps one should have seen it coming – the terrorist attacks on foreign tourists, the abrupt stopping of certain exploration projects. But I could not accept such an abrupt stop to *my* project…. Overcoming my shock, I vehemently protested: the three of us came to Egypt just for that, based on an explicit promise from you to let us in, I told Hawass, how can you go back on your word?"

"Speaking to his deputy and to Abbas in Arabic, Hawass finally asked me and Wally to wait outside. A short while later Abbas came out. Hawass was very embarrassed, he said; so he will let you in – **but no pictures;** we must leave the cameras behind – there must not be any photographic record of this visit. I tried to protest, but Abbas said that Hawass overruled his deputy for this compromise: Go in without cameras, or not at all. So be it, I told Abbas. We went out to the car, and the Egyptian aid, riding with us to the Pyramid, collected all the cameras and lock them in the car's trunk."

"We entered the Pyramid through the familiar entrance, going all the way up through the majestic Grand Gallery. Where it ends, a large flat stone block is known as the "Great Step" forms a platform in front of the anti-chamber that leads to the Kings Chamber. Reaching it and stopping there, we saw that above us the workmen were standing on a ledge; from there, we assumed, the way would lead further up to the Crawlway leading to Davidson's Chamber, and then Vyse's vertical Forced Passage into the upper Relieving Chambers. Hawass's deputy shouted to them and they lowered to him a letter; he climbed up, spoke to them, looked around, and climbed back down. All is ready for you, he said; we were to use this ladder to climb up to where the workmen were, and then we would continue further up by means of additional ladders; it had to be done one at a time, he explained, because the ledge and the way up from it are narrow. And then he left."

"It looked like a flimsy and unsafe arrangement to me; so Wally volunteered to go up first. After Wally climbed from the ledge up to the next ladder, Abbas went up, and called out to me from the ledge, encouraging me to follow. As he turned to climb further up, I reached for the ladder and was about to take the first step up. At that moment *I suddenly felt a mighty blow to my head: a large and heavy piece of wood, dropped from higher up, hit me smack on my head and knocked me down. Warmblood began to pour down from the top of my head, and I was certain that my skull had been cracked."* (Authors italics)

"I cried out in pain. Abbas, back on the ledge, shouted to me: What happened? "My skull is cracked, I am bleeding!" I shouted. He climbed down, grabbed hold of me, and half supporting, half carried me as I staggered, rushes me out to our car, ordering his manager to drive back to the hotel. There is a doctor there, he said. The handkerchief I was holding to my head was soaking with blood; blood was spilling on my clothing. I was sure it was my end, and myriad thoughts of finality raced through my mind."

"It took forever – so it seemed to me – to reach the hotel clinic. The doctor, American trained and speaking English, examined me, cleaned the wound, and bandaged it. I think it's just superficial, he said, the blow just cut the skin on your head; but it's advisable to take x-rays and make sure there is no internal concussion. Also, he said, you need a Tetanus shot, since what hit you could have been infected. He advised Abbas to take me to the hospital without delay."

"We returned to the lobby, where the anxious local manager of Abbas was waiting. Steadier and less apprehensive, I asked for a cup of coffee. We sat down to evaluate the situation. I kept asking Abbas what had happened, who dropped the piece of wood on me. He said he did not know; it was an accident. Was it? I said – it had nothing to do with the newspaper article? I don't think I am safe in Egypt, I said. I think I'd better get back to New York right away, I told Abbas – **tonight.**"

"At the end of my Fateful Day – the day I almost got killed inside the Great Pyramid – I was leaving empty-handed; and the

Great Pyramid, defiant, continued to keep its secrets."

Comment: If this does not drive home the point that some of the "Egyptian authorities" will go to any extreme to protect their most sacred secret, that being, they know, absolutely, without an Angstrom of doubt, that their ancient Egyptian co-patriots **did not bill the pyramids and they will continue to do whatever they have to do to keep the world from knowing!**

What is most disappointing and frustrating to me, is that I know of no one (and I could be wrong) writing about, talking about, or any segment of a national television program or newspaper edifying or elucidating, anything close to what I have just described in the above segment. One can refer to Zechariah Sitchin's "accident" as an attempt to kill him. One could also refer to Zechariah Sitchin's "accident" as an assassination attempt. In my opinion, Mr. Sitchin's "accident," to describe it as an assassination attempt, would be a euphemism for attempted murder.

ONE LAST THING – There are more than enough "professional" peoples out there who are familiar with Mr. Zechariah Sitchin's, 14 books that he is written, collectively known as, "The Earth Chronicles." They are intelligent, knowledgeable, well-educated, and shall I say, possessing more than a healthy financial status. Here is my challenge to them, *pick up the gauntlet* left by the incomparable Zechariah Sitchin. I ask any one of them, individually or collectively, to go after *ONE THING* and that is: *find a way to carbon date the red paint inside the Great Pyramid!*

I, myself have the financial means to travel to Egypt and have the red paint carbon dated. But I do not have is the means of obtaining authority to enter the Great Pyramid as an Individual, nor do I have the physical abilities to do extensive traveling, walking, or the ability to climb a ladder. Otherwise, I would have, years ago, been knocking on Zahi Hawass' Great Pyramid door. `I kid you not!`

For those of you who remain naysayers, nabob's and obstinate deniers of the writings of the **Anunnaki's** ancient Sumerian Texts, the brilliant translations, transgramations, interpretations and analyzation of those ancient texts, by Mr. Zechariah Sitchin, you force me firstly, to take umbrance and secondly, you force me to ask you to saddle-up your unicorn, mount your unicorn backward, and ride off into the sunset of augmented, self-induced ignorance. You can plead ignorance but you cannot plead stupidity: ***IT'S THE ANUNNAKI THAT BUILT THE GREAT PYRAMID – STUPID!***

On Tuesday morning August 28, 2018, I decided to watch a previously recorded Ancient Aliens program which first aired on June 2, 2017 entitled "The Science Wars," describing the program to the viewer as, "A study of scientific discoveries, artifacts, and evidence that could point to extraterrestrial origins, *but that the academic community denies.*

The irony here lies in the fact that the producers of Ancient Aliens are the ones that are in a state of denial as they let people like William Henry and Eric von Daniken, and others, present themselves as authorities in the particular area of discussion.

The other irony is that I watched this program two days after writing the above information, about Zechariah Sitchin's dogged efforts to successfully prove who built the Great Pyramid, showing undoubtedly that it was not the Egyptians. The program informs us:

In Giza Egypt, we are told that the Great Pyramid was built as a tomb for King Khufu around 2500 BC. The dating of the pyramid is associated with Khufu because around 2500 BC was the period in time of Khufu's reign. The "evidence" provided by Richard Howard Vyse that he found the cartouche of King Khufu in one of the upper chambers of the Great Pyramid. Therefore, if Khufu rained about 2500 BC that is the timeframe for his building of the Great Pyramid, and that has been unchallenged until now.

In Vyse's Journal "*new evidence*" has been found which is now questioning his discovery. The suggestion is that he may have forged the name of Khufu himself. In a previous journal, Vyse writes "there is nothing in the chambers resembling hieroglyphics." In his published book 3 years later he writes "I could only make out one cartouche." After the contradicting evidence was exposed in 2014 (totally false statement) to Dresden University archaeology students "smuggled" a sample of the paint used in the King Khufu markings and had it analyzed by a German lab. The sample was too small to be radiocarbon dated, however, "they determine something shocking," the pigment was not painted onto the original stone block but a later plaster repair. Meaning the cartouche was not original to the great pyramid construction but added to a much later date. He may have forged the name Khufu on the chamber wall thereby establishing an inaccurate date for the structure.

Now let's go back and look at this "SHOCKING NEW EVI-DENCE," which is to say if you have read the above information that I have presented in this chapter you can easily determine there is absolutely nothing shocking and there is no new evidence. Zechariah Sitchin wrote his book "Journeys of the Mythical Past," in 2007 and the first chapter, entitled, "The Great Pyramid Forgery, consisting of 35 pages, revealing that he and he alone is the person responsible for exposing Vyse's intended forgery! Now Ancient Aliens, in 2017 decide they need an hour-long program claiming that new evidence has been discovered, when in fact what they present is proxied information which has been in publication for more than a decade.

Please note that the two Dresden University archaeology students remain *unnamed*. If they had made it to one of the upper chambers of the Great Pyramid and done nothing else, they would be world renown and famous for penetrating the security of the Egyptian authorities! Further, they, surreptitiously, "SMUGGLED," out of one of the upper chambers of the Great Pyramid, a sample of the red paint used to inscribe the name, Khufu. To this particular program from Ancient Aliens, the information provided, in my opinion, is nothing more than **bloviated balderdash**! In my opinion, it would be literally impossible to surreptitiously smuggle anything out of the *upper chambers,* of the Great Pyramid because the Egyptian Authorities and ruling Egyptian government simply would not allow that. Let us not forget that an attempt was made on the life of Mr. Zechariah Sitchin to prevent him from acquiring a sample of that same red paint. Now let us add in the fact that the two unnamed students do not have enough knowledge about radiocarbon dating to get a proper sample size. And this is what some television programs have deteriorated too?

Further, in the same program, they reveal A seventh century BC text known as "The Inventory Stela," unearthed in 1858, detail repairs made by Pharaoh Khufu, including work on the Sphinx. The question then becomes, how could Khufu be repairing the Sphinx, that was supposedly constructed by his son, which would more than suggest that the Sphinx itself had already been built prior to the reign of Khufu.

I have myself in this book have covered the importance of "The Inventory Stela," and specifically how it relates to proving who built the Great Pyramid. Mr. Sitchin has revealed his research relating to the Stela, decades ago, in several of his books. The point is that the importance of "The Inventory Stela," is an " old hat," revelation.

Now, let us do some walking down The Yellow Brick Road.

Following in the same program Mr. Eric von Danica relates that it was Enoch who built the Great Pyramid because "the Flood was coming and the Great Pyramid would serve as a repository for the knowledge that he not only learned in heaven but all of the earthly knowledge as well." Then Mr. William Henry offers the statement, "perhaps they were built by otherworldly beings such as angels." My comment here would be, "Who woulda thunk it? I have to think that some of the authors and a few Ancient Alien pundits have been in too many parades, where the horses and livestock are placed at the beginning of the parade, and they have, via necessity, spent too much time dodging road apples.

Chapter 8: The Great Flood

The Lost Book of Enki Page 205-8

Now, this is the account of Earth's tribulations before the deluge,

By the conjugations of Igigi (biblical Nefilim, Those who came down) and the Earthling

daughters was Enlil greatly disturbed,

By Marduk's espousal of an Earthling female Enlil was much distraught.

In his eyes the Anunnaki mission to Earth had been perverted,

To him the howling, shouting Earthling masses an anathema became;

Oppressive the pronouncements of the Earthlings have become,

The conjugations of sleep deprived me! So did Enlil to the other leaders say.

Both Ninmah and Enki plead with Enlil to help the beings that they had fashioned. Ninmah wanted to teach the Earthlings how to solve their medical problems. "Let us the Earthlings curing teach, how themselves to remedy to learn! So did Ninmah say. And Enki relates to Enlil, "Let us the Earthlings pond-and-canal-building teach, let them from the seas fish and sustenance obtained!"

This by decree I forbid! Enlil to Enki said. Let the Earthlings by hunger and pestilence perish!

For one Shar (3600 years) the Earthlings ate the grasses of the fields,

For the second Shar, the third Shar, the vengeance of Enlil they suffered.

Comment: The ancient astronaut theorists tell us that the reason for the Great Flood was that God was so displeased with Man, whom he had created, that he brought on the flood specifically to eliminate mankind from the face of the earth. The Bible puts it this way:

Genesis 6:5,6,7 " The Lord saw how great was man's wickedness on earth, and how every plan devised by his mind was nothing but evil all the time." "And the Lord regretted that He had made man on earth, and His heart was saddened." "The Lord said, I will blot out from the earth the men whom I created."

Genesis 6:11, 12, 13, 14, "The earth became corrupt before God; the earth was filled with injustice." "When God saw how corrupt the earth was, for all flesh had corrupted its ways on earth, God said to Noah, "I have decided to put an end to all flesh, for the earth is filled with lawlessness because of them I am about to destroy them with the earth. Make yourself an Ark of gopher wood;"

The ancient text tells us that for three Shars (10,800 years) the Earthlings suffered the vengeance of Enlil. So relating to the ancient texts revelations, what we see is, the Earthlings were disdained by Enlil, yet *after 10,800 years the great flood had not happened!* What will be revealed, in short order, will show that *the great flood was caused by a cosmological circumstance beyond anyone's control!* That cosmological circumstance happens to be the effect and results of the planet Nibiru coming into our solar system and nearing its' perigee.

In those days the Anunnaki, for their own surviving were concerned;

Their own rations were diminished, by Earth's changes they themselves afflicted became.

On Earth as on Lahmu the seasons their regularity lost. For one Shar, for two Shars, from

Nibiru the heavenly circuits were studied,

Oddities in the planetary destinies from Nibiru were observed.

On the Sun's face black spots were appearing, from its face flames shot up;

Kishar (Saturn) was also misbehaving, its host its footings lost, dizzying were their circuits.

The Hammered Bracelet (Asteroid Belt) was by unseen netforces pulled and pushed,

For reasons unfathomed the Sun its family was upsetting;

On Nibiru the savant's alarms raised, in the public squares the people gathered;

On Earth the tribulations were increasing, fear and famine their heads reared.

For three Shars, for four Shars the instruments the Whiteland facing were observed.

By Nergal and Erishkigal *odd rumblings* in the White lands (Antarctic) snows were recorded:

The snow ice that the Whiteland covers to sliding has taken! So did the day from Abzu's

(Enki's domain in Southeast Africa) trip report.

In the Land beyond the Seas, Ninurta (Sun of Enlil) in his haven for telling instruments
established,

Quakes and gestures at the *Earth's bottom* with the instruments he noticed.

An odd matter is afoot! So did Enlil to Anu on Nibiru words of alarm send.

For the fifth Shar, for the sixth Shar the phenomena gained strength,
On Nibiru the savants an alarm it raised, of calamities to the King

they forewarnings gave:

The *next time* Nibiru the Sun be nearing, Earth to Nibiru's net force exposed shall be,

From the net force of Nibiru Earth in the heavens protection shall not have,

Kishar (Saturn) and his host agitated shall be, Lahmu (Venus) shall also shake and wobble;

In Earth's great Below, the snow-ice of the Whiteland (Antarctica) its footing is losing;

The next time Nibiru the closest to Earth shall approach,

The snow-ice of the Whiteland's surface, shall come a-sliding.

A watery calamity it shall cause: **By a huge wave, a Deluge, the Earth will be overwhelmed!**

Comment: This ancient text tells us, from the time that Enlil, being so perturbed with the Earthlings, to the time of the Great Flood, was seven Shars. Each Shar, being approximately 3600 years, multiplied by seven, equals 25,200 years. This poignantly proves that the Great Flood was not caused by the God of the Bible, or Enlil in this ancient text, for the purpose of destroying mankind, or in Enlil's case the Earthlings.

The great flood was caused by cosmological circumstance, that being Nibiru's return to our inner solar system nearing its perigee. The Anunnaki recorded each Shar and scientifically measured its effect upon Earth to the point of knowing that the seventh Shar would dislodge the ice mass from the Antarctic and cause the Great Flood! Remember also that this was at the end of the Ice Age some 13,000 years ago.

To add scientific credence and credibility to the ancient text one might ask the question, could the volume of ice sliding off the landmass of Antarctica into the ocean cause massive flooding of the Earth? I'll let you be the judge.

1 cubic foot of ice at 30°C which is the average temperature of

Antarctica equals 57.2 lbs.

One square mile equals 27,878,400 sq. Ft., times 57.2 lbs. brings up an error on my calculator. But the answer is right at 15,946,000,444 pounds.

The averaged ice on the landmass of Antarctica today is 1.2 miles, (6200 feet) in thickness. And that equates to 5,400,000 sq.mi.. I'll let those of you out there who are math heads figure it out. To further complicate the issue and to boggle one's mind, today's scientist tells us that at the end of the Ice Age, around 13,000 years ago, the ice mass averaged 5 miles deep.

Another factor, which might lend itself to a better comprehension of the ecological effects of the melting ice of Antarctica. It isn't going to melt but if it did, it would be over a slow period of time, *the Sea would rise by 200 feet.*

Now, let us consider another factor that would most certainly lend scientific credence to the ancient text, one that most people are not aware of:

Ancient texts tell us that the great flood came from the South Pole. One should be aware that the great flood could not possibly have come from the North Pole! Why, because the ice mass at the North Pole *forms 'in the water' and not atop of a landmass!*

Encompassed in the Ancient Texts are more than several versions of the same Great Flood. I chose the Babylonian Legend of the Deluge for several reasons: the first is that in my opinion, having read them all, it is the most accurate. The second being is that it is the most readable and more comprehensible than most. The most important reason I chose this particular interpretation of the Ancient Text, is that it follows very closely to the words written by Enki himself in his own dictated words which can be found in "The Autobiography of an Extraterrestrial God." 26 different nations recognize that statement as identifying "The Lost Book of Enki," interpreted by the incomparable Zechariah Sitchin. It should be noted that Zechariah Sitchin translated more than 620 of the available Ancient Texts.

E. A. Wallace Budge

THE BABYLONIAN STORY OF THE DELUSION AS TOLD BY ASSYRIAN TABLETS FROM NINEVEH

1. Gilgamesh said unto him, to Uta–Napishtim the remote:

2. "I am looking at thee, Uta –Napishtim.
3. That person is not altered; even as am I so are thou.
4. Verily, nothing about thee is changed; even as am I so hard thou.
5. A heart to do battle doth make thee complete,
6. Yet at rest (?) Thou dost lie upon thy back.
7. How then hast thou stood the company of the gods and sought life?"

There upon Uta-Napishtim related to Gilgamesh the Story of the Deluge and the Eleventh Tablet continues thus.
8. xxxxxxxxxxxxx said unto him, to Gilgamesh;
9. I will reveal unto thee, bold Gilgamesh, a hidden mystery,
10. And a secret matter of the gods I will declare unto thee.
11. Shurippak, a city which thou thyself knowest,
12. On (the bank) of the river Putatti (Euphrates) is situated,
13. That city is old; and the gods (dwelling) within it
14. Their hearts induced windstorm (a-bu-bi)
15. There was their father Anu,
16. Their counselor, the warrior Enlil,
17. Their messenger En-urta (and)
18. There prince Ennugi.
19. Nin-igi-ku, Ea, (Enki) was with them (in council) and
20. Reported their word to the house of reeds."

(FIRST SPEECH OF EA (ENKI) TO UTA-NAPISHTIM WHO IS SLEEPING IN A REED HUT)

21. O House of reeds, O House of reeds! Oh Wall. Oh Wall!
22. O House of reeds, here! O Wall, understand!
23. Oh man of Shuripak, son of Ubar-Tutu,
24. Throwdown the house, build a ship,
25. Forsake wealth, seek after life,
26. Hate possessions, save thy life,
27. Bring all seed of life into the ship.

28. The ship which thou shalt build,
29. The dimensions thereof shall be measured,
30. The breadth and the length thereof shall be the same.
31. Then lunch it up on the ocean.

(UTA-NAPISHTIM'S ANSWER TO EA)

32. I understood and I said unto Ea, my Lord:
33. See, my Lord, that which thou hast ordered,
34. I regard with reverence, and will perform it,
35. But what shall I say to the town, to the multitude, and to the elders?

(SECOND SPEECH OF EA."
36. Ea opened his mouth and spake
37. And said unto his servant, myself,
38. Thus, man, shalt thou say unto them:
39. Ill- will have the god Enlil formed against me,
40. Therefore I can no longer dwell. In your city,
41. And never more will I turn my continents upon – the son of Enlil.
42. I will descend into the ocean to dwell with my lord Ea.
43. But upon you he will reign riches
44. A catch of birds, a catch of fish
45.... an (abundant) harvest,
46.... The sender of...
47.... shall make hail (to fall upon you).

(THE BUILDING OF THE SHIP.

48. As soon as (something of dawn) broke...
   (Lines 49-- 54 broken away.)
55. The child... brought bitumen,
56. The strong (man)... brought what was needed.
57. On the fifth day I laid down its shape.
58. According to the plan its walls were 10 gar, (i.e. 120 cubits) high,
59. And the width of his deck (?) was equally 10 gar.
60. I laid down the shape of his four-part and marked it out.

61. I covered (?) It six times,
63. It's interior I divided into nine,
64. Caulking I drove into the middle of it.
65. I provided a steering pole, and cast in all that was needful.
66. Six sar of bitumen I poured over the whole (?),
67. Three sar of pitch I poured into the middle.
68. The men who bear loads brought three-sar of oil,
69. Besides a sar of oil which the tackling (?) consumed,
70. In two sar of oil which the boatman hid.
71. I slaughtered oxen for the (work) people,
72. I slough sheep every day.
73. Beer, sesame wine, oil and wine
74. I made the people drink as if they were water from the river.
75. I celebrated a feast as if it had been New Year's Day.
76. I opened (a box of ointment), I laid my hands in unguent.
77 Before the sunset (?) the ship was finished.
78. (Sense)… was difficult.
79. The shipbuilders brought the… of the ship, above and below,
80. … two – thirds of it.
81. With everything that I possessed I loaded it (i.e., the ship).
82. With everything that I possessed of silver I loaded it.
83 With everything that I possessed of gold I loaded it.
84. With all that I possessed of all the seed of life I loaded it.
85. I made to go up into the ship all my family and kinsfolk,
86. The cattle of the field, the beasts of the field, the beasts of the field, all handicraftsmen I made them go up into it.
87. The god Shamash had appointed me a time (saying)
88. The sender of….. will at eventide make a hail to fall;
89. Then enter into the ship and shut my door.
90. The appointed time drew nigh;
91. The sender of…… will make a hail to fall at eventide.
92. I watched the aspect of the (approaching) storm,
93. Terror possessed me to look upon it,
94. I went into the ship and shut my door.
95. To the pilot of the ship, Puzar-Enlil the sailor.
96. I committed the great house (i.e., ship), together with the contents thereof.

(THE ABUBU (CYCLONE) AND ITS EFFECTS DE-

SCRIBED.)

97. As soon as something of dawn shown in the sky
98. A black cloud from the foundation of heaven came up.
99. Inside it the god Adad thundered,
100. The gods Nabu and Sharru (i.e., Marduk) went before,
101. Marching as messengers over high land and plain,
102. Irragal (Nergal) tore out the post of the ship,
103. En-urta went on, he made the storm to descend.
104. The **Anunnaki** (1) brandished their torches,
105. With their glare they lighted up the land.
106. The whirlwind (or, cyclone) of Adad swept up to heaven.
107. Every gleam of light which turned into darkness.
108. .... the land..... as if had laid it waste.
109. A whole day long (the flood descended).

(1. The star-gods of the southern sky.)

110. Swiftly it mounted up....... (the water) reached to the mountains
111. (The water) attacked the people like a battle.
112. Brother saw not brother.
113. Men could not be known (or, recognized) and heaven.
114. The gods were terrified at the cyclone.
115. They shrank back and went up into the heaven of Anu.
116. The gods crouched like a dog and cowered by the wall.
117. The goddess Ishtar cried out like a woman in travail.
118. The lady of the Gods lamented with a sweet voice (saying):

(ISHTAR'S LAMENT.)

119. May that former day be turned into mud,
120. Because I commanded evil among the company of the gods.
121. How could I commanded evil among the company of the gods,
122. Command the battle for the destruction of my people?
123. Did I of myself bring forth my people
124. That they might feel that sea like little fishes?

(UTA-NAPISHTIM STORY CONTINUED.)

125. The gods, the **Anunnaki** wailed with her,

126. The gods about themselves, and set down weeping.

127. Their lips were shut tight (in distress)....

128. For six days and nights

129. The wind, the storm raged and the cyclone overwhelmed the land.

130. When the seventh day came the cyclone ceased, the storm and battle

131. which had fought like an army.

132. The sea became quiet, the grievous wind went down, the cyclone ceased.

133. I looked on the day and voices were stilled,

134. And all mankind were turned into mud.

135. The land had been laid flat like a terrace.

136 I opened the air- hole and the light fell upon my cheek,

137. I bowed myself, I set down, I cried,

138. My tears poured down over my cheeks.

139. I looked over the quarters of the world, (two) the limits of the ocean.

140. At 12 points islands appeared.

141. The ship grounded on the mountain of Nisir.

142. The mountain of Nisir held the ship, it let it not move.

143. The first day, the second day, the mountain of Nisir held the ship and let it not move.

144. The third day, the fourth day, the mountain of Nisir held the ship and let it not move.

145. The fifth day, the sixth day, the mountain of Nisir held the ship and let it not move.

146. When the seven day had come

147. I brought out a dove and let her go free.

148. The dove flew away and (then) came back;

. 149. Because she had no place to alight on she came back.

150. I brought out a swallow and let her go free.

151. The swallow flew away and (then) came back;

152. Because she had no place to alight on she came back.

153. I brought out a raven and let her go free.

154. The raven flew away, she saw the sinking water.

155. She ate, she waded (?), she rose (?), she came not back.

156. Then I brought out (everything) to the four winds and made a sacrifice;

157. I sent out an offering on the peak of the mountain.

158. Seven by seven I set out the vessels,

159. Under them I piled reeds, cedarwood and myrtle (?).

160. The gods smelt the savour,

161. The gods smelt the sweet savour.

162. The gods gathered together like flies over him that's sacrificed.

(SPEECH OF ISHTAR, LADY OF THE GODS.)

163. Now the Lady of the Gods game nigh,

164. She lifted up the priceless jewels which Anu had made according to her desire, (saying)

165 O ye gods here present, as I shall never forget the sapphire jewels of my neck

166. So shall I ever think about these days, and shall forget them nevermore!

167. Let the gods come to the offering,

168. But let not Enlil come to the offering,

169. Because he took not thought and made the cyclone,

170. And delivered my people over to destruction,"

(THE ANGER OF ENLIL)

171. Now when Enlil came nigh

172. He saw the ship; then was Enlil wroth

173. And he was filled with anger against the gods, the Igigi (saying): (1)

174. Hath any being escaped with his life?

175. He shall not remain alive a, a man among the destruction

(SPEECH OF EN-URTA)

176. Then En-urta opened his mouth and spake

177. And said unto the warrior Enlil:

178. Who besides the god Ea can make a plan?

179. The god Ea knoweth everything that is done.

180. The god Ea opened his mouth and spake
181. And said unto the warrior Enlil,
182. O Prince among the gods, the warrior,
183. How, how couldst thou, not taking thought, make a cyclone?
184. He who is sinful, on him lay his sin,
185. He who transgresseth, on him lay his transgression.
186. But be merciful that (everything) be not destroyed be long-suffering that (man not be blotted out).

(1. The star gods of the northern heaven."

187. Instead of thy making a cyclone,
188. Would that the lion had come and diminished mankind.
189. Instead of thy making a cyclone
190. Would that the wolf had come and diminished mankind.
191. Instead of thy making a cyclone
192. Would that a famine had risen and (laid waste) the land.
193. Instead of thy making a cyclone
194. Would that Irra (the Plague god) had risen up and (laid waste) the land.
195. As for me I have not revealed the secret of the great gods.
196. I made Atra-hasis to see a vision, and thus he heard the secret of the gods.
197. Now therefore take counsel concerning him.

(ENLIL DEIFIED UTA-NIPISHTIM AND HIS WIFE.)

198. Then the God Enlil went up into the ship,
199. He seized me by the hand and brought me forth.
200. He brought forth my wife and made her to kneel by my side.
201. He touched our brows, he stood between us, he blessed us (saving),
202. Formally Uta-pishtim was a man merely,
203. But now let Uta-pishtim and his wife be like unto us gods.
204. Uta-pishtim shall dwell far off, at the mouth of the rivers.

(UTA-PISHTIM ENDS HIS STORY OF THE DELUGE)

205. And they took me away to a place afar off, and made me dwell

at the mouth of the rivers.

Comments: It should be noted here, as I have noted in my reading of the ancient texts, whether it be Sumerian, Akkadian, Babylonian, Assyrian, Phoenician, Canaanite, or Ugaritic, etc. etc. the lead character in all of these different texts, including Stela, cylinder seals and/ or Palettes: *the lead characters are always the Anunnaki.* So for the reader to have a clearer understanding of who the Anunnaki are, here, I shall identify them, using what I consider to be the most indispensable guide and informative book relating to the studying of the ancient text. That being "THE EARTH CHRONICLES HANDBOOK," by Mr. Zechariah Sitchin.

The pantheon of Anunnaki, those holding the authority and power of leadership, consisting of only 12 members, Anu, Enlil, and Enki are the three most important of the nine.

Anu (= `The Heavenly One'): The ruler on the planet Nibiru when its astronauts came to Earth. As head of the pantheon, his numerical strength was 60.

En.lil (= `Lord of the Command'): The son of Anu by his spouse and half-sister Antu, and those the Legal Air to Nibiru's throne; his numerical rank was 50.

En.ki (=`Lord of Earth'); Another epithet was E.A (=` Whose abode is water'): The leader at the first group of 50 Anunnaki who arrived on earth, splashing down in the Persian Gulf. His numerical rank was 40. Note that he is referred to, in line 19, as Nin-igi-ku.

Uta-Napishtim (= 'His day Is Life'): the name, in the Akkadian renditions, of the hero of the Deluge of who the Anunnaki are. In a previously written ancient text, his epithet was Ziusudra (=`His Life days Prolonged'): The`Noah'of the biblical Deluge tale.

Ennugi (god of water) His primary Anunnaki function was to dig canals.

Ninurta, (=`Hunter and Plow man '): The firstborn son of Enlil by

Enlil's half-sister Ninharsag, and therefore in line to succeed Enlil and his rank of 50. Mentioned in the above text, on line 17, as En-urta.

Shamash (Akkadian equals `Sun'): Whose other epithet was Utu (=` The shining one'): A grandson of Enlil, his pantheon rank number was 20. As the second generation born on Earth.

Nabu (=` He Who Speaks For'): Marduk's son (see line 100.,Shar-ru (i.e. Marduk) by his Earthling wife Sarpanit.

Adad (also Hadad and the Sumerian Ishkur) Enlil's youngest son. See line 19 of the text.

Nergal (=`Great Watcher'): A son of Enki, half-brother of Marduk. After carrying out the nuclear attack on Sodom, Gomorrah, and three other cities, He was given the epithet *Erra (=` The Annihilator') on line 102 he is named Irragal.*

Ishtar/In.anna (=`An's Lady'): Born on earth with her twin brother Utu/Shamash.

Atra-hasis/Uta-Napishtim (see line 196.)

Whether the ancient texts are interpreted by EA Wallace budge or George Smith Or Zechariah Sitchin and others, all of them infuse and allocate erroneously to the ancient text, the word religion. Their reasoning seems to be if we, modern-day man, living in the 17th
through the 21st century are religious, then those who lived before us, centuries and millennia ago obviously had to be religious. That pseudo-infusion is false.

Nowhere in the ancient texts will you find that the Anunnaki relating themselves in any way to religion. In fact, it's just the opposite! They ubiquitously referred to, (in all ancient texts) the "Father of All," or "The Creator of All," and without the slightest bit of ambiguity, the Anunnaki defined those two names as "THE SUN." They tell us in, "The Emerald Tablets of Thoth," that we are made of Stardust! And I ask the reader, where have you ever heard that statement before? Remember that Carl Sagan and other scientists have made the same statement in the past and current scientists and future scientists have and will make it in the future. The Anunnaki, also in the ancient texts, repeatedly tell us that they "Evolved," on the planet Nibiru.

What do the Anunnaki do when they become frightened, distressed and loaded with anxiety when they incur a most extreme and life-threatening situation that they have no control over? Starting at line 109.

A whole day long (the flooded descended.)
Swiftly it mounted up (the water) reached to the mountains.
The gods were terrified at the cyclone.
The gods crouched like a dog and cowered by the wall.
The goddess Ishtar cried out like a woman in travail.
The lady of the gods lamented with a sweet voice.
The gods, the Anunnaki wailed with her.
The gods bowed themselves, and sat down weeping.
I bowed myself, I set down, I cried,
My tears poured down my cheeks.

The ancient texts are replete with their own written words, describing themselves, the Anunnaki, as having the same emotional reactions to different given situations as we do today i.e., love, hate, jealousy, fear, conniving, shame, cowardice, bravery, terrified, warlike, autocratic, dictatorial, sadness, happiness, depression, hubris, and all of it, especially relating to the top leadership positions of the 12 Anunnaki individuals, their concern for ignominy.

Again in all the ancient texts that I have read, no matter the situation, the Anunnaki never turn to a supreme deity or being for help. The reason being is, that they know, they have only themselves to turn to.

Further when Uta-Napishtim is angry with the Anunnaki god Enlil, what does he do?

Starting at line 39: Ill will hath the god Enlil formed against me,
Therefore I can no longer dwell in your city,
And never more like turn my countenance upon the soil of Enlil.

In the above three sentences, Uta-Napishtim tells us that he does not like living under the geographic realm controlled by the Anunnaki god Enlil and that forces me to live under the geographic realm controlled by the Anunnaki god Enki.

If we look at the opinions of modern-day authors, researchers, theorists and too many scientists, the cause of the Great Flood was caused by God, meteors, or comments. For example:

A theorist on an Ancient Alien program tells us, "Gods sent the ancient flood to wipe out all of humanity." The incongruity here lies in the plurality of "Gods."

Sabrina Magliocco Ph.D., a Folklorist at the California State University at Northbridge, using the Bible as a reference tells us "Humans had not been behaving properly." "They had been violating God's laws."

Kathleen McGowan Coppens – author/researcher tells us, "God became so disgusted with his creation that he repented making them."

Andrew Collins, the author of "Genesis of the Gods," tells us: "A conflagration caused by a Comet colliding with Earth, sent fiery debris down on the Northern atmosphere." "A fragment of the comet in our Northern atmosphere vaporized the ice sheets." And he follows that up by saying that the firestones that fell on her Northern atmosphere caused the Great Flood; that firestones, caused by the fragmentation of the comet's collision with Earth, fell for "40 days and 40 nights like the Bible tells us."

Now we can look at a frequent visitor and contributor's on several of the Ancient Aliens programs, that being Rabbi Ariel Bar Tzadok of Kosher Torah, who tells us, in subjunctive mood of course, – If a comet would swing around behind the Sun, colliding with a certain part of the ocean, that would rip it out. "The flood was clearly contrived." "It was sent by higher powers to correct things on Earth." "The Earth had become corrupt and the flood was sent as an assault on humanity."

My comment to the reader would be to re-read the ancient texts which I have already printed out for you, and you can make your own decision. To put it another way, *I retort and you decide.*

David Wilcox author of "The Synchronicity Key," tells us that the flood had, "Possible extraterrestrial cause." That statement is pounding a fist on the truth's door! I would only change the word, extraterrestrial, to the writings of the Ancient Text's Anunnaki.

Chapter 9: Memoirs and Prophecies of and ET God – Enki

How smitten is the land, its people delivered to the Evil Wind, its stables abandoned, its sheepfolds emptied?

How smitten are the cities, their people piled up as dead corpses affected by the Evil Wind?

How smitten are the fields, their vegetation withered, touched by the Evil Wind?

How smitten are the rivers, nothing swims anymore, pure sparkling waters turned to poison?

Of its black-headed people, Sumer is emptied, gone is all life;

Of its cattle and sheep Sumer is emptied, silent is the hum of churning milk.

In its glorious cities, only the wind howls; death is the only smell.

COMMENTS: Reading Ancient Texts and in particular the "Erra Epos", and the "Lamentation of the description of Ur" will render to any reasonable mind, the subject matter in question, is definitively describing the aftermath of a Nuclear Holocaust. The EVIL WIND referred to is the Nuclear Cloud fallout, carrying death and devastation in its path.

Nibiru is its name

A great planet, reddish in radiance; around the Sun an elongated circuit Nibiru makes.

For a time in the cold is Nibiru engulfed; for part of its circuit by the Sun strongly is it heated.

A thick atmosphere Nibiru envelopes, by volcanic eruptions constantly fed.

All manner of life this atmosphere sustains; without it there would be only perishing!

In the cold period the inner heat of Nibiru it keeps about the planet, like a warm coat that is constantly renewed.

In the hot period it shields Nibiru from the Sun's scorching rays.

COMMENT: How can a planet in its apogee being so far from the Sun, maintain a source of heat?

The Twin Planets so-referred to in the Ancient Texts, Jupiter and Saturn, (Kishar and Anshar), carry with them more than a few similarities. Saturn maintains an atmosphere similar to Jupiter although Saturn is more than one million miles further from the Sun.

When nearest to the Sun's quarters, a festival of the warmth was celebrated (perigee)

When to its far abode Nibiru was distanced, the festival of coolness was decreed (apogee)

In the atmosphere a breaching has occurred; that was their finding.

Volcanoes, the atmosphere's forebears, less belching were spitting up!

Nibiru's air has thinner been made, the protective shield has ?!

To remedy the afflictions ways he sought; of Nibiru's heavenly circuit he made such study.

In its loop, of the Sun's family five members it embraced, planets of dazzling beauty.

Other children of the Sun, four in number, from intrusion the bracelet shielded.

The atmospheres of the five greeters Enshar set out to study.

In its repeating circuit, the five in Nibiru's loop carefully were examined.

What atmospheres they possessed by observation and with celestial chariots intensely were examined.

Beyond the fifth planet, the utmost danger was lurking, so indeed he knew.

The Hammered Bracelet ahead was reining, to demolish it was awaiting!

COMMENTS: The Sun's five family members; Mercury, Venus,

Earth, Mars, Jupiter.

Children of the Sun, four in number, outside the asteroid belt, Saturn, Uranus, Neptune Pluto.

One was to use a metal, gold was its name. On Nibiru was greatly rare; within the Hammered Bracelet, it was abundant.

It was the only substance that to the finest powder could be ground; lofted high to heaven, suspended it could remain.

Let celestial boats be constructed, he decided, to seek the gold in the Hammered Bracelet, he decided.

By the Hammered Bracelets, the boats were crushed; none of them returned.

Into a missile-throwing chariot Alalu climbed; its hatch behind him he closed.

The forepart chamber he entered; the commander's seat he occupied.

That-Which-Shows-the-Way he lit up, with bluish aura the chamber filling.

The Fire Stones he stirred up: their hum like music was enthralling

The chariot's Great Cracker he enlivened, a reddish brilliance it was casting.

COMMENT: We can envision a modern-day astronaut launching his missile loaded spacecraft.

To Anshar, (Saturn) the Foremost Prince of the heavens, the course was a-turning.

By the speeding chariot Alalu the ensnarling pull of Anshar could tell. (gravitational pull)

The giant Kishar, (Jupiter) foremost of the Firm Planets, its size was overwhelming.

Swirling stormes obscured its face, colored spots they moved about;

A host beyond counting, some quickly, some slowly, the celestial god encircled.

Troublesome were their ways, back and forth they were surging.
Kishar itself a spell was casting, divine lightings it was thrusting.
As Alalu looked on, his course became upset,
His direction was distracted, his doings confused.
Then the deepness darkening began to depart: Kishar on his destiny continued to circuit.
Slowly moving, its veil from the shining Sun it lifted; the One from the Beginning came fully into view.
Beyond the fifth planet, the utmost danger was lurking, so indeed he knew.

COMMENTS: Coming in from the outer planets, Alalu encountered Saturn first, then Jupiter and then the asteroid belt, AKA the Hammered Bracelet. Jupiter, as it states, is our largest planet, and we know today that Jupiter has storm spots as large as our planet Earth which we describe as colored and swirling. Coming around the backside of Jupiter's circuit, the Sun comes into view and correctly identifies the Sun as The One From the Beginning. Irrefutable science........ wouldn't you agree?

Of rocks and boulders was it together hammered, like orphans with no mother they banded together.
Nibiru's probing chariots like praying lions they devoured.
The chariot of Alalu toward the Hammered Bracelet was headlong moving,
The ferocious boulders in close combat to boldly face
Alalu the Fire Stones in his chariot more strongly stirred up,
That Which Shows the Way with steady hands he directed.
Toward them Alalu a death-dealing missile from the chariot let loose;
Then another and another against the enemy the terror weapons he thrust.
Like by a spell the Hammered Bracelet a doorway to the king it opened.

Then snow-hued Earth appeared, the seventh in the celestial count.
Toward the planet Alalu set his course to a destination most invit-

ing.

Smaller than Nibiru was its alluring ball, weaker than Nibiru's was its attracting net. (gravity)

Its atmosphere thinner than Nibiru's was clouds were within it swirling

Below the Earth to three regions was divided: Snow white at the top and on the bottom, blue and brown in between.

Deftly Alalu spread the chariots arresting wings around the Earth's ball to circle.

COMMENT: The same as a modern-day orbit procedure.

In the middle region drylands and watery oceans he could discern.

The Beam That Penetrates downward he directed, Earth's innards to detect.

Gold, much gold the beam has indicated; it was beneath the dark-hued region, in the waters too!

In the Eagles seat Alalu was not stirring; to fate's hands the chariot he trusted

Fully caught in Earth attracting net, the chariot was moving faster.

Its spread wings became aglow; Earth's atmosphere like an oven was.

Then the chariot shook, emitting a mortifying thunder.

With abruptness the chariot crashed, with a suddenness altogether stopping.

COMMENT: Reentry and sonic boom. Spread wings aglow due to friction of Earth's atmosphere.
What a classic description!

At the planet of gold Alalu victoriously arrived, his chariot with thunder crashing.

He put on an Eagle's helmet, he put on a Fishes suit.

The chariots hatch he opened; at the open hatch he stopped to wonder.

A pole from the chariot he extended; with a tester it was equipped.

It breathed the planet's air; compatibility it indicated!

The chariot's hatch he opened, at the open hatch he took a breath.

Another breath he took, then another and another; the air of KI indeed was compatible!

Without an Eagle's helmet, without a Fishes suit, to the ground himself he lowered.

The brightness outside was blinding; the rays of the Sun were overpowering!

Into the chariot he returned, a mask for his eyes he donned.

He picked up the carried weapon, he picked up the handy sampler.

Into the pond the sampler he lowered; for drinking the water was good

A sound hissing he could hear; a slithering body by the poolside was moving!

His carried weapon he seized, a blast of its ray toward the hissing he directed.

The moving stopped the hissing was ended.

Into deeper waters he waded, the Tester into the waters he inserted.

Then Alalus' heartbeat stopped: There is gold in the waters, the tester is telling!

Back to the chariot he made his way, the Fish's suit off he took, the commander's seat he occupied.

The Tablet of Destinies that knows all circuits he enlivened to Nibiru's circuit to find the direction.

The Speaker of Words he uttered, thus he was saying:

The words of the great Alalu to Anu on Nibiru are directed.

On another world am I, the gold of salvation I have found.

The third Tablet

The words of Anu Alalu's chariot did reach; Alalu them quickly answered:

Alalu the words merit pondered, to transmit his secrets he agreed;

Of the Tester its crystal innards he removed, from the Sampler its crystal heart he took out;

Into the Speaker he the crystals inserted, all the findings to transmit.

With heavy heart Ea(Enki) the chariot entered, to soar up the command he gave.

The celestial chariot he deftly guided; from Nibiru it powerfully soared, toward

the distant Sun he it directed.

Little Gaga (Pluto) came out to greet them, a welcome to the heroes it was extending.

Toward the heavenly An (Uranus), the third in planetary counts, the chariot continued.

On its side was An lying, his host of moons about him were whirling.

The Testers beams the presence of water was revealing; a stop if needed to Ea it was indicating.

Soon the ensnarling pull of Anshar (Saturn) they could tell, his colored rings with fear they admired.

The giant Kishar (Jupiter) foremost of firm planets, was next to be encountered.

Her net pull was overpowering, with great skill did Anzu the chariots course divert.

Beyond the fifth planer the Hammered Bracelet was lurking!

The water thruster to prepare. Toward the host of turning boulders the chariot was rushing.

The word of EA was given, With a force of a thousand heroes the stream of water was thrust.

But as one bolder fled, another in its stead was attacking;

A multitude beyond count was their number, a host for the splitting of Tiamat revenge seeking!

And then at last the path was cleared; it's unharmed the chariot would continue!

A cry of joy the heroes sounded; double was the joy as the sight of the Sun was now unveiled.

Waters to feed the chariots Fiery Stones for the remaining journey were not sufficient!

There is water on Lahmu, (Mars) EA was saying.

The planet's net is not great, its pull is to handle easy, Anzu was saying.

A sight to behold was Lahmu, snow white was its cap, snow white were its sandals.

On command the heroes That Which Water Sucks extended, the chariots bowels with the lakes waters to fill.

The waters were good for drinking, the air was insufficient.

With its vigor replenished the chariot soared up to benevolent Lahmu farewell biding.

COMMENTS: AS this section correctly states, the gravitational pull of a given planet is, in general, proportional to its size and mass. Clearly, water is used as a source of fuel. One of the major problems of space travel is we can't load enough fuel on a craft to get the craft to distant planets without having to refuel. The major source of fuel would necessarily come from an external source like the Sun.

The Anunnaki evidently have the technological knowledge to separate Hydrogen from water and use it as a fuel source. Now the planets that have water become a "Cosmic Gas Station", if you will.

Uranus still lies on its side 58°.

Modern Science has determined that 8 ounces of water, contains enough Hydrogen, once separated, to provide elect power to New York City for more than 24 hours. Helium-3 is somewhat abundant on the surface of the moon. A "spacecraft" loaded with Helium-3 could power all of America for one full year!

The chariot must be slowed or in Earth's thick atmosphere it shall perish! Anzu to Ea declared.

Around Earth's companion, the Moon, make slowing circled Ea to him suggested.

They circled the Moon; by the vanquishing Nibiru in the Celestial Battle it prostrate and scarred was lying.

Having the chariot thus slowed down, toward the seventh planet Anzu the chariot directed.

Once, twice the Earth's globe he made the chariot circle, ever closer to the Firm Land he lowered it.

Snow hued was two thirds of the planet, dark hued was its middle.

They could see the oceans, they could see the Firm Lands; for the signal beacon from Alalu they were searching.

When an ocean touched dry land, where four rivers were swallowed by marshes, Alalu's signal was beaconed.

Two heavy and large the chariot is for the marshes! Anzu was declaring.

The Earth's pulling net, too powerful for on dry land to descend it is! Anzu to Ea announced.

Splash down! Splash down in the ocean's waters! Ea to Anzu shouted.

Around the planet Anzu made one more circuit, the chariot with much care toward the ocean's edge he lowered.

The chariot's lungs he filled with air; into the waters down it splashed, into the depths it was not sinking.

From the Speaker a voice was heard: To Earth be welcomed! Alalu was saying.

By his beamed words the direction of his whereabouts was determined.

Toward the place Anzu the chariot directed, floating as a boat it was upon the waters moving.

Anzu a Beam-That- Kills from the chariot brought over, a Speaker-That-Words-Beams at Ea's abode he set up.

Ea the task of gold from the waters obtaining started.
Thus were the metals that were in the waters in the vessel collected.
In the vessels metals were collected!
Iron there was, much copper there was; of gold there no abundance.

A month did EA the Moons circuit call, Month to its circuit he gave the name.

The Sun, every six Months to earth another season gave; Winter and Summer did EA by names them call.

There was Winter and there was Summer; By Year of Earth did Ea the full circuit call.

ERIDU.

Now this is the account of how Eridu on Earth was established
By evetime, complete was the encampment! the heroes gathered.
Ea (Enki), and Alalu, and Anzu the doings considered; all that was done indeed was good!
And it was evening, and it was morning, the sixth day.

On the seventh day the heroes in the encampment were assembled, to them Ea spoke these words:

A hazardous journey, we have taken, from Nibiru to the seventh planet, a dangerous way we traversed.

At Earth, we with success arrived, much good we attained, an encampment we established.

Let this be a day of rest; the seventh day hereafter a day of resting always to be!

Let this place, henceforth by the name. Eridu be called, Home in the Faraway. The meaning there of will be!

12th P 35p

COMMENT: The ancients texts reveals the building of Eridu, took place some 445,000 years ago. The heroes, or astronauts from the planet Nibiru, looking for gold and building their Home in the Faraway.

In time Eridu became the starting place of the first great civilization of the Sumerians. The city of Eridu was discovered by archaeologists in 1919. They unearthed a temple dedicated to Ea (Enki), a temple that had been rebuilt again and again. Continuing the excavation to the inevitable discovery of virgin soil, and the discovery of the first Temple built for Enki, circa 3800 B.C!.

In the surrounding area and villages, the archaeologist found ***indisputable proof of the earliest civilization***, validating and verifying the written words of ***the Extraterrestrial god, Enki!***

Tablet 4

With confidence was Abgal the chariot guiding;

Around Kingu, the Moon, he made a circuit, by its net powers speed to gain.

(N.A.S.A. personnel describe this as a "Slingshot effect."

A thousand leagues, ten thousand leagues toward Lahmu he journeyed,

Deftly did Abgal Ea's crystals make aglow, the opened paths to locate.

In the Abzu the soil they tested. Gold there was indeed:

with much soil and rocks it was commixed,

Refined as in the waters it was not, in an admixture it was hiding.

Along the way there is the Lahmu planet,
with waters and an atmosphere it is endowed.
Enki, asEa, they're on made a pause;
of it as a way station have I been thinking.
Its net force is less than that of Earth forceful,
an advantage in wisdom to be considered.

An Earth Splinter with cleverness Enki designed,
on Nibiru that it be fashioned he requested,
Therewith in the Earth to make a gash,
its innards reach by way of tunnels;
That-Which-Crunches and That- Which-Crushes he also designed,

To snow covered mountains on the Edin's north side he took a liking,
The tallest trees he ever saw grew there in a cedar forest. (Lebanon)
There above a mountain valley with power beams the surfaced he flattened. (there are still artificially flattened areas there)
Great stones from the hillside the heroes quarried and to size cut.
To uphold the platform with sky ships they carried and emplaced them.
With satisfaction did Enlil the handiwork consider,
A work beyond belief indeed it was, a rupture of everlasting!

COMMENT: There is only one geographical location and source for a cedar forest with what Enlil describes as "The tallest trees he ever saw," Baalbek, Lebanon. In our opinion, what is being built, as described in the above paragraph, is at least the beginning of Baalbek's Landing Place.

Indeed it was just as Enlil described it, "beyond belief a structure of everlasting!" *The massive stone platform still exists,* called Baalbek, the place of the biblical Canaanite, Anunnaki god Ba'al

There are three massive stone blocks placed side-by-side forming a strategic part of the massive platform each weighing about 1,100 *tons.* An impossibility for modern man or machine to move. We know that the stone blocks came from a quarry about a mile away from the building site as one colossal stone (1100 tons) remains today protruding from the mountainside half- quarried.

As the ancient text described it *"Great stones from the hillside the heroes quarried and to size cut. To uphold the platform with sky ships they carried and emplaced them."*

The Landing place, Baalbek, was built in the pre-diluvial days. Here is how the Anunnaki described it after the flood.

All that in the Olden Times in the Edin, in the Abzu had existed under the mud was buried!

Eridu, Nibiru-ki, Shurubak, Sippar, all were gone, completely vanished;

With wet in the Cedar Mountains in the great stone platform in the sunlight glistened,

The Landing Place, in the Olden Times established, was still standing after the flood!

And it still stands today!

FACE ON MARS

Inside what of Alalu remained they found;

He who once on Nibiru was a pile of bones was in a cave and now!

For the first time in our annals, a king not on Nibiru has died, not on Nibiru was he buried!

So did Ninmah say. Let him in peace for a eternity rest! she was saying.

They the cave entrance again with stones covered;

The image of Alalu upon the great rock Mountain with beams they carved.

They showed him a wearing an Eagles helmet: his face they made uncovered.

Let the image of Alalu forever gaze toward Nibiru that he ruled,

Toward the Earth whose gold he discovered!

COMMENT: In our opinion, this description is of the Face on Mars, is a tomb honoring Alalu.

With a bright metal, silver is its name, it is embellished,

With a deep blue stone, lapis lazuli, it is adorned;

COMMENT: Lapis lazuli (sapphire) is a stone frequently mentioned in the Bible.

In Nibiru-ki Enlil the Bond Heaven-Earth established, a sight to
see it was.
At its center a heavenward tall pillar the sky itself was reaching,
On a platform that cannot be overturned it was placed;
Therewith the words of Enki all settlements encompassed, on Lah-
mu and in Nibiru they were heard.
From there beams were raised the heart of all the lands they could
search ;
Its eyes could skin all the lands, its net unwanted approach impos-
sible made.
In its lofty house a crown like chamber was the center, to distant
heavens it peered;
Toward the horizon was its gaze, the heavenly zenith it perfected.
And it's dark hollowed chamber, by twelve emblems was the family
of the Sun marked,
On ME's were these secret formulas of Sun and Moon,
Nibiru and Earth, and eight celestial gods recorded.
The Tablets of Destinies in the chamber their hues emitted,
With him Enlil all comings and goings oversaw.

COMMENT: That's what you could describe as a security system
for their communications center.

To death by execution the seven judged Anzu;
With a killing ray Anzu's life breath was extinguished.
Let his body to the vultures be left! Ninurta said.

The essences|(DNA) in the ME's Ninmah carefully considered,
One bit she took from one, one a bit she took out from another,
Then in the crystal bowl the oval of an Earth female she insemi-
nated
There was conception, at the appropriate time there was birth giv-
ing!
This one more in the likeness of the Anunnaki was;
In the Hammered Bracelet, (asteroid belt) turmoils are occurring!
Upon the Earth, brimstone from the skies are falling.
Pitiless demons havoc causing, violently the Earth they approached,
Into flaming fires in the skies they were bursting.
Like stony missiles the Earth they were attacking,

Kingu, Earth's Moon, and Lahmu (Mars) too by these havocs were afflicted,
The faces of all three with countless scars were covered!

One league was its head, fifty leagues in length it was, awesome with its tail
By day the skies of Earth it darkened,
By night upon the face of the Moon a spell of darkness it cast.
To intercept the dragon in its path Kingu was making haste:
By its foundations was Kingu shaken, from the impact did the Moon quake and shake.
The stony missiles upon the Earth and Lahmu ceased their reigning.

Nearby the Earth a companion it has, the Moon it is!
Smaller in its net pull, ascent and descent thereon the little effort will require.

Do not be hasty, my son! So was Enki to Marduk saying.
Are you not by the celestial dance of Earth and the Moon and Sun Enchanted?
Unobstructed from here is the viewing, the quarter of the Sun is at Hand,
The Earth like a globe in the void by nothing is hanging.

Let us stay, the circuits observe, how the Moon circles the Earth,
How the Earth its circuits around the Sun is making!
By his father's words Marduk was persuaded; in the rocketship they made their dwelling.
For one circuit of Earth, for three circuits on the Moon they remained;
Its motions about the Earth they measured the duration of a month they calculated.
For six circuits of Earth, for twelve circuits about the Sun, Earth's year they measured.
How the two were entwined, causing the luminaries to disappear they recorded
Then to the (1) Sun's quarter they attention gave, the paths of. (2) Mummu (Mercury)

and(3) Lahamu (Venus) they studied.

With the (4) Earth and the (5) Moon, (6) Lahmu (Mars) the Sun's second quarter constituted,

Six were the celestials of the Lower Waters So was Enki to Marduk explaining.

Six were the Celestials s of the Upper Waters,., beyond the bar, the Hammered Bracelet, they were:

(7) Anshar (Saturn) (8) Kishar (Jupiter), (9)Anu (Uranus) and (10)Nudimmud (Neptune), (11) Gaga (Pluto) and (12)Nibiru.

12 they were in all, of 12 did the Sun and its family make the count.

COMMENT: Is this not proof that the Anunnaki, the Nephilim of the Bible had full knowledge of our solar system dating back more than 2000 B.C. This example is only one of many depictions of our solar system conveyed to us in writing from the ancient texts. Hence the masterful work of Zachariah Sitchin's, The 12ᵗʰ Planet. Unchallenged and undisputed now for more than 40 years.

By the motions of Nibiru, of the Sun not a descendant, the width of the great band he outlined.

And the expense of the deep evidence, the stars did father and son observe:

By their proximity and groupings was Enki fascinated.

By the circuit of the heavens, from horizon to horizon, he drew images of twelve constellations.

To each one he designated a station, by the names they were to be called.

To it twelve constellations by their shapes he also allotted.

Therein too the stars into twelve constellations he assembled.

Henceforth when Nibiru nears and departs, from Earth by the stars stations its course shall be known

So will the Earth's position designated as around the Sun it travels!

The start of the cycle, of Celestial Time the measure, Enki to Marduk indicated.

Of the family of the Son and the twelve celestial gods Enki him (Adapa) was teaching,

And how the months by the Moon were counted and the years by the Sun,

And how by Nibiru the Shars were counted, and how you count of Enki were combined,

A constellation to each one how Enki assigned, 12 stations in a grand circle he arranged,

How to honor the twelve Anunnaki great leaders by names the stations were called.

Contrary to popular opinion we did not obtain our knowledge of the heavens from the Greeks. Here Enki creates, formulates, designates (and names in many ancient texts) the stations and positions of our Zodiac, from Greek meaning Animal Circle.

The Egyptians themselves were familiar with our constellations which they, in turn, derived from the Anunnaki. The names the Egyptians used to describe each of the12 constellations are the same names of the constellations we use today. It all goes back to Sumer!

Ningishzidda his hand on the neck of Adapa put; in an instant was Adapa quiet.

(For levity, I thought I'd throw in a little Star Trek)

On the Suns face black spots were appearing, from his face flames shot up;

(This cannot be observed with the naked eye)

The next time Nibiru the Sun shall be nearing, Earth Nibiru's net force exposed shall be

Lahmu (Mars) in its circuits on the Sun's other side shall a station take.

From the net force Nibiru Earth in the heavens protection shall not have,

Kishar (Jupiter) and its host agitated shall be, Lahamu (Venus) shall also shake and wobble;

In Earth's great Below, the snow and ice of the White land its footing is losing;

The next time Nibiru the closest to Earth shall approach,

The snow ice of the White lands surface shall come, a- sliding.

A watery calamity it shall cause: By a huge wave, a Deluge, the

Earth will be overwhelmed!

On that day, on that unforgettable day, the Deluge with a roar began;

And the White land, at the Earth's bottom, the Earth's foundation were shaking;

Then with a roar of a thousand thunders equal, off its foundations, the ice sheets slipped,

By Nibiru's unseen net force it was pulled away, into the south sea crashing.

One sheet of ice into another ice sheet was smashing,

The White lands surface like a broken eggshell was crumbling.

All at once a tidal wave arose, the very skies was the wall of waters reaching.

Now we know that the Deluge of the Bible was not caused by 40 days and 40 nights of rain.

The ancient texts explain why it happened and how it happened.

WHO BUILT THE PYRAMIDS PARTIAL

Artificial peaks there on we can raise! So did Ningishzidda (Thoth) to the leaders say.

On a tablet the image of a smooth-sided, skyward rising peaks for them he drew.

If it can be done, let it be so! Enlil with approval said. Let them also as beacons serve!

Ningishzidda a scale model built,

The rising angles and four smooth sides with it he perfected.

Next to it a larger peak he placed, its side to Earths four corners he set ;

By the Anunnaki with their tools of power, were its stones cut and erected.

Beside it in a precise location, the peak that was its twin he placed;

With galleries and chambers for pulsating crystals he designed it.

When this artful peak to the heavens rose to place upon it the cap-stone the leaders were invited.

Of electrum, an admixture by Gibil fashioned, was the Apex Stone made.

The sunlight to the horizon it reflected, by night like a pillar of fire it was,

The power of all the crystals to the heavens in a beam it focused.

When the artful works, by Ningishzidda (Thoth) designed, were completed and ready.

Ekur, (Pyramid) House Which Like a Mountain Is, they named it, a beacon to the heavens it was.

Now you know who built the Pyramids, the Anunnaki which Enki (Ea) and Ningishzidda (Thoth) conceived of and designed. In "The Emerald Tablets of Thoth" he states plainly that he built the Pyramids ***using anti-gravity machines.*** That's clear enough for us.

Enki to Enlil words of suggestions said: When in future days it will be asked:

When and by whom has this marvel been fashioned?

Let us beside the Twin Peaks a monument to create, the Age of the Lion (Sphinx) let it announce,

The image of Ningishzidda, the peaks' designer, let its face be,

Let it precisely towards the Place of the Celestial Chariots gaze

To further elucidate your knowledge of the Anunnaki, they also built the Sphinx and the original face on the Spinks belonged to none other than Thoth. Later the face was changed to a son of Thoth, Asar/Osiris.

TABLET 11

With the waters did the Celestial Chariots obtained their thrust power, in waters I splashed down;

(Just in case you missed my previous statement that the Anunnaki evidently could separate the hydrogen molecules from the oxygen and use it for fuel.)

At its entrance Marduk the sliding stone blocks lowered; from one and all admission they barred

Into the Ekur (Pyramid) Inanna and Ishkur Ninurta followed; what next to do that contemplated.

Let the encased hiding chamber be Marduk's stone coffin! To them Iskur said.

To three blocking stones, ready for download gliding, Iskur their attention drew

Let slow death, by alive being buried, be Marduk's sentence! Inanna her consent gave.

At the end of the Gallery, the three the blocking stones let loose,

Each one of them one stone for plugging slip down, Marduk as in a tomb was sealed.

The sliding stone and the three blocking stones by Archaeologists and Scientists.

In a hollowed out chest the heart of the Ekur pulsated, its net force by five compartments was enhance.

With his baton Ninurta the stone chest struck; with a resonating sound it responded.

It's Gug Stone, that the direction determined, Ninurta ordered to be taken out, to a place of his choice carried.

Coming down the grand Gallery, Ninurta the twenty-seven pairs of Nibiru crystals examined.

To replace the incapacitated beacon a mountain near the Place of the Celestial Chariots was chosen.

Within its innards the salvaged crystals were rearranged.

Upon its peak the Gug Stone of Directing, was installed;

.As clearly stated, the Pyramids were not built nor used as a tomb for the Pharaohs.

His Tablets of Destinies did Enlil there keep, with his weapons it was protected:

The Lifted Eye that scans the lands, the Lifted Beam that penetrates all.

In the courtyard, in its own enclosure, Enlil's fast-stepping Skybird (helicopter) was kept.

How to a place for melting and refining metals it was made Ninurta explained.

How a new metal from stones was extracted he showed them: Anak, Anunnocki -made he called it.

How by combining it with the abundant copper a strong metal he invented, he showed them.

In the Age of the Bull, to Enlil dedicated, was the count of the Earth years begun.

This is the start of our year one obviously **relates to the Hebrew calendar**.

In Kishi were the black-headed people with numbers to calculate taught,
Heavenly Nisiba writing them taught, heavenly Ninkashi ___beer making them___ showed.

My kind of Anunnocki gals.

For Inanna a celestial constellation to her which assigned:
Beforehand with her brother Utu the Station of the Twins she shared
Henceforth as a gift from Ninharsag, her Constellation of the Maiden to Inanna was allotted;

TABLET 13

Let Gilgamesh to the Landing Place go! Utu in the end agreed.
To guide and protect him, Ninharsag a double of Gilgamesh fashioned
Enkidu, As by Enki Created was he called, of a womb he was not born, blood in his veins was not.

Evidently, Enki had created an android?

In a dream vision to Enlil, Galzu prophesies :
One who himself as Supreme God has declared supremacy on earth will seize.

The dream vision prophesy was fulfilled by Marduk. Not only did he declare himself the Supreme God over all the Anunnaki, but he also changed the names of the festivals and rituals to include his name. Enuma Elish, which was read every year during the Festival he changed the name of the celestial god, the planet Nibiru, to the planet Marduk. He ruled over the Anunnaki as the Supreme God. Scholars and authors accredit his actions in the ancient texts as attributing to the conceptual formation of Monotheism by the biblical scribes. We concur.

NUCLEAR? NO DOUBT

Those seven Weapons of Terror, in a mountain they abide! To them Enki said.

In a cavity inside the Earth they dwell, with the terror to clad them is required!

When Ninurta at the weapons place arrived, Nergal from the cavity had already been brought out,

As their ME's from the long slumber he awakened, and each one of these seven Nergal a task name made:

The One Without Rival the first weapon he called, he The Blazing Flame he named to the second,

The One Who with Terror Crumbles he called the third, Mountain Melter the fourth he called,

Wind That the Rim of the World Seeks he named the fifth, the One Who Above and Below No One Spares was the sixth,

At the seventh with monstrous venom was filled, Vaporizer of Living Things he called it.

With Anu's blessing were the seven Nerdgal and Ninurta given, therewith to destruction wreck.

A thousand and seven hundred and thirty-six was the count of Earth years then.

The Mount and the plain, in the heart of the Fourth Region, Ninurta from the skies surveyed.

Then the first terror weapon from the skies Ninurta let loose;

The top of Mount Mashu with a flash it sliced off, the mount's innards in an instant it melted.

Above the Place of the Celestial Chariots the second weapon he

209

unleashed,

With a brilliance of seven suns the plain's rocks into a gushing wound were made,

The Earth shook crumbled, the heavens after the brilliance were darkened;

With burnt and crushed stones was the plane of the chariots covered,

Of all the forests that the plain that had surrounded only tree stems are left standing.

It is done! Ninurta from the sky ship, his Black Divine Bird, words shouted.

Over the five cities, one after the other, Erra upon each from the skies a terror weapon sent,

With fire and brimstone's they were upheavaled, all that lived there to vapor was turned.

By the awesome weapons were the mountains toppled, where the sea waters were barred the bolt broke open,

Down into the valley the sea's waters poured, by the waters was the valley flooded;

When upon the cities' ashes the waters poured, steam to the heavens was rising

It is done! Erra in his sky ship shouted. In Nergal's heart there was no more vengeance.

By a darkening of the skies were the brilliances followed, then a storm to blow began.

Swirling within a dark cloud, gloom from the skies an Evil Wind carried,

As the day wore on, the Son on the horizon with the darkness it obliterated,

At night time a dreaded brilliance skirted its edges, the Moon at its rising it made disappear.

The dark brown cloud eastward it directed, towards the settled lands did the cloud spread;

Wherever it reached, death to all that lives mercilessly it delivered;

Unstoppable the Evil Wind death to all delivers!

From their cities the gods did flee, like frightened birds from their nests escaping they were.

The people of the lands by the Evil Storms hand were clutched; futile was the running.

Stealthy was the death, like a ghost the fields and cities it attacked;

The highest wall, the thickest walls, like floodwaters it passed,

No door could shut it out, no bolt could turn it back.

Those behind the locked doors hid inside their houses like flies were felled

Those who to the streets fled, and in the streets were their corpses piled up.

Cough and phlegm the chests filled, the mouth with foam and spittle filled up

Slowly over the lands the Evil Wind blew, from East to West over the plains and mountains it traveled;

Everything that lived, behind it was dead and dying, people and cattle, all alike perished

The waters were poisoned, in the fields all vegetation withered.

From Eridu in the South to Sippar in the north did the Evil Wind the land overwhelm

Babili, where Marduk supremacy declared, by the Evil Wind was spared.

Let the Future of the Past the judge be!

These are the words of Enki, Firstborn of Anu of Nibiru.

No doubt remains in our minds, that the above paragraphs describe a Nuclear Holocaust,

followed by radiation fallout. If doubt remains in the reader's mind .....read

the ancient texts Erra Epos.

Chapter 10: Ancient Use of Nuclear Weapons

The ancient texts tell us that the Sumerian civilization sprang up in Sumer circa 3800 BC. Those same texts tell us that the Sumerian civilization came to an abrupt end in 3000 BC. The beginning and the end of that civilization are excepted, undisputed and factually documented from texts such as The Era Epos, The Attestation of Endubsar, and The Lamentation Texts, of which there is an existing text lamenting the destruction of each Sumerian city.

The questions posed by these ancient texts were not that Sumer existed, and Sumer was destroyed, but how were the cities and other areas, targeted by the Anunnaki, destroyed in a very short, same time period? No one knew, until one man, Zechariah Sitchin, the man I will always refer to, with undying respect and admiration, as the "Godfather of the Ancient Texts," committed his brilliant mind and brilliant abstract IQ, to solve the enigma. I will begin with The Attestation of Endubsar:

THE FIRST TABLET

The words of the Lord Enki, firstborn son of Anu, who reigns on Nibiru,

With heavy spirit laments; laments that are bitter fill my heart.

How smitten is the land, its people delivered to the Evil Wind, it stables abandoned, its sheep foals emptied.

How smitten are the cities, their people piled up as dead corpses, afflicted by the Evil Wind.

How smitten are the fields, their vegetation withered, touched by the Evil Wind.

How smitten are the rivers, nothing swims anymore, pure sparkling waters turned into poison.

Of its black headed people, humor is emptied, gone is all life;

Of its cattle and sheep Schumer is emptied, silent is the hum of churning milk.

In its glorious cities, only the wind howls; death is the only smell.

The temples and whose heads to heaven arose by their gods have been abandoned.

Of Lordship and kingship command there is none; scepter and tiara are gone.

On the banks of the two great rivers, once lush and life-giving, only weeds grow.

No one treads the highways, no one seeks out the roads; flourishing Schumer is like an abandoned desert.

How smitten is the land, home of gods and men!

On that land a calamity fell, one unknown to man.

A calamity that Mankind had never before seen, one that could not be withstood.

On all lands, from West to East, a disruptive land of terror was placed. The gods, and their cities, were helpless as men!

An Evil Wind, a storm born in a distant plane, a Great Calamity wrought in its path.

A death dealing wind born in the west its way to the east has made, it's course set by fate.

A storm, devouring as the deluge, by wind and not by water a destroyer; by poisoned air, not tidal waves,
    expanded.

By fate not destiny, was it engendered; the great gods in their counsel, the Great Calamity had caused.

By Enlil and Ninharsag it was permitted; I alone for a halt was beseeching.

Day and night to accept what the heavens decree I argued, to no avail!

Ninurta, Enlil's warrior son, and Nergal, my very own son, poisoned weapons in the Great Plains then unleashed.

That an Evil Wind show followed the brilliance we knew not! They now cry in agony.

That the death dealing storm, born in the West, its course to the east shall make, who could foretell! The gods now bemoan.

In their holy cities, the gods stood disbelieving as the Evil Wind toward Schumer made its way.
One after another the gods fled their cities, their temples abandoned to the wind.
In my city, Eridu, as the poisoned cloud approach, I could do nothing to stop it.
Escape to the open steppe! to the people I gave instructions; with Ninki, my spouse, the city I abandoned.

In his city Nippur, place of the Bond Heaven-Earth, Enlil could do nothing to stop it.

The Evil Wind against Nippur was on rushing. In his celestial boat, Enlil and his spouse hurriedly took off.

In Ur, Shumer's city of kingship, Nannar to his father Enlil for help cried;

In the place of the Temple that to heaven in seven steps rises, Nannar the hand of fate refuses to heed it.

My father who begot me, great God who to Ur had granted kingship, turn the Evil Wind away! Nannar pleaded.

Great God who decrees the fates, let Ur and its people be spared, your praises to continue! Nannar appealed.

Enlil answered his son Nannar: Noble son, your wondrous city kingship was granted; eternal reign it was not granted.

Take hold of your spouse Ningal, flee the city! Even I who decree fates, it's destiny I cannot bend!

Thus did Enlil my brother speak; alas, alas, not a destiny it was!
A calamity none greater since the deluge gods and Earthlings has befallen; alas, not a destiny it was!

The great deluge was destined to happen; the Great Calamity of the death dealing storm was not.

By the breach of a vow, by a Council decision it was caused; by Weapons of Terror was it created.

By a decision, not destiny, were the poisoned weapons unleashed; by deliberation was the lot cast.

Against Marduk, my firstborn, did the two sons destruction direct; vengeance was in their hearts.

Ascendancy is not Marduk's to grasp! Enlil's firstborn shouted.

With weapons I shall oppose him, Ninurta said.

Of people he raised an army, Babili as Earth's naval to declare! Nargal, Marduk's brother, so shouted.

In the Council of the great gods, words of venom were spread.

Ishkur, Enlil's youngest, punishment demanded; in my lands to whore after him the people he made! He said.

Utu, son of Nannar, at Marduk's son Nabu his wrath directed: The Place of the Celestial Chariots he tried to seize!

Inanna, twin of Utu, was furious of all; the punishment of Marduk for the killing of her beloved Dumuzi she still demanded.

Only with weapons will Marduk be stopped! Ninurta, Enlil's first-born, shouted.

Utu about protecting the Place of the Celestial Chariots was concerned; in Marduk's hands it must not fall! So he said.

Nergal, Lord of the Lower Domain, ferociously was demanding: Let the olden Weapons of Terror for obliteration be used!

At my own son I gazed it in disbelief: For brother against brother the terror weapons have been forsworn!

In the silence Enlil opened his mouth: Punishment there must be; like birds without wings the evildoers shall be,

Marduk and Nabu us of heritage are depriving; let them of the Place of Celestial Chariots be deprived!

Let the place be scorched to oblivion! Ninurta shouted, the One Who Scorches let me be!

Excited, Nergal stood up and shouted: Let the evildoers cities also be upheaveled,

The Earthlings, by us created, must not be harmed; the righteous with the sinners must not be perished, I forcefully said.

Ninharsag, my creating helpmate, was consenting; The matter is between the gods alone to settle, the people must not be harmed.
Anu, from the celestial abode, to the discussions was giving much

heed.

Anu, who determines fates, from the celestial abode his voice made heard:

Let the Weapons of Terror be this once used, let the place of the rocket ships be obliterated, let the people be spared.

Let Ninurta the Scorcher be, let Nergal be the Annihilator! So did Enlil the decision announce.

To them, a secret of the gods I shall reveal; the hiding place of the terror weapons to them I shall disclose.

LAMENTATION FOR THE DESTRUCTION
OF UR (Selected Verses)

In its lofty gates, where they were want
to Promenade, dead bodies lay about…
Where the festivities of the land took place,
the people lay in heaps…
The young were lying in their mothers' laps
like fish carried out of the waters…
The counsel of the land was dissipated.

In the storehouses that abounded in the land,
fires were kindled…
The ox in its stable has not been attended,
 gone is its herdsman…
The sheep in his fold has not been attended,
gone is its shepherd boy…
In the rivers of the city dust has gathered,

The Temple of Ur has been given over
to the wind…
The song has been turned into weeping…
Ur has been given over to tears.

On that day,

When heaven was crushed
and the Earth was smitten,
it's face obliterated by the maelstrom--
When the skies were darkened
and the cupboard as a shadow--

A great storm from heaven...
A land- annihilating storm...
An evil wind, like a rushing torrent...
A battling storm joined by a scorching heat...
By day it deprived the land of the bright sun,
in the evening the stars did not shine...

The people, terrified, could hardly breathe;
The Evil Wind clutched them,
does not grant them another day...
Mouths were drenched in blood,
heads wallowed in blood...
The face was made pale by the Evil Wind.

It caused cities to be desolated,
It caused houses to become desolate,
It caused stalls to become desolate,
the sheepfolds to be emptied...
Sumer's rivers it made flow
with the water that is bitter;
it's cultivated feels grow weeds,
it's pastors grow withering plants.

Ningal, the Anunnaki goddess of Ur, relates her sense of foreboding doom.
Verse 7

And then verily, to the assembly, where the crowd had not yet risen,

while the Anunnaki, binding themselves (to uphold the decision),
were still seated,

I dragged my feet and I stretched out my arms,

Truly I shed my tears in front of On/Anu.

Truly I myself mourned in front of Enlil:

Verse 8

"May my city not be destroyed!" I said indeed to them.

"May Ur not be destroyed!" I said indeed to them.

"And may its people not be killed!" I said indeed to them.

But An/Anu never bent towards those words,

Verse 9

(Behold,) they gave instruction that the city be destroyed,

(behold,) they gave instruction that Ur be destroyed,

and as its destiny decreed that its inhabitants be killed.

Verse 10

Enlil called the storm. The people mourn.

Disputed evil wins. The people mourn.

Verse 12

(Great) fires he lit that heralded the storm. The people mourn.

And lift on either bank of furious winds the searing heat of the desert.
Like flaming heat of noon this fire scorched.

Verse 13

The storm ordered by Enlil in hate, the storm which wears away the country,

covered Ur like a cloth, veiled it like a linen sheet.

Verse 14

On that day did the storm leave the city; that city was in ruin.

O father Nanna, that town was left in ruin. The people mourn.

On that day did the storm leave the country. The people mourn.

It's peoples, not potsherds, littered the approaches.

The walls were gaping; the high gates, the roads, were piled with dead.

In the wide streets, where feasting crowds (once) gathered, jumbled they lay.

In all the streets and roadways bodies lay.

In open feels that used to fill with dancers, the people lay in heaps.

Verse 15

The country's blood now filled its holes, like metal in a mold;

bodies dissolved-like butter left in the sun.

The Lament of Sumer and Urim   (Selected Verses)

To overturn the appointed times, to obliterate the divine plans, the storms gathered to strike like a flood.

An, Enlil, Enki and Ninmah have decided its fate-- to destroy the

city, to destroy the house, to destroy the cattle
   pen, to level the sheepfold;

to take kingship away from the Land, to cast the eye of the storm
on all the land, to obliterate the divine plans by the order of An and
Enlil;

so is to obliterate the divine powers of Sumer,

that on the two parallel banks of the Tigris and of the Euphrates
bad weeds should grow,

that the city and its settled surroundings should be razed to ruin-;
that it's numerous black headed people should be slaughtered;

to decimate the animals of the open country, to finish off all living
things,

its' fate cannot be changed. Who will overturn it? It is the command of An and Enlil. Who can oppose it?

Turmoil descended upon the land, something that no one had ever
known, something unseen, which had no name, something that could
not be fathomed.

The people, in their fear, breathed only with difficulty. The storm
immobilized them, the storm did not let them return.

The dark time was roasted by hailstones and flames. The bright
time was wiped out by a shadow.

On that day, heaven rumbled, the earth trembled, the storm
worked without respite.

Large trees were uprooted, the forest growth was ripped out. The
orchards were stripped of their fruit.

There were corpses floating in the Euphrates.

On the feels fine range grew no more, people had nothing to eat. The orchards were scorched like an oven, it's open country was scattered.

Ninmul cried bitter tears over her destroyed city. "Oh my city, whose charms can no longer satisfy me," she cried bitterly.

On that day, the storm forced people to live in darkness.

In Urim no one went to fetch food, no one went to fetch water. Those who went to fetch food, went away from the food and will not return.

Those who went to fetch water, went away from the water and will not return.

In Urim, its people rushed around like water being poured from a well. Their strength ebbed away, they could not even go on their way.

It's people, like fish being grabbed in a pond, sought to escape. It's young and old lay spread about, no one could rise.

As the day grew dark, the eye of the sun was eclipsing.

Urim, like a city raked by hoe, is to be counted as a ruin-mound.

The judgment uttered by the assembly cannot be reversed.

The word of An and Enlil knows no overturning.

Urim was indeed given kingship but it was not given an eternal reign.

There is lamentation in the haunted city, mourning reeds grow there.
Indeed the storm that blew over Sumer, but also over the foreign lands.

It has blown over Tidman. It has blown over Gitium. It has blown over Ansan. It leveled Ansan like a blowing evil wind.

O mankind........, princess over, by lamentation and crying!

O Nanna! O your city! O your house! O your people!

Comment: The nuclear weapons were used in five cities, two of the most important cities, Sumer and Ur have been described in the two above translations. There was a total of seven nuclear bombs dropped. The other two sites were the Anunnaki's Spaceport in the Sinai Peninsula in the Anunnaki Command Center at Mount Mashu.

Every city west of the Dead Sea felt the devastating effects of, what we today call, radiation fallout. The Anunnaki obviously refers to radiation fallout as the Evil Wind.

THE CASE OF THE EVIL WIND
Climate Study Corroborates Sumer's Nuclear Fate

At the end of the third millennium, B. C. the great Sumerian civilization came to an abrupt end. Its sudden demise was bewailed in numerous lamentation texts that have been discovered by archaeologists. The texts ascribed the calamity to an Evil Wind that came blowing from the west (from the direction of the Mediterranean Sea)-a deadly cloud that caused excruciating death to all living beings, people and animals alike, that withered plants and poisoned the waters.

In The Wars of Gods and Men (third book of The Earth Chronicles series), Zechariah Sitchin saw an ex-elimination of the sudden death in a long text known to scholars as The Era Epos, that described a chain of events that ultimately led to the use of "Weapons of Terror" in a conflict between opposing clans of the Anunnaki ("Those who from Heaven to Earth Came").

Based on the descriptions of the weapons in the Era Epos and in the Lamentation Texts, Zechariah Sitchin concluded that the weapons of terror were nuclear weapons. Used to obliterate the spaceport that then existed in the Sinai Peninsula (and the "sinning cities" such as Sodom and Gomorrah", the nuclear cloud then was carried by the prevailing winds eastward, causing death and desolation to the Lands between the Rivers (Mesopotamia"-- the empire of Sumer and Akkad.

Besides claiming the nuclear weapons were first used on Earth, not in the 1940s in Hiroshima but thousands of years earlier in the Near East, Zechariah also pinpointed the date: 2024 B. C.!

SCIENTIFIC CORROBORATION NOW COMES ALONG

That the civilization that sprang out in Sumer circa 3800 BC-reaching unparalleled the heights under the last dynasty, the Third Dynasty of Ur (Abraham's city)--had come to an abrupt end near the end of the third millennium BC has been an accepted and well-documented fact. That the end was abrupt, was also certain. What scholars deemed is still lacking was an explanation: How, what caused it?

Beginning in 1999, archaeologists and scholars specializing in the Near East saw mounting evidence that the demise of Sumer and Akkad (Sumer's northern extension) coincided with an abrupt climate change. And the initial study by Harvey Weiss and Timothy C. Wieskel of Harvard University was reinforced by a subsequent study (Geology, April 2000) by H. M. Cullen at a from the Lamont Doherty Earth Observatory of Columbia University, the University of Utah, the Lawrence Livermore national laboratory, and the Institute of fur Geowissenschaftens, Germany. Based on studies of unexplained aridity and windblown dust storms and radiocarbon datings, they reported that their readings indicated a date of 4025 years ago (plus or minus a margin of 125 years)

A precise date corroborated!

Those and similar climate change studies, relating the climate conditions to the rise and fall of civilizations in the Old as well as the New Worlds, were summed up in a major study published in the prestigious journal Science in its 27 April 2001 issue. Authored by Peter B. deMenocal of the Lamont-Doherty Earth Observatory of Columbia University, the study paid particular attention to sedimentary remains of Tephra; the tail rock fragments confirmed the date of 4025 years, before present.

And 4025 years, before the present year A. D. 2001-- is exactly

2024 BC, as Zechariah Sitchin had determined in his 1985 book!

The Tephra Mystery

The reliance on the latest study on the Tephra evidence is doubly significant.

While the previous studies spoke of, "windblown dust," this latest study focuses on a material called Tephra. And what is Tephra? It is defined in geology textbooks thus:

> When a volcano erupts, it will sometimes eject material such as rock fragments into the atmosphere. This material is known as Tephra.

These burnt through pieces of blackened gravel-like rock mostly fall near their volcanic source, but ash-like particles can be carried by prevailing winds over many miles and can stay aloft for more than a year.

The area in the Sinai Peninsula where the destroyed spaceport had been indeed covered--- to this day-- with grave – like burnt through this blackened stones but as Zechariah Sitchin has pointed out in his book; there are **NO VOLCANOES** in the Sinai Peninsula. In the Sinai Peninsula, the source of the wind carried dust remains a mystery. And the only explanation for these broken and blackened stones in the Sinai and the windblown desolation in Mesopotamia can be the tail of the Era Epos, (reflected in the biblical tale of the upheaval of Sodom and Gomorrah): not an eruption by a nonexistent volcano, but the use of nuclear weapons in 2024 B. C.

C- Z. Sitchin November 2001

The Seven Weapons of Nuclear Destruction:
From the Attestation of Endubsar, 13th tablet.P-380

Those seven Weapons of Terror, in a mountain they abide! To them Enlil said.

In a cavity inside the earth they dwell, with the terror to clad them is required!

Then the secret of how the weapons from their deep sleep awakened, Enlil to them did reveal.

When Ninurta at the weapon's place arrived, Nergal from the cavity had already them brought out,

As their ME's from a long slumber he awakened, to each one of the seven Nergal a taskname gave:

The One without Rival the first weapon he called, the Blazing Flame he named the second,

The One Who Would Terror Crumbles he called the third, Mountain Melter the fourth he called,

Wind That the Rim of the World Seeks he named the fifth, the One Who above and below No One Spares was the sixth,

The seventh with monstrous venom was filled, Vaporizer of Living Things he called it.

A thousand and 36 was the count of Earth years then.

To Mount Mashu Ninurta departed, behind him Nergal followed.

The Mount and the plane, in the heart of the Fourth Region, Ninurta from the skies surveyed.

Then the first terror weapon from the skies Ninurta let loose;

The top of Mount Mashu with a flash it sliced off, the mount's inners in an instant it melted.

Above the Place of the Celestial Chariots the second weapon he unleashed,

With a brilliance of seven suns the plain's rocks into a gushing wound were made,

The Earth shook and crumbled, the heavens after the brilliance were darkened;

With burnt and crushed stones was the plane of the chariots covered,

Of all the forests that the plane had surrounded, only tree stems were left standing.

Over the five cities, one after the other, Erra upon each from the skies a terror weapon sent.

The five cities of the Valley he finished off, to desolation they were overturned.

With fire and brimstones they were upheaveled, all that lived there to vapor was turned.

By the awesome weapons were mountains toppled, where the sea waters were barred the bolt broke open,

Down into the valley the seas waters poured, by the watchers was the alley flooded;

When on the cities' ashes the waters poured, steam to the heavens was rising.

By a darkening of the skies were the brilliance is followed, then, a storm to blow began.

Swirling within a dark cloud, gloom from the skies an Evil Wind carried,

As the day wore on, the Sun on the horizon with darkness it obliterated,

At nighttime a dreaded brilliance skirted its edges, the Moon at its rising it made disappear.

The dark Brown cloud eastward it directed, toward the settled lands did the cloud spread;

Wherever it reached, death to all that lives mercilessly it delivered;

From the Valley of No Pity, by the brilliance is spawned, toward Schumer the death was carried.xxxxxxxxxxxxxxxxxxxx

Stealthy was the death, like a ghost the fields and cities it attacked;

No door could shift it out, no bolt could turn it back.

Those who behind closed doors hid inside their homes like flies were felled,

Those who to the streets fled, in the streets were their corpses piled up.

Cough and phlegm the chests filled, the mouths with spittle and foam filled up;

As the Evil Wind the people unseen engulfed, their mouths were drenched with blood.

Everything that lived, behind it was dead and dying, people and cattle, all alike perished.

Comment: For anyone reading these Sumerian texts with any kind of a reasonable logical mind, one cannot help but determine, with an empirical degree of certainty, that the written words of the Sumerian texts have clearly defined the use of nuclear weapons and their effect thereof. What you have read here is a classic description of the use of nuclear weapons **clearly defined and described thousands of years ago!**

My efforts now will be geared toward *nailing the coffin of hubris closed*! It was more than three decades ago *(1985)* that the Godfather of the Sumerian Texts, Zechariah Sitchin clearly wrote in "The Earth Chronicles", that not only did the Anunnaki use nuclear weapons, *he gave the date of their use! That date was 4025 years* ago. The testing and **studies were done in 2001,** with three different archaeological groups. *Zechariah Sitchin's specific date for the use of nuclear weapons in the Sinai Peninsula, as written in his 1985 book, was 2024 BC! That date has now been scientifically corroborated!*

Further: Scientists have now determined that there can only be two sources of Tephra, nuclear explosions and erupting volcanoes that eject material rocks and fragments into the atmosphere. When a volcano erupts they burn through pieces of blackened rock and ash-like particles can be carried by prevailing winds, staying aloft for more than a year. As Zechariah Sitchin points out in his book, "The Wars of Gods and Men", "The Erra Epos", tells us that the Anunnaki's nuclear bombs were dropped in the area of the Sinai Peninsula, including what was then the Anunnaki spaceport. *We know, to this day, that the Anunnaki spaceport is covered with what can only be described as Tephra!*

From the count of the Hebrew calendar, the year 1736 BC (2024 BC) did this holocaust occur. To describe nuclear weapons and their use, with the resulting holocaust and nuclear fallout, its destruction so vivid and clear the authors, of the ancient texts, Enki, Enlil, Ninurta, Ningishzidda, Thoth, Nergal, Ninmah, etc. etc., A.K.A. the Anunnaki, most indubitably had the scientific knowledge and ability to carry out the above. So shall it be written, so shall it be done!

Babylonian text CT-XU1-44/46

Selective Sentences Book 42

Ishum to the mount most supreme set his course;

the awesome seven weapons without parallel trailed behind him.

At the amount most supreme the hero arrived,

he raised his hand the mount was smashed....

In its forest not a tree was left standing.

Even the crocodiles he made to wither,

as with the fire he scorched the animals,

banned its grains to become dust,....

Who rained fire and stones upon the `adversaries'.

He who scorches with fire and he of the evil wind, together performed their evil,

the two made the gods to flee, made them flee the scorching.

NUCLEAR HOLOCAUST---- THE LOST BOOK OF ENKI
Page 310, 11

On that day, on that fateful day, Enlil to Ninurta the signal sent;

To Mount Mashu Ninurta departed, behind him Nergal followed.

Then the first terror weapon from the skies Ninurta to let loose;

The **top of Mount Mashu with a flash it sliced off, the mount's innards in an instant it melted.**

Above the Place of the Celestial Chariots the second weapon he unleashed,

With **a brilliance of seven Suns the plain's rocks into a gushing** *wound were made.*

The earth shook and crumbled, **the heavens after the brilliance were darkened**.

Of all the forest that the plane had surrounded, *only tree stems were left standing.*

It is done! Ninurta from the sky ship, his Black Divine Bird, words shouted.

Comment: A classic description of the use of nuclear weapons.

NUCLEAR FALLOUT

THE LOST BOOK OF ENKI Page 11, 12

Surveying their evil handiwork, the two heroes by what they saw were puzzled:

By a darkening of the skies were the brilliances followed, then a storm began to blow.

Swirling within a dark cloud, gloom from the skies an Evil Wind they carried,

As the day wore on, the Sun on the horizon with darkness it obliterated,

At nighttime a dreaded brilliance skirted its edges, the Moon and it's rising it made disappear.

The dark Brown cloud eastward it directed, toward the settled lands did the cloud spread;

Wherever it reached, death to all that lives mercilessly it delivered.

From the Valley of No Pity, by the brilliances spawned, towards Shumer the death was carried.

Two Enlil and Enki, Ninurta and Nergal the alarm sounded:

Unstoppable the evil Wind death to all delivers!

From their cities the gods did flee, like frightened birds from their nests escaping they were,

Stealthy was the death, like a ghost in the fields and cities it attacked;

No door could shut it out, no bolt could turn it back.

Those who fell behind locked doors hid inside their houses *like flies were felled,*

Those who in the streets fled in the streets where *their corpses piled up.*

Cough and phlegm the chests filled, the mouths with spittle and foam filled up;

As the Evil Wind the people unseen engulfed, their mouths were filled and drenched with blood.

Everything that lived, behind it was dead and dying, people and cattle, all alike perished.

The waters were poisoned, in the fields all vegetation withered.

From A redo in the South to Sip are in the North did the Evil Wind the land overwhelm;

Babili, where Marduk supremacy declared, by the Evil Wind was spared.

Comment: A classic description of death to all that lives, caused by radiation fallout and radiation poisoning.

Mahabharata Book 8 Karna Parva

As bright as the thousand suns

Rose in all its splendor…

A perpendicular explosion

with its billowing smoke clouds…

…the cloud of smoke

rising after its first explosion

formed into expanding round circles

like the opening of giant parasols

It was an unknown weapon, an iron thunderbolt,

 a gigantic messenger of death, which reduced to ashes

 the entire race of the Vrishnis and the Andhakas.

When the next day came, Samva actually brought forth

 an iron bolt through which all the individuals

 in the race of the Vhrishnis and the Andhakas

 destruction of the Vrishnis and the Andhakas,

 Samva brought forth, through that curse,

a fierce iron bolt that looked like a gigantic messenger

of death. The fact was duly reported to the King.

In distress of mind, the King (Ugrasena) caused that iron bolt

to be reduced to a fine powder.

Men were employed to cast the powder into the sea.

Mausala Parva Section 2

Hurled a single projectile charged with the power

of the Universe. An incandescent column of

smoke and flame, as bright as 10,000 suns, rose with all its splendor.

It was an unknown weapon, an iron thunderbolt, a gigantic

messenger of death, which reduced to ashes the entire race

of the Vrishnis and the Andhakas.

Hair and nails fell out; Pottery broke without apparent cause,

and the birds turned white.

… After a few hours all foodstuffs were infected…

… To escape from this fire the soldiers threw

themselves in streams to wash themselves and their equipment.

Dense arrows of flame, like a great shower, issued

forth upon creation, encompassing the enemy…

A thick gloom swiftly settled upon the Pandava hosts.

All points of the compass were lost in darkness.

Fierce wind began to blow upward, showering dust and gravel.

Birds croaked madly...the very elements seemed disturbed.

The earth shook, scorched by the terrible violent heat of this weapon.

Elephants burst into flame and ran to and fro in a frenzy...

over a vast area, other animals crumpled to the ground and died.

From all points of the compass the arrows of flame

  rained continuously and fiercely.

Churka flying in a vimana of great power, hurled at the triple city

  a missile weighed with all the force of the universe.

An incandescent column of smoke and flame in all its' splendor...

By the heat and ran to and fro in a trumpeting frenzy

  to self protection from the terrible violence.

The rivers boiled and those that dived into them perished miserably.

Animals crumpled to the ground and died.

The armies of the enemy were mown down when

  the raging of the elements reach them.

The raging of the blaze made forests collapse

in rows as if in a forest fire.

The elephants made fearful trumpeting and

sank dead to the ground over a vast area.

Horses and chariots were burned up,

and the scene looked like the aftermath of a conflagration.

Thousands of chariots and horses were destroyed and then

a deep silence settled over the land and sea.

The wind began to blow and the earth grew bright.

It was a terrible sight to see.
The corpses of the fallen were so mutilated by the

terrible heat that they looked other than humans.

Never before have we seen such a terrible weapon,

never have we even heard of such a ghastly weapon.

It was an unknown weapon, an iron thunderbolt,

a gigantic messenger of death that reduced to ashes

the entire race of the Vrishnis and the Andhakas.

The corpses were so burnt as to be unrecognizable.

The Ramayana
It was a weapon so powerful

that it could destroy the earth in an instant-

A great soaring sound in smoke and flames—

and it sits on death…

Comment: Here I offer a 1-2-3 punch from ancient text sources other than the Sumerian text. And I would have to say for those that are still in denial of the millennia-old usage of nuclear weapons, I would have to offer this, "There is no education in the second kick of a mule." Even if we advanced the timeline, relating to the use of nuclear weapons, to 1900 A. D., You still cannot deny that the ancient text descriptions of the use of nuclear weapons, required an empirical experience, to so aptly describe a nuclear event.

Chapter 11: Ancient Science and Knowledge

Science knowledge....all go back to Sumer, the birthplace of civilization. Astronomy Astrology, Cosmology, writing, mathematics, the wheel, botany, medicine, surgery, Genetics, theology, schooling, formal education dating to 3600 B.C. and the list goes on.

SPACE TRAVEL - ASTRONAUTS

"With waters did the Celestial Chariots obtain their thrust power."
Autobiography of Enki

The ancient Sumerian texts are replete with stories of their spacecraft and interplanetary craft, helicopters, rocket ships (Shems, MU) divine birds, etc. The Igigi were in constant orbit of Earth, 200 of them traveled from Mars to Earth to attend Marduk's wedding to an Earthling female named Saparnet. There were wars between the gods themselves in contesting their battles. Many of the Anunnaki gods just prior to the ensuing Great Flood lifting off with a thunderous roar launching themselves into orbit around Earth to wait out the flood.

Did the gods of old, really do all those things as described in the ancient texts? To answer a question with a question, one might ask, "If they could not conceivably do the things they write about, how could they have enough knowledge to describe the different events in writings more than 4000 years old!?

If we start from the beginning and describe the first contact made between Earth and the Anunnocki we find Alalu setting his course for Earth, which he describes from space as snow- hued, and Nibiru as a ball in voidness hanging.

The first planet he encounters is Gaga (Pluto) which he refers to as the one who shows the way. Approaching Anshar (Saturn) he described it as the Formost Prince of the heavens, then Kishar (Jupiter) which he describes as foremost of the Firm Planets, with swirling storms obscuring its place.

Beyond the fifth planet, Alalu anticipates the danger of the approaching Hammered Bracelet, the asteroid belt. The rocks and boulders posed an imminent danger as other probing chariots from Nibiru had previously been destroyed.

Alalu fired several missiles destroying the boulders, and clearing his path to the asteroid belt. He then views a red-brown planet the sixth in the count (Mars) then Earth seventh product appears. It is smaller than Nibiru and has a weaker gravitational pull; Snow White at the top and on the bottom, (Ice Age) blue and brown in between.

"Deftly Alulu spread the chariots arresting wings around the Earth's ball to circle."

Fully caught in the Earth's attracting net, the chariot was moving faster

Its spread wings became aglow; Earth's atmosphere like an oven was

The chariot shook, admitting a mortifying thunder.

COMMENT: Alalu describes the planets in an accurate way of a traveler in space. He is knowledgeable relating to gravity. He describes slowing his descent into reentry by spreading the chariots arresting wings. Caught in the Earth's gravitational pull his craft gains speed, the wings are a glow as a result of friction caused by Earths' atmosphere. To cap it off he describes a sonic boom.

And it goes on from there. He used an instrument to test the air for the viability of breathing, prior to removing his Space Helmet. He uses another instrument inserting into the waters searching for gold, and he finds it. With a ray emitting weapon he kills an encroaching snake.

Although this is a lesser rated example of the Scientific knowledge of the Anunnaki, the reader should readily admit the sophistication of knowledge, especially when we know that these words were written more than 6000 years ago! And how could someone describe the above events, void of an empirical relationship with the subject matter?

Would it not be interesting to find something that the Anunnocki used for space travel? Perhaps a helmet, some type of related clothing, equipment or even a craft of some kind, not something ambiguous as caveman drawings which perhaps could be interpreted as a Being with a space helmet on, but something extraordinary that can be identified as being used by these celestial gods for flight and/or Planetary travel

From the ancient ruins of the Royal Library of Nineveh, a Sumerian clay tablet depicting what is in our opinion a Flight Plan. Referred to, by R.H.M. Bosanquet and A.H. Sayce as a planisphere, a spherical shaped disk serving as a flight map.

The circular disc was divided into eight sections. Each section was determined to represent 45° totaling 360°. Celestial bodies were named in each of the eight segments

L.W. King made a meticulous copy of this most puzzling circular disc in 1912. J. Oppert P. Jensen, Dr. Fritz Hommel, and Ernest F. Weidner all adding their individual contributions in deciphering the perplexing plaque. Interest waned and the planisphere was put aside and forgotten. Then.....

In 1976, after 30 years of inexorable research" The 12ᵗʰ Planet", the first book of the Earth Chronicles was published, the ineffable works of author Zachariah Sitchin. In his words....

The tablet's inscriptions assume a completely different aspect if we try to read them not as Assyrian word -signs, but as Sumerian word -syllables; for there can hardly be any doubt that the tablet represents and Assyrian copy of an early Sumerian original. When we look at one of the segments (which we can number 1)meaningless syllables.......

na na na na   a na   a na nu(along the descending line)

sha sha sha sha sha sha (along the circumference)
sham sham bur kur kur (along the horizontal line)

Literally, spring to meaningfulness if we enter the Sumerian meaning of the word-syllables.

"What unfolds here is a *route map.*, marking the way by which the god Enlil "went via the planets," accompanied by some operating instructions. The line inclined at 45° appears to indicate a line of a spaceships descent from a point which is "high high high high," through "vapor clouds" and a lower zone that is vaporless, towards the horizon point where the skies and the ground meat."

"In the skies near the horizontal line, the instructions to the astronauts make sense: They are told to "set set set" their instruments for the final approach; then as they near the ground, "Rockets Rockets" are fired to slow the craft, which apparently should be raised ("piled up") before reaching the landing point because it has been passed over high or rugged terrain ("mountain mountain").

"The information provided in this segment clearly pertains to a space voyage by Enlil himself. In this first segment we are given a precise geometric sketch of two triangles connected by a line that turns at an angle. the line represents a route, or the inscription clearly states that the sketch shows how the "deity Enlil went by the planets."

"The starting point is the triangle on the left, representing the farther reaches of the solar system: the target area is on the right, for all the segments converge towards the landing point."

"The triangle on the left, drawn with its base open, is akin to a known sign in Near Eastern pictographic writing; its meaning can be read as "the ruler's domain, the mountainous land." The triangle on the right is identified by the inscription shu-ut il Enlil ("Way of the God Enlil"); the term, as we know, denotes Earth's northern skies. Both good

"The angled line, then, connect what we believe to have been the 12th Planet -- "the ruler's domain, the mountainous land" -- with Earth's skies. The route passes between two celestial bodies-- Dilgan and Apin."

"Some scholars have maintained that these were names of distant stars or parts of constellations. If modern manned and unmanned spacecraft navigate by a painting a "fix" on pre-determined bright stars, a similar navigational technique for the Nefilim cannot be ruled out."

"Yet the notion that the two names stand for such faraway stars somehow does not agree with the meaning of their names: DIL.GAN meant, literally, "the first station"; and APIN, "where the right course is set."

"The meanings of the names indicate way stations, points passed by. We tend to agree with such authorities as Thompson, Epping, and Strassmaier, who identified Apin as the planet Mars. If so, the meaning of the sketch becomes clear: The route between the Planet of Kingship and the skies above Earth passed between Jupiter ("the first station") and Mars ("where the right course is set").

"Evidence, that this is a space map and flight manual shows up

in all the other undamaged segments too. Continuing in a counter-clockwise direction the legible portion of the next segment bears the inscription:
"take take take

cast cast cast cast

complete complete."

"The third segment, where a portion of the unusual elliptical shape is seen, and legible inscriptions include "kakkab SIB.ZI.AN.NA..... envoy of AN.NA>...deity ISHTAR," and the intriguing sentence Deity NI.NI. supervisor of descent."

"In the fourth segment, which contains what appears to be direction on how to establish original destination according to a certain group of stars, the descending line is specifically identified as the skyline: The word sky is repeated 11 times under the line.

Does this segment represent a flight phase nearer Earth, nearer the landing spot? This might indeed be the import of the legend or with the horizontal line:

"hills hills hills hills

top top top top

city city city city."

"The inscription in the center says: "kakkab MASH.TAB.BA (Gemini) whose encounter is fixed; kakkab SIB.ZI.AN.NA (Jupiter) provides knowledge."

"Yes, as appears to be the case, these segments are arranged in an approach sequence, then one can almost share the excitement of the Nefilim as they approach Earth's spaceport. The next segment, again identifying in the descending line as "sky sky sky," also announces :
our light   our light   our light

change   change   change   change

Observed path and the high ground

… flat land…

The horizontal line contains, for the first time, figures:

rocket   rocket
rocket   rise   glide

40 40 40
40 40 20 22 22

"The upper line of the next segment no longer states: "sky sky"; instead it calls for "channel   channel100 100 100 100 100 100 100." A pattern is discernible in this largely damaged segment. Along one of the lines, the inscription says: "Ashshur," which can mean "He who sees" or "seeing."

The seventh segment is too damaged to add to our examination; the few discernible syllables mean "distant distant sight sight and the instructional words are "press down. "The eighth and final segment, however, is almost complete. **Directional line, arrows, and the inscription marks a path between two planets.** Instructions to "pile up mountain mountain," show four sets of crossers, inscribed twice "fuel water grain" and twice "vapor water grain."

"Was this a segment dealing with preparations for the flight toward Earth, or one minute dealing with stocking up for the return flight to rejoin the Twelfth Planet? The latter may have been the case, for the line it with the sharp arrow pointing toward the landing site on Earth has at its other end another "arrow" and pointing in the opposite direction, and bearing the legend "Return." (Fig. 124)

"In the planisphere, we have just deciphered, we indeed see such a route map, A. "plan of Heaven -- Earth." In sign language and in words, **the Nephilim have sketched for us the root from their planet to ours.**"

Otherwise inexplicable texts, dealing with the celestial distances also makes sense if we read them in terms of space travel from the Twelfth Planet. One such text, found in the ruins at Nippur and believed to be some 4000 years old, is now kept at the Hilprect Collection at the University of Jena, in Germany. O. Neugebauer (The Exact

Sciences in Antiquity) established that the tablet was undoubtedly a copy "from an original composition which is older," it gives ratios of celestial distances starting from the Moon to Earth and then through space and six other planets.

The second part of the text appears to have provided the mathematical formulas for solving whatever the inter-planetary problem was.

There has never been full agreement among scholars as to the correct reading of the measurement units in this part of the text (a new reading was suggested to us in a letter from Dr. J. Oelsner, custodian of the Hilprect Collection at Jena). **It is clear, however, that the second part of the text, measured distances from SHU.PA (Pluto)**

Only the Nefilim, traversing the planetary orbits, could have worked out these formulas; only they needed such data.

The ancient texts frequently relate stories of the Anunnocki gods ascending and descending to and from heaven, of traversing the Earth with ease, from the 8thTablet of Enki...

In his Bird of Heaven Ninurta to be took himself,

to the Land of Wandering he flew.

Over the Lands he roamed,

From the skies for Ka'in (Biblical Cain) each search.
And when he found him,
like on Eagles wings Ka'in to Adapa he brought.

Sitchin goes on to explain in his book, from the ancient texts, describing Inanna as "crossing heaven, crossing earth", and prior to her journeys, donning seven objects...

1. The SHU.GAR.RA he put on her head.
2. Measuring pendants, on her ears.
3. Chains of small blue stones, around her neck.
4. Twin "stones," on her shoulders.
5. A golden cylinder, in her hands.
6. Straps, clasping her breast.
7. The PALA garment, clothed around her body.

He then identifies the seven items on a 4000-year-old statue of Inanna named The Goddess with a Vase as she is shown holding a cylindrical object "golden cylinder", in her hands

The SHU.GAR.RA helmut he translates literally as "that which makes go far into the universe" and PALA as "ruler's garment"

A. hymn to Ianna, clearly indicates that the mu was the vehicle in which the gods roamed the skies far and high:

Lady of Heaven:

She puts on the Garment of Heaven;

She valiantly ascends toward Heaven.

Over all the peopled lands

She flies in her **MU**

To the heights of Heaven joyfully wings.

Over all the resting places

She flies in her **MU**.

The primary meaning of MU, "that which rises straight" and Sitchin goes on to explain...

"Sumerian texts describing Sippar relate that it had a central part, hidden and protected by mighty walls. Within those walls stood the Temple of Utu "a house which is like a house of Heavens" In an inner courtyard of the temple, also protected by high walls, stood "erected upwards, the mighty APIN" ("an object that plows through," according to the translators).

A drawing found at the temple mound of Anu, at Uruk, depicts such an object. We would have been hard put a few decades ago to guess what this object was, but now regretfully recognize it as a multi-stage space rocket at the top of which rests the comical MU, or command cabin.

That the *Mu* could hover in Earth's skies on its own, or fly over Earth's land when attached to a *gir*, or become the command module a top aide multistage apin is testimony to the engineering ingenuity of the gods of Sumer, the Gods of Heaven and Earth.

Finally, let us look at the pictographic sign for "gods" in Sumerian. The term was a two-syllable word: DIN.GAR. We have already seen that the symbol for GIR was: a two-stage rocket with fins. DIN the first syllable, meant "righteous," "pure," "bright.". Put together, then, DIN.GAR as "gods" or "divine beings" conveyed to the meaning "the righteous ones of the bright, pointed objects" or, more explicitly, "the pure ones of the blazing rockets."

The pictographic sign for din was this: (draw rocket see page 158), easily bringing to mind a powerful jet engine spewing flames from the end part and a front part that is puzzlingly open. But the puzzle turns to amazement if we spell "dingar" by combining the two pictographs. The tail of the finlike *gir* fits perfectly into the opening in the front of *din!*

The astounding result is a picture of a rocket-propelled space ship with a landing craft docked into it perfectly-- just as the lunar module was docked with the Apollo 11 spaceship! It is indeed a three-stage vehicle, with each part fitting neatly into the other: the thrust portion containing the engine, the midsection containing supplies and equipment, and the cylindrical "sky chamber" housing that people named *dingar*-- the gods of antiquity, the astronauts of millennia ago.

Can there be any doubt that the ancient peoples, in calling their deities "Gods of Haven't and Earth," meant literally that they were people from elsewhere would come to Earth from the heavens?

The evidence thus far submitted regarding the ancient gods and their vehicles should leave no further doubt that they were once indeed living beings of flesh and blood, people who literally came down to Earth from the heavens.

THE GREAT FLOOD AND NOAH'S ARK

We've already discussed the Great Flood and Noah's Ark in the "Where it came from" chapter; however I will review the salient features of the story.

Ziusudra is instructed by Enki to build a MA.GUR.GUR, a boat that can survive the initial onslaught of overpowering water by tossing and turning. *A* sulili in Sumerian, *a soleth* in Hebrew, or *elippu tebiti* meaning sunken ship, in short Ziusudra was told to build a submarine.

Ziasudra is told to take aboard the "seed" and "essence" (DNA) of all that is needed.

Modern-day Engineers have stated unequivocally that the Arc that Noah was told to build with specific length, height, and width instructions, could not support its own weight, nor contend with the enormity of the flood..

Which would you render the more feasible, more logical, the more scientific approach? God telling Noah you have seven days to build a boat that won't make it out of its moorings and load on by twos, (by seven if you are a clean animal) all animals, insects, and marine life that exists in the world ?....., or.... Take the "SEED " of man, animal, and plant, that the Anunnocki would prepare in advance and take ALL THAT IS NEEDED, aboard a scientifically built submarine?

Of the subject matter we have been describing, the celestial knowledge markedly demonstrated in the ancient texts can be described as wondrously amazing and intriguing. There are many scholars and authors of the ancient texts that I could quote; however, we chose, as we have done previously, the authoritative and documented writings of Zachariah, Sitchin. A man who has dedicated most of his life, since early manhood, searching for documented truth in the ancient texts and we think he found it.

From The Stairway to Heaven   09,19,39p

It was first ever in Sumer-- not centuries later in Greece, as has been thought-- that the stars were identified, grouped together into constellations, given names, and located in the heavens. All the constellations we now recognize in the northern skies and most of the constellations of the southern skies are listed in Sumerian astronomical tablets--in their correct order and by the names which we have been using to this very day!

Of the greatest importance were the constellations which appear to ring the plane or band in which the planets orbit the Sun. Called by the Sumerians UL.HE ("The Shiny Herd")-- which the Greeks adopted as the *zodiakos kyklos* ("Animal Circle") and we still call Zodiac--they were arranged in twelve groups, to form the twelve Houses of the Zodiac.

Not only the names by which these star groups were called up by the Sumerians--Bull *(Taurus)* Twins *(Gemini)*, The Pincer *(Cancer)*, Lion *(Leo)* and so exactly on--but even there for real depictions have remained in unchanged through the millennia. The much later Egyptian Zodiac representations were almost identical to the Sumarium ones.

In addition to the concept of spherical astronomy that we employ to this very day (including the notions of a celestial axis, poles, elliptic, equinoxes and the like) which were already perfected in Sumerian times, there was also the astounding familiarity with the phenomenon of Precession. As we now know, there is an illusion of retardation in Earth's orbit as an observer from Earth pinpoints the Sun on a fixed date (such as the first day of spring) against the Zodiac constellations that act as a backdrop in space. Caused by the fact that the Earth's axis is inclined relative to its plane of orbit around the Sun, this retardation of Precession is infinitesimal in terms of human life spans: in the seventy-two years, the shift in the Zodiac backdrop is a mere 1° of the 360° Celestial Circle.

Since the Zodiac circle surrounding the band and in which Earth (and other planets) orbits around the Sun was divided into an arbitrary twelve Houses, each takes up to one-twelfth of the full circle or a celestial space of 30°. It thus takes Earth 2160 years (72 x30) to retard through the full span of a Zodiac House. In other words, if an astronomer on Earth has been observing (as is now done) the spring day when the Sun began to rise against the constellation or House of Pisces, his descendants and one thousand 160 years later would observe the event with the Sun against the backdrop of the adjutant constellation, the "House" of Aquarius.

No single man, perhaps even no single nation, could have possibly observed, noted and understood the phenomena in antiquity. Yet the evidence is irrefutable: The Sumerians, who began their time -- counting or calendar in the Age of Taurus (which began circa 4400 B.C.), were aware of and recorded in their astronomical lists the previous precessional shifts to Gemini (circa 6500 B.C.), Cancer (circa 8700 B.C.) and Leo (circa 10,900 B.C.)! Needless to say, it was duly recognized circa 2200 B.C. that the first day of spring-- New Year to the peoples of Mesopotamia--retarded a full 30° and shifted to the constellation of "Age" of Aries, the Ram (KU.MAL in Sumerian).

It has been recognized by some of the earlier scholars who combine their knowledge of Egyptology/Assyriology with astronomy, that the textual and pictorial depictions employed the Zodiac Age as a grand celestial calendar, whereby events on Earth were related to the grander scale of the heavens. The knowledge has been employed in more recent times as a means of prehistoric and historic chronological aid in such studies as that by G. de Santillana and H. von Dechend (Hamlet's Mill). There is no doubt, for example, that the Lion like Spinks south of Heliopolis, or the Ram- like Sphinxes guarding the temples of Karnak, depicted the Zodiac ages in which the events they stood for had occurred, or in which the gods or kings represented had been supreme.

AUTOBIOGRAPHY OF ENKI TABLET 8

By the name Enki-ME, (the biblical Enoch) by Enki ME Understanding, in the annals. he was called.

Wise and intelligent he was, numbers, he quickly understood,

About the heavens and all matters celestial, he was constantly curious.

To him, the Lord Enki took a liking, secrets once to Adapa revealed to him and he told.

Of the family of the Sun and the twelve Celestial Gods Enki him was Teaching,

And how the months by the Moon were counted and the years by the Sun,

And how by Nibiru the Shars were counted, and how they count by Enki were combined,

How the Lord Enki the circle of the heavens to twelve parts divided,

A constellation, and each one, how Enki assigned, twelve stations in a grand circle he arranged,

How to honor the twelve Anunnaki great leaders by names, the stations were called.

To explore the heavens Enki-ME was eager; two celestial journeys he did make.

SUMERIAN CONSTELLATIONS   12ᵗʰ P   471p

1.GU.AN.NA("heavenly bull"), Taurus
2. MASH.TAB.BA ("Twins"), Gemini
3.DUB("pincers,") Cancer
4.UR.GULA (" lion"), Leo
5.AB.SIN ("her father was Sin"), Maiden, Virgo
6.ZI.BA.AN.NA ("heavenly fate"), the scales of Libra
7.GIR.TAB ("which claws and cuts"), Scorpio
8.PA.BIL ("defender"), the Archer, Sagittarius
 9.SUHUR.MASH ("goat-fish"), Capricorn
10.GU ("Lord of the waters"), the Water Bearer, Aquarius
11.SIM.MAH ("fishes"), Pisces
12.KU.MAL "(field dweller"), the Ram, Aries

COMMENT: Look familiar? It should, as previously stated, we use those identifications today.

VAT 7847   The12ᵗʰ Planet   781p

This Sumerian Tablet today is found in the Berlin Museum, the Constellations are listed starting with Leo, clearly indicating the date of circa 11,000 B.C.

PHASES OF THE MOON succF -ENUMA ELISH TABLET--5

The Moon-god he caused to shine forth, the night he interested in him.
He appointed him, a being of the night, to determine the days;
Every month without ceasing with a crown he covered him, saying:
"At the beginning of the month, when thou shineth upon the land,
Thou commandest the horns to determine six days,
And on the seventh day to divide the crown.
On the 14ᵗʰ-day thou shalt stand opposite, the half....
When the Sun-god on the foundation of heaven...thee,
And on the.... day thou shalt stand opposite, and the Sun-god shall.....
... thou shalt cause to draw nigh, and thou shalt judge the night.

COMMENT: As a consequence of the Celestial Battles between Nibiru/Marduk, Tiamat, and their assigned satellites, Enuma Elish expresses the relationship between the Earth, its Moon, and the Phases of the Moon

At the month start rising with luminous horns to signify six days, reaching a crescent on the seventh day. Mid-month slanting opposite the Sun (full moon) then diminishing in light approaching the Sun in waning until months end, standing against the Sun.

The Sumerian Enuma Elish, (Ea, Enki, being the suspected author) clearly describes the orbital relationship of the Moon in orbit of Earth and Earth, in orbit of the Sun.

"The Moon-god "he caused to shine" (he) being the planet Nibiru/ Marduk the Celestial Lord responsible for the planet Tiamat and satellite collisions that resulted in the current position and orbits of Earth and our Moon.

The Bible and Genesis 1: 4, 14 assigns that "creation" to an entity God. Clearly, Enuma Elish tells us that Tiamat was split in half, not by Nibiru/Marduk but by the planet's satellites. One half becoming the Hammered out Bracelet (asteroid belt) the other half Earth; congruently placing our moon (Kingu), an independent celestial body (not cleaved from Tiamat) in Earths orbit.

THE PHENOMENON OF PRECESSION When Time Began52p
Gen. Rev 512p

·The phenomenon of precession undoubtedly was known by the Sumerians in ancient times, as stated by H. V. Hilprecht. His study of thousands of mathematical texts from the library of Ashurbanipal concluded the number 12,960,000 was in literal fact an Astronomical number, (including other pertinent calculations) derived from multiplying 500, the cycle of 500 Great years of completed processional shifts by 25,920 (a shift from House to House in the Zodiac required. 2,160 years x12 complete House cycles= 25,920) equals 12,960,000.

·The ultimate question is who would have the need or use for the knowledge of precession? The answer is not mankind but the gods, the Anunnaki gods, "Those from heaven to earth came"

·In 1822 John Landser credited the Chaldeans with the ancient knowledge of precession and the Zodiacal ages dating back 3800 B.C.

Precession of the equinoxes definition-The earlier occurrence of the equinoxes in each successive sidereal year because of a slow retrograde motion of the ecliptic, caused by the gravitational force of the Sun and the Moon upon the Earth and by the gravitational force of the planets upon the earth's orbit:a complete revolution of the equinoxes requires about 26,000 years.

AKKADIAN SEAL VA/243   The 12th Planet   781p Fig.99,981p

If I were asked to choose, what I considered to be the "sine qua non " of ancient writings, stalas, scrolls, papyrus, artifacts, scripts or texts, the selection would be most difficult, yet inevitably it would be the above Seal VA/243.

The choices are literally startling when you consider the scientific knowledge of the Anunnaki revealed to us through the ancient texts. One must consider their knowledge of our solar system, astronomy cosmology, genetics, the establishment and naming of our constellations, the building of the pyramids literally all over the world and last but not least their knowledge and use of the phenomenon of Precession.

VA/243 represents the last piece of the puzzle, when placed in the position, provides the stark mental realization, clarification, and understanding *that there is another planet in our solar system.*

The schematic drawing depicts 11 globes encircling a larger "star" our Sun. The Globes are relative in size and position (in the elliptical) which clearly depict our solar system. The closest to the Sun is Mercury, Venus, Earth, and its moon, Mars, then a strange anomaly, an unidentifiable globe positioned between Mars and Jupiter, which is larger than all of the known planets of our solar system excepting Jupiter and Saturn.

Zachariah Sitchin, after his masterful, erudite30 year documentation and dogged research of the ancient texts wrote his first book, published in 1976, entitled The 12th Planet. He provides therein millennia-old evidence of (a strange anomaly, an unidentifiable globe positioned between Mars and Jupiter) the existence of the planet Nibiru, the 12th Planet. Of great importance, to the reader of the 12th planet, *the book stands unchallenged as of this day! And in our opinion remained so.*

The other anomaly shown in the schematic, referred to in the ancient text, Enuma Elish, is Gaga, an emissary (in the orbit) of Anshar (Saturn). Nibiru and its satellites entered our solar system in its clockwise (retrograde) orbit, the opposite direction, counter-clockwise, of our solar system. When positioned close to the rings of Anshar, their gravitational force captures Gaga. After the Celestial Battle Gaga's resulting destiny becomes a celestial planet (Pluto), in an erratic orbit of the Sun positioned for the most part outside that of Ea (Neptune).

Anshar opened his mouth, and
unto Gaga, his minister, spake the word,
O Gaga, thou minister that rejoices my spirit
Unto Lahmu and Lahamu will I send thee
Go Gaga, stand before them,
And all that I tell thee, repeat unto them, and say:
Ansar, your son hath sent me.
Gaga went, and took his way
Nibiru opened his mouth and unto Ea (Neptune) he spake
That which he had conceived in his heart he imparted unto him.

The 12th Planet is a must-read providing a comprehensive and specifically detailed explanation of the above subject matter.

THE EMERALD TABLETS OF THOTH

Man is a star bound to a body,
Until in the end, he is freed through his strife.

Strange, beyond knowledge, were some of the planets,
great and gigantic, beyond dreams of men
Shapes there were, moving in Order,
great and majestic as stars in the night;
mounting in harmony, ordered equilibrium,
symbols of the Cosmic, like unto Law.
Just as the stars in time a lose their brilliance,
like passing from them into the great source.

Formed forth ye, from the primal ether,
filled with the brilliance that flows from the source,
 bound by the ether coalesced around,
yet ever it flames until at last it is free.

COMMENT. Birth and life of a star.

There exists the brothers of light.
Powers have they, mighty and potent.
Knowing the LAW, the planets obey.
Work they ever in harmony and order,
 freeing the man-stole from its bondage of night.

Everything created is based on ORDER:
LAW rules the space where the INFINITE dwells.
Forth from the equilibrium came the great cycles,
moving in harmony toward Infinity's end.
Know ye O man, that far in the space-time,
INFINITY itself shall pass into change.

Learned I of the Masters of cycles.
Time after time, stood I before them
listening to words that came not with sound.
(Telepathy ?)

Far have I been on my journey through space-time.
In that space where time exists not. (at the speed of light)
Few there are who have succeeded in passing the Barrier.

Chapter 12: Space Flight of the Anunnaki

Would it not be interesting to find something that the Anunna-ki used for space travel? Perhaps a helmet, some type of route-related clothing, equipment or even a craft of some kind, not something ambiguous as caveman drawings which perhaps could be interpreted as a being with a space helmet on but something extraordinary it can be identified as being used by the celestial gods for flight and/or Planetary travel.

From the ancient ruins of the Royal Library of Nineveh, a Sumerian clay tablet depicting, what is in our opinion, a flight plan. Referred to, by R.H.M. Bosanquet and A.H. Sayce as a planisphere, aspherical shaped disk serving as a flight map.

The circular disk was divided into eight sections. Each section was determined to represent 45° totaling 360°. Celestial bodies were named each of the eight segments. L. W. King made a meticulous copy of this most puzzling circular disk in 1912. J.OPPERT, P. Jensen, Dr. Fritz Hamill and Ernest F Weidner all adding their individual contributions in deciphering the perplexing plaque. Interest waned and the planisphere was put aside and forgotten. Then In 1976, after 30 years of inexorable research, "The 12th Planet," the First Book of the Earth Chronicles was published, the ineffable works of "The Godfather of the Sumerian Texts", author Zacharias Sitchin relates in his words...

"The tablets inscriptions assume a completely different aspect if we try to read them not as Assyrian word-signs, but as Sumerian word-syllables; for there can hardly be any doubt that the tablet represents an Assyrian copy of an early Sumerian original. When we look at one of the segments (which we can number 1) meaningless syllables

na na na na   a na   a na nu (along the descending line)

sha sha sha sha sha sha (along the circumference)

sham sham bur kur kur (along the horizontal line)

Literally, spring to meaningfulness if we enter the Sumerian meaning of the word-syllables." (figure 123 page 249: also see fig.122 page

248)

"What follows here is a *route map,* marking the way by which the god Enlil "went via the planets," accompanied by some operating instructions. The line inclined at 45° appears to indicate a line of a spaceships descent from a point which is "high high high high," through "vapor clouds" at a lower zone that is vaporless has, towards the horizon point where the skies and the ground meet. "

"In the skies near the horizontal line, the instructions to the astronauts makes sense: They are told to "set set set" their instruments for the final approach; then as they near the ground, "Rockets Rockets" are fired to slow the craft, which apparently should be raised ("piled up") before reaching the landing point because it has passed over high or rugged terrain and ("mountain mountain")".

The information provided in this segment clearly pertains to a space voyage by Enlil himself. In the first segment, we are given a precise geometric sketch of two triangles connected by a line that turns at an angle. The line represents a route, or the inscription clearly states that the sketch shows how the "deity Enlil went by the planets."

The starting point is the triangle on the left, representing the farther reaches of the solar system: the target area is on the right, for all the segments converge towards the landing point.

The triangle on the left, drawn with its open base, is akin to a known sign in Near Eastern pictograms and writing; its meaning can be read as "the ruler's domain, the mountainous land that." The triangle on the right is identified by the inscription shu-ut il Enlil ("Way of the god Enlil"; the term as we know, denotes Earth's northern skies.

Some scholars have maintained that these were names of distant stars or parts of constellations. If modern manned and unmanned spacecraft navigate by painting a "fix" on predetermined bright stars, a similar navigational technique of the Nephilim cannot be ruled out."

"Evidence, that this is a space map and the flight manual shows up in all the other undamaged segments, too.

"In the fourth segment, which contains what appears to be directions on how to establish original destination according to a certain group of stars, the descending line is specifically identified as the skyline: The word sky is repeated 11 times under the line."

", as appears to be the case, the segments are arranged in an approach sequence, then one can almost share the excitement of the Ne-

filim as they approach Earth's spaceport. The next segment, again identifying as the descending line as "sky sky sky" also announces:"

our light   our light   our light

change   change   change   change

Observed path and the high ground

... flat land.... "The seventh segment is too damaged to add to our
examination; the few discernible syllables mean distant distant   sight
sight   and the instructional words are "press down." The eighth and
final segment however, is almost complete. Directional wind, arrows,
and **the inscription mark a path between two planets." "**
Was this a segment dealing with preparations for the flight toward
Earth, or one dealing with stocking up for the return flight to rejoin
the 12th planet? The latter may have been the case, for the line with
the sharp arrow pointing toward the landing site on Earth has at its
other end another "arrow" and pointing in the opposite direction, **and
bearing the legend, Return.**

To add some more depth to the above subject matter relating to
spaceflight of the Anunnaki, the following is from Mr. Sitchin's website:
Searching for? Life?

So what exactly is NASA searching for?

"Though only indirectly, with a wink or a Mona Lisa smile, NA-
SA's leaders say **that**? Where there was water there could be life.? Officially, they are all just searching for evidence of water. If water is still
there, it would make it so much more feasible to achieve the vision-?
declared by Pres. George W. Bush?-of sending people from Earth to
Mars. A dream of the future!"

THE SUMERIAN EVIDENCE

The evidence for that was recorded -In words and illustrations- by the Sumerians, whose civilization blossomed out in Mesopotamia (now mostly Iraq) some six thousand years ago.

"They did not claim the achievement of visiting Mars for themselves. Rather, they wrote on their clay tablets about the Anunnaki (Those who from Heaven to Earth came?) who came to Earth from their planet Nibiru, a 12th member of our solar system (counting, as they did, the Sun, Moon and ten planets whose great Elliptical Orbit around the Sun lasts some 3600 (Earth-) years. The many ancient texts, unearthed by archaeologists, that deal with the Anunnaki, their comings and goings and the astronomical knowledge (among other sciences) that they bequeathed to Mankind, have been revealed and explained in my series of books, beginning with The 12th Planet."

"Moreover, the texts have been accompanied by illustrations found on clay tablets or drawn on cylinder seals. In the text, dealing with the actual space travel between the planets, Earth was designated as the seventh planet? which indeed it is but only if one counts from outside-in, where Pluto would be the first, Neptune the second, Uranus and Saturn third and fourth, Jupiter the fifth, Mars the sixth and Earth the seventh. In those texts, Mars was called the Way Station? A stopover place between Nibiru and the Earth."

"And, amazingly but true, a circular tablet they can be seen on display in the British Museum in London, describes in eight segments various aspects of space travel between the Anunnaki's planet Nibiru and the Seventh Planet (Earth) Fig. 122 – page 247 in the 12th Planet. One segment, in particular, enlarged here for clarity, (Fig. 123 – page 249 in The 12th Planet). shows (and s that the route traveled by Enlil (Lord of the Command)) entailed passage by seven planets; it is also called for a route diversion between the planet DILGAN (Jupiter) and APIN (Mars):"

PLACEMENT OF FIGURE 122 ON THE LEFT AND 123 ON THE RIGHT.

Mars is a way station

"In their texts, the Sumerian' s wrote that the Anunnaki traveled to Earth in groups of fifty. The first team, under the leadership of E-A(? Whose name is water?), splashed down in the waters of the Persian Gulf, waded ashore, and established ERIDU (? Home in the Faraway?). In time, 600 and Anunnaki were deployed on earth and another 300 operated spacecraft between Earth and Mars? Yes, Mars!"

Pictorial evidence of the Earth-Mars connection is provided by a depiction on a cylinder seal (now kept at the Hermitage Museum in St. Petersburg, Russia)? Fig. 121 in The 12th Planet:

INSERT CYLINDER SEAL DEPICTION

"It depicts an astronaut (Eagleman) on Earth (the planet marked by the seven dots, accompanied by the crescent of the Moon) and an astronaut on Mars (the six-pointed star symbol)?-the latter depicted as one of the Fishmen? class of astronauts, those equipped to splashdown in waters. nbsp; Between the two planets an object is depicted, that could only be a spacecraft, with extended panels and antennas."

A Space Base on Mars

"To maintain, over thousands of years, a space base on Mars required water for survival. The Fishman's attire on Mars suggests bodies of waters on Mars. Moreover, as detailed in my latest book The Lost Book of Enki (Lord Earth, A later title for Ea), water was used by the Anunnaki to propel their spacecraft, and the availability of water on Mars made it a suitable way-station."

"The Anunnaki, I have concluded in my book, used Mars not just for a quick stopover; they created a permanent space base on Mars, complete with structures and roads. In Genesis Revisited I reproduced numerous photographs taken by NASA?s Mariner-9 in 1972 and Vi-

king-1 Orbiter in 1976 that clearly showed a variety of artificial structures there. Some of them are were in the Cydonia area with its famed
Face."

"Not only such ancient evidence but NASA?s <u>own</u> photographs
from the 1970s onward indicated the presence of water on Mars. A
search for watery evidence is thus, no great innovation."

<u>Searching Or Avoiding</u>

"The current search for evidence of water on Mars is hinted as an
indirect effort to find evidence for life
  on Mars. But as in a previous attempt to test Martian soil (that was
deemed unsuccessful), the current one looks again, at best, for evidence
of <u>microbial</u> life. This impels one to ask: Why Is NASA<u> not</u> sending
its rovers to such areas as Cydonia, where its own photographs have
shown remains of artificial structures such as the Face."

"As exciting as a discovery that<u> microbes</u> had been on Mars would
be- Isn't the avoidance of closer looks at areas with structures (and the
Face) indicative of a desire to<u> not find</u> real life on Mars-the life represented by<u> intelligent beings</u> who fashioned us to look to be like them?"

"For those who launch the space missions, the word? Extraterrestrials? Remain taboo."
C. Z.Sitchin 2004

Chapter 13: Enki's Flight to Earth

The words of Anu, Alalu's chariot did reach; Alalu them quickly answered:

Alalu the words merit pondered, to transmit his secrets he agreed; ·

Of the Tester its crystal innards he removed, from the Sampler its crystal heart he took out;

Into the Speaker he the crystals inserted, all the findings to transmit.

With heavy heart Ea (Enki) the chariot entered, to shore up the command he gave.

The celestial chariot he deftly guided; from Nibiru, it powerfully soared toward the distant Sun he directed.

Little Gaga (Pluto) came out to greet them, a welcome to the heroes it was expanding.

Toward the Heavenly An (Uranus), the third in planetary counts, the chariot continued.

On Its side was An lying, (*Uranus still lies on the side* 58°) His host of moons about him were whirling.

The Testers beams the presence of water was revealing; a stop if needed to Ea it was indicating

Soon the ensnarling pull of Anshar (Saturn) they could tell, his colored rings with fear they admired.

The giant Kishar (Jupiter) foremost of firm planets, was next to be encountered.

Her net Pull was overpowering, with great skill did Anzu the chariot's course divert.

Beyond the fifth planet with the Hammered Bracelet was lurking!

The water thruster to prepare. Toward the host of turning boulders the chariot was rushing.

The word of Ea was given, with a force of a thousand heroes the stream of water was thrust.

But as one boulder fled, another in its stead was attacking;

A multitude beyond count was their number, a host of the splitting of Tiamat revenge seeking!

Comment: When we look at Alalu's flight which is been previously described, the problems encountered during their flight are the same. They both are on their way to Earth, they both have to fight off the tremendous boulders in the Asteroid Belt and they both make it quite evident that they are traveling at stupendous speeds.

And then at last the path was cleared; its unharmed chariot would continue!

A cry of joy the heroes sounded; double was the joy as the site of the Sun was now unveiled.

Waters to feed the chariots Fiery Stones for the remaining journey was not sufficient!

There was water on Lahmu, (Mars) Ea was saying.

The planet's pull is not great, it's pull is to handle easy, Anzu was saying.

A sight to behold was Lahmu, snow white was its cap, snow white where its sandals.

On command the heroes That Which Water Sucks extended, the chariot's bowels with the lake's waters to fill.

The waters were good for drinking, the air was insufficient.

With its vigor replenished the chariot soared up to benevolent Lahmu farewell bidding.

Comments: As this section correctly states, the gravitational pull of a given planet is, in general, proportional to its size and mass. Clearly, water is used as a source of fuel. One of the major problems spacecraft have is that we can't load enough fuel on a craft to get the craft to distant planets without having to refuel. Evidently, the Anunnaki, Alalu and Enki, have the technological knowledge to separate Hydrogen from water and use it as a fuel source. Now the planets, that have water, become a "Cosmic Gas Station," if you will. Another source of power is Helium-3 which is somewhat abundant on the surface of the moon. A "spacecraft" loaded with Helium-3 would power *all of America for one full year!*

The chariot must be slowed or in Earth's thick atmosphere it shall perish! Anzu to Ea declared.

Around Earth's companion, the moon, make slowing circled Ea to him suggested.

They circled the Moon; by the vanquishing Nibiru in the Celestial Battle it prostrate and scarred was lying.

Once, twice the Earth's globe he made the chariot circle, even closer to the Firm Land he lowered it.

Snow hewed was two thirds of the planet, dark hued was its middle.

They could see the oceans, they could see the Firm Lands for the signal beacon from Alalu they were searching.

When a notion touched dry land, there were four rivers were swallowed by marshes, Alalu signal was beaconed.

Comment: The Bible mentions the "four rivers," two of those rivers were the Tigris and the Euphrates and the other two have since been identified. The point being is, this information tells us where the Anunnaki astronauts were intent on landing their spacecraft and that geographic location was Iraq, just south of where the Tigris and Euphrates rivers meet.

Too heavy and large the chariot is for the marshes! Anzu was declaring.

The Earth's pulling net, too powerful for on dryland to descend it is! Anzu to Ea announced.

Splash down! Splash down in the ocean waters! Ea to Anzu shouted.

Around the planet Anzu made one more circuit, the chariot with much care toward the ocean's age he lowered.

The chariots lungs he filled with air; into the waters down it splashed, into the depths it was not sinking.

From the Speaker a voice was heard: To Earth he welcomed! Alalu was saying.

By his beamed words the direction of his whereabouts were determined.

Toward the place, Anzu the chariot directed, floating as a boat it was upon the waters moving.

Chapter 14: Anzu and Ea's Trip to Earth from Nibiru

From The Attestation of Endubsar   Third Tablet   Pages 68 to 73

The ancient Sumerian tales are replete with stories of the spacecraft and interplanetary craft, helicopters, rocket ships, (Shem, MU,) divine birds, etc. etc.... Igigi were in constant orbit of Earth, 200 of them traveled from Mars to Earth to attend Marduk's wedding to an Earthling female name Saparnet. Wars between the gods themselves used these rocket ships and interplanetary craft, in contesting their battles. Many of the Anunnaki gods just prior to the ensuing Great Flood lifting off with a thunderous roar launching themselves into orbit around Earth to wait out the flood.

Did the gods of old, really do all these things as described in the ancient text? To answer a question with a question, one might ask, "If they could not conceivably do the things they write about, how could they have enough knowledge to describe the different esoteric events in writings more than 4000 years old? To put it more direct, they have to have an empirical relationship with the subject matter in order to put those words in writing!

· Ancient text continued:

Now this is the account of the journey to the seventh planet,

With heavy heart Ea's chariot he entered, to soar up the command he gave.

The commander's seat by Anzu, not Ea, was occupied;

Anzu, not Ea was the chariots commander;

The celestial chariot he deftly guided; from Nibiru it powerfully soared, toward the distant Sun he it directed.

10 leagues, 100 leagues the chariot was coursing,

1000 leagues the chariot was journeying.

Little Gaga (Pluto) came out to greet them,

a welcome to the heroes it was extending.

Two blue hued Antu, the beautiful enchantress, it showed the way.

Toward the heavenly An, the third in planetary counts,

the chariot continued.

On his side An was lying, his host of moons about him were hurling.

To continue the journey was Ea saying, toward Anshar,

the heavens foremost prince, he was directing.

Soon the ensnaring poll of Anshar (Saturn) they could tell,
his colored rings with fear they admired.

The giant Kishar, foremost of firm planets, was next to be encountered.

Her net's pull was overpowering; with great skill did Anzu the chariots course divert.

Slowly Kishar moved away, for the chariot the next enemy to encounter:

Beyond the fifth planet the Hammered Bracelet was lurking.

Comment: This is again is an in-flight demonstration of what one would encounter coming in retrograde, into our solar system. Pluto,

Neptune, Uranus, Saturn, Jupiter, heading into the Asteroid Belt.

Ea his handiwork to set a-whirring commanded the Water Thruster to prepare.

Toward the host of turning boulders that chariot was rushing,

Ea word by he was given, with the force a thousand heroes the stream of water was thrust.

A multitude beyond count was their number, a host for the splitting of Tiamat revenge seeking!

Again and again toward the host of boulders streams of water were directed;

And then at last the path was clear; unharmed that chariot could continue!

Comment: Again, understanding that the Asteroid Belt's average distance between 'boulders' is 600,000 miles and the width being 4,200,000 miles, the speed of the Anunnaki's craft, even to our scientists today, would be unfathomable!

Amidst the elation Anzu the alarm sounded: For the path to have fashioned, excessive waters were consumed,

Waters to feed the chariots Fiery Stones for the remaining journey were not sufficient!

In the dark deepness the sixth planet (Mars) they could see, the Sun's rays it was reflecting.

There is water on Lahmu, (Mars) Ea was saying.

Deftly Anzu the chariot toward Lahmu directed;

reaching the celestial god, around it he that chariot made circle.

On command the heroes That Which Water Sucks extended,

the chariots bowels with the lakes waters to fill.

Comment: Here, we can clearly discern that the spacecraft of the Anunnaki _uses water for fuel!_ The question then becomes, is it scientifically feasible to use water as a fuel source? The answer is a definite yes! We know that one 8 ounce glass of water, has enough hydrogen to power New York City for 48 hours. This is an excellent example whereby our modern-day Science has not caught up with ancient knowledge. Further, they put the _spacecraft in orbit around Mars!_

Let's go back to the year 2002 when the magazine Atlantis Rising announced on Its November/December 2002 cover, introducing Zechariah Sitchin's article "The Ancients and the Power of Water":

WATER: THE ULTIMATE PROPELLANT

Will water be the fuel of the future to power aircraft and spacecraft?

If so, mankind will be employing a "technology of the gods" and, as in other fields, modern science will be only catching up with ancient knowledge.

The news of the possible use of water- an abundant and clean resource- as the "fuel" for jet propulsion comes from the Tokyo Institute of Technology that has been developing technologies for powering small unpiloted planes by subjecting their "engines" to laser beams fired from the ground or from satellites. And what has been hailed as a great success, the Tokyo team reported in the June 10 issue of Applied Physics that they made a tiny paper "plane" fly by subjecting its "motor" of aluminum plates to laser beams. Causing minute amounts of metal to vaporize, a jet stream was achieved that cause the plane to soar.

The experiment thus attained the trick of creating an ejected jet of some mass that push the plane forward. In regular jet planes, the jet is created by burning petroleum fuel and ejecting the hot gas. In the

Tokyo experiment, the heat was provided by the laser beam, the jet by the evaporated aluminum. To scale the propulsion system up to full size, Takashi Yabe, head of the Tokyo team, propose using <u>water</u> as the propellant. "Water can be harvested from the atmosphere as the plane flies," he said. Reporting the experiment and the water -use idea, the journal <u>New Scientist (</u>15 June 2002)

"Water an Intriguing Fuel"

Reporting this series of experiments,<u> The New York Times</u> science editor Kenneth Chang stated that "water is the more intriguing fuel. The paper airplane received only a single push before the water propellant was used up, but Dr. Yabe speculated that a larger plane using this technology could continuously replenish the water from the error, "so we don't need to carry large amounts of water," he said.

A Technology of the Anunnaki

"I admit to having broadly grin when I read the above news reports because, in my latest book,<u> The Lost Book of Enki,</u> I describe the use of water for the propulsion of the spacecraft of the Anunnaki (Those Who from Heaven to Earth Came" in Sumerian)."

"Enki, the great chief scientist of the Anunnaki, was the leader of the first team of Anunnaki to come to Earth. His name, EN.KI meant "Lord of Earth" in Sumerian. But that title was granted to him only later, after the arrival of his half-brother Enlil (EN.LIL= "Lord of the Command"). Of the original Epithet-name of Enki was E.A., commonly taken to mean "He whose home is water." He is depicted by the Sumerians as a seated deity outpouring streams of water. He was the prototype of the Water Bearer <u>Aquarius</u> and his zodiacal constellation."

"At first, I accepted the explanation that his epithet reflected his love of waters, for sailing and fishing. As the scope of my research and writings expanded, increasingly involving the "technologies of the gods," I was increasingly astounded to discover that modern science is only catching up with ancient knowledge. This was true and astronomy, then in genetics, and now in space propulsion."

The Role of Mars

"The Sumerian incredible knowledge of the heavens applied not only to the recognition of all the planets we know of today (plus Nibiru) but also to their descriptions and roles. Thus, Mars was spoken of as The Way Station. NASA's own photographs from the 1970s, shown in my book Genesis Revisited, reveal the remains of artificial structures on Mars. But the argument has been that Mars could not have served as an astronauts base because it is a lifeless, atmosphere- less and a dry, waterless planet."

"So Mars could not only sub stain a Way station: it could serve to resupply the spacecraft of the Anunnaki with their fuel: Water."

"

C. Z. Sitchin 2002

Ancient Text Continued:

While the chariot was getting its fill of waters, Ea and Anzu the whereabouts examined.

With Tester and Sampler all the matters they ascertained:
The waters were good for drinking, the air was insufficient.

With its vigor replenished the chariot soared up, to benevolent Lahmu farewell bidding.
Beyond the seventh planet was making its circuit; Earth and its companion the chariot were inviting!

The chariot must be slowed or in Earth's thick atmosphere it shall perish! Anzu to Ea declared

Around Earth's companion, the Moon, make slowing circles! Ea to him suggested.

Having the chariot thus slowed down, toward the seventh planet Anzu the chariot direct.

Once, twice the Earth's globe he made the chariot circle, even closer to the Firm Land he lowered it.

Snow hued was two thirds of the planet, dark hued was its middle. (Seemingly this would indicate, at the time of arrival, Earth was experiencing an Ice Age!)

The Earth's pulling net, too powerful for on dry land to descend it is! Anzu to Ea announced.

Splashdown! Splashdown in the ocean waters! Ea to Anzu shouted.

Around the planet Anzu made one more circuit, the chariot with much care toward the ocean's edge he lowered.

The chariots lungs he filled with air; into the waters down it splashed, into the depths it was not sinking.

As dryland he was approaching, green meadows he could see.

Then his feet touched firm ground; he stood up and by walking he continued.

Alalu toward him came running; his son by marriage he powerfully embraced.

Welcome to a different planet! Alalu to Ea said.

Comment: Relating to the commentary, "Snow hued was two thirds of the planet." We know from the ancient text that the Anunnaki arrived here on earth some 445,000 years ago. The ancient text also tells us that the above events happened during the ninth Shar of the planet Nibiru. A Shar is equal to one orbit, of the planet Nibiru around our Sun, taking some 3600 years. Subtracting nine Shars or 32,400 years from the arrival date of 445,000 years ago we can accurately date the above events to being 412,600 years ago.

Chapter 15: Alalu's Flight

The Attestation of Endubsar – Second Tablet – page 41 – 46

To snow-hued Earth Alalu set his course; by a secret from the Beginning he chose his destination.

Riding like an eagle, Alalu the heavens scanned; below, Nibiru was a ball in a voidness hanging.

Alluring was its figure, its radiance emblazoned the surrounding heavens.

It's a measure was enormous, it's belchings fire blazed forth.

He looked down again; the wide breach turned into a small tub.

He looked again, Nibiru's great ball turned into a small fruit;

The next time he looked, in the wide dark sea Nibiru disappeared.

100 leagues, 1000 leagues the chariot was coursing; 10,000 leagues the chariot was journeying.

In the expanse of the heavens, the celestials emissary was him greeting!

Little Gaga, (Pluto) the One Who Shows the Way, by its circuit allowing was greeting, to him a welcome extending.

Me by the celestial gods he is welcomed! So was his understanding.

Comment: Here Alalu is in his spacecraft, traveling at great speeds, from Nibiru, coming into our solar system. (A league in the ancient texts equates to 3.52 miles) Accordingly, he is now able to view the planet, Pluto.

In his chariot Alalu followed Gaga's path; to the second god (Ea/Neptune) of the heavens it was directing.

Soon celestial Antu, (Uranus) its name by King Enshar was given, in the deep darkness was looming;

Blue as pure waters was her hue; of the Upper Waters she was the commencement.

As his spouses double, by a greenish blueness was An distinguished

Alalu by the sights and beauty was enchanted; to course at a distance he continued.

To the two celestials Alalu bade a fond farewell, the path of Gaga still discerning.

To Anshar, (Saturn) the Foremost Prince of the Heavens, the course was a turning.

My the speeding chariot, Alalu the ensnaring pull of Enshar could tell;

With bright rings of dazzling colors the chariot it was enchanting!

Comment: Saturn is reverently referred to, in the Ancient Texts as the 'Foremost Prince of the Heavens'. The word, 'Foremost', is not referring to size, as Saturn is not the largest planet in our solar system; the reference is to the gaseous planet itself encircled with its vast "bright rings of dazzling colors."

Perhaps even more significant is the text Ancient Text pointing out the colors of Neptune, which we did not discover until 1846. "Blue as pure waters was her hue;" "As his spouses double, by a greenish blueness was Anshar distinguished."

NASA launched Voyager 1 and 2 in August of 1977. In August 1989, some 12 years later, the unmanned spacecraft Voyager 2, flew by distant Neptune. The following is taken from Zechariah Sitchin's Genesis Revisited: Is Modern Science Catching up with Ancient Knowledge? Page 6.

"But two months *before* the August encounter, I had written an article for a number of U. S., European, and South American monthlies contradicting the long-held notions: Neptune *was* known in antiquity, I wrote; and the discoveries that were about to be made would only confirm ancient knowledge. Neptune, I predicted, would be blue-green, watery, and have patches the color of "swamp-like vegetation!"

"The electronic signals from Voyager 2 confirmed all that and more. They revealed a beautiful blue-green, aquamarine planet embraced by an atmosphere of helium, hydrogen, and methane gases, swept by swirling, high-velocity winds that make Earth's hurricanes look timid. Below this atmosphere, there appears mysterious giant "smudges" whose coloration is sometimes darker blue and sometimes greenish-yellow, perhaps depending on the angle at which the sunlight strikes them."

A site most awesome then to him appeared: In the faraway heavens the family's bright star he discerned!

A site most frightening the revelation follows:

A giant monster, in its destiny (orbit), moving, upon the Sun a darkening cast; Kishar (Jupiter) its creator swallowed!

The giant Kishar, Foremost of the Firm Planets, Its size was overwhelming.

Swirling storms obscured its face, colored spots they moved about;

Kishar itself a spell was casting, divine lightings it was thrusting.

Then the darkness darkening began to depart: Kishar on his destiny continued to circuit.

Slowly moving, its veil from the shining Son it lifted; the One from the Beginning came fully into view.

Comment: What has been described herein this Ancient Text is an *indisputable* eclipse of the Sun by the planet Jupiter! The statement "Swirling storms obscured its face, colored spots they moved about;" Almost everyone on the face of this Earth has seen NASA's pictures from Voyager and other launches. We have here in this Ancient Text, a perfect *empirical description* of the planet Jupiter as we knew it _from the 1980s!_ These ancient astronauts, a.k.a. (the Anunnaki) have known of our solar system and have been part of our solar system _for many millennia!_ It is impossible to put these kind of descriptions in writing without an empirical relationship with the subject matter. This kind of empirical information is replete throughout the Ancient Texts.

I want to coin a new word here that relates to those scientific minds and all others that remain in a state of denial relating to the historical value of the Ancient Texts, that word is insananity, meaning, insanely inane!

Beyond the fifth planet (Jupiter) the utmost danger was lurking, so indeed he knew.

The Hammered Bracelet (Asteroid Belt) ahead was reigning, to demolish it was awaiting.

Of rocks and boulders was it together hammered, like orphans with no mother they banded together.

Surging back and forth, a bygone destiny they followed;

The chariot of Alalu towards the Hammered Bracelet was headlong moving,

The ferocious boulders in close combat to boldly face.

Alalu in the Fire Stones in his chariot more strongly stirred up,

That Which Shows the Way with steady hands he directed.

The ominous boulders against the chariot charged forward, like an enemy in battle attacking.

Toward them Alalu a death dealing missile from the chariot let loose;

Then another and another against the enemy the terror weapons he thrust.

As frightened warriors the boulders turned back, a path for Alalu granting.

Like a spell the Hammered Bracelet a doorway to the King it opened.

By the bracelets ferocity he was not defeated, his mission was not ended.

Comment: To lend credibility to Alalu's described passing through the Asteroid Belt: NASA has calculated that the average distance between all of the stone objects comprising the Asteroid Belt is 600,000 miles. They have also mathematically calculated, that the chance of a launched satellite or missile, colliding with any object in the Asteroid Belt is infinitesimally small. It is of no concern to them, therefore it seems quite logical that Alalu's spacecraft is traveling at a stupendous speed. The sentences, "The ominous boulders against the chariot charged forward." "Then another and another." "By the bracelets ferocity he was not defeated." support my statement.

In the distance, the Sun's fiery ball its brilliance was sending forth;

Before it, a red brown planet (Mars) on its circuit was coursing; the sixth in the count of celestial gods it was.

Then the snow hewed Earth appeared, the seventh in the celestial count.

Towards the planet Alalu set his course, to a destination most inviting.

Smaller than Nibiru was this alluring ball, weaker than Nibiru was its attracting net.

Its atmosphere thinner than Nibiru's was, clouds were within it swirling.

Below, the Earth to three regions was divided:

Snow white at the top and on the bottom, blue and brown in between.
It's

Comment: The ancient text has depicted accurate travel through our solar system coming in retrograde. The first planet encountered was Pluto, (Gaga) the next Neptune, (Ea) the next Uranus, (Anu) then Saturn, (Anshar) then Jupiter, (Kishar) then, fighting his way through the Asteroid Belt, encountering Mars (Lahmu) and finally its destination comes into view, Earth. (Ki) Earth is described, *as can only be described as viewed from space!*

"Then the snow hewed Earth appeared." Snowcaps on the North and South Pole.

Smaller than Nibiru was an alluring ball. Scientists at NASA have determined that Nibiru is between three and five times the size of Earth, therefore Earth being smaller.

"Weaker than Nibiru was its attracting net. The gravitational pull of the Earth would be 3 to 5 times weaker than Nibiru's.

"Snow-white at the top and on the bottom, blue and brown in between." As I previously pointed out this description of Earth, *from the Ancient Texts, could only be described as viewed from space!*

Deftly Alalu spread the chariot's arresting wings around the Earth's ball to circle.

In the middle region drylands and watery oceans he could discern.

The Beam That Penetrates downward he directed, Earth's innards to detect.

Gold, much gold, the beam has indicated;

Fully caught in Earth's attracting net, the chariot was moving faster.

Its spread wings become aglow; Earth's atmosphere like an oven was.

Then the chariot shook, emitting a mortifying thunder.

With abruptness the chariot crashed, with a sudden altogether stopping.

Senseless from the shaking, stunned by the crash, Alalu was without moving.

Then he opened his eyes and knew he was among the living;

At the planet of gold he gloriously arrived.

Comment: Spreading the chariot arresting wings was done to *place the spacecraft into orbit!*
Fully caught in Earth's attracting net, the chariot was moving faster, obviously relates to *gravitational pull!*
It spread wings become aglow; Earth's atmosphere like an oven was. *A classic description of re-entry!*
Then the chariot shook, emitting a mortifying thunder. *A classic description of a sonic boom!*
Need I say more relating to proving this chapter of the ancient text?

Chapter 16: Months, Winter, Summer,= One Year

The Lost Book of Enki Page 79

In the nighttimes the Moon waxed and waned; by the name Month Ea its circuit call:

At half crown the seventh day it announced; a day to rest it was.

At Midway by a fullness was the Moon distinguished; then it paused to become diminished.

With the Sun's course was the Moon's circuit appearing, with Earth's circuit it was its face revealing.

Fascinated by the Moon's motion was Ea, its attachment as Kingu (Moon) to Ki (Earth) he contemplated:

What purpose did the attachment serve, what heavenly sign was it giving?

A Month did Ea the Moons circuit call, Month to its circuit he gave the name.

For one Month, for two Months, in the chariot were the waters separated;

The Sun, every six Months, to Earth another season gave; Winter and Summer did I by names them call.

There was Winter and there was Summer; by Year of Earth did Ea the full circuit call.

Comment: Here we have Ea, determining the different phases of the Moon. A circuit he named a month and determining every six months the Sun (moving north to south and back again) gave us Winter and Summer, accumulating those two periods, to a full circuit (orbit) of the Earth around the Sun. Based on the accuracy given to us by the ancient text, Ea's mathematical calculations were done more than 400,000 years ago!

Chapter 17: Christopher Dunn/The Giza Power Plant Statements

The Giza Power Plant Statements 1998

P-49-I have some very strong opinions regarding the level of manufacturing expertise practiced and by the Egyptians. They were not primitive by any means, and their craftsmanship and precision should be an extreme challenge to duplicate today.

P 56 In preparation for his book 5/5/ 2000 Ice: The Ultimate Disaster, Richard Noone asked Merle Booker, technical director of the Indiana Limestone Inst. of America, to prepare a study of what it would take to quarry, fabricate, and ship enough limestone to duplicate the Great Pyramid. Using the most modern quarrying equipment available for cutting, lifting, and transporting the stone, Booker estimated that the present-day Indiana limestone industry would need to triple its output, and it would take the entire industry, which as I have said includes 33 quarries, 27 years to fill the order for 131,467,940 ft. of stone. Then we would be faced with the task of putting the limestone blocks in place. (Not to mention that limestone is much easier to work with than granite or diorite.

P-57 When I informed him of the minute variation of the foundation of the great pyramid, he expressed disbelief and agreed with me that in this particular phase of construction, the builders of the pyramid exhibited a state of the art that would be considered advanced by modern standards.

P-59 The Great Pyramid was the most accurately aligned structure in the world until the building of the Paris Observatory.

P – 60 Although the incorporation of pi into the shape of the Great Pyramid has been attributed by some to be pure chance, the fact that such an angle was discovered in the casting stones suggests that the builders were at least knowledgeable in the science of mathematics, trigonometry, and geometry.

P-62 Considering the immense size of the Great Pyramid, the precision with which it was built, the materials that were used, and the uniqueness of its interior passages in chambers, we are faced with a structure that has no parallel in modern times.

P-63 – When Told That Giant Limestone Casting Stones, Which Were Cut to within 1/100 of an Inch, Were Cut with Hammer and Chisel, a Typical Response Was a Shake of the Head.

P – 64 It could always be said that those who built the Great Pyramid did not really know what they were doing and that the end result of their labors was achieved purely through trial and error – the Great Pyramids precision was just a stroke of luck. Yes, I know that reasoning sounds ridiculous *but it has been suggested by Egyptologists and other researchers, actually more than a few times.*

P – 67 I have noticed many inconsistencies between what the Egyptologists have taught regarding the tools that were supposedly used in the evidence that can be drawn from the masonry itself. In other words, the stones of the Great Pyramid tell me a different story then they have other observers. The stones tell me that they were cut *using machine power,* not manpower as other Egyptologists theorize.

P – 70 The tools displayed by Egyptologists as instruments for the creation of many of these incredible artifacts are physically incapable of reproducing them. P – 71 So why do modern Egyptologists insist that this work was accomplished with a few primitive copper instruments?

P – 72 evidence proving that the ancient Egyptians used tools such as straight saws, circular saws, and even lathes *have been recognized for over a century.*

P 74 I.E.S. Edwards, British Egyptologist and the world's foremost expert on pyramids said, "Quarrymen of the Pyramid Age would have accused Greek historian Strabo of an understatement as they hacked at the stubborn granite of Aswan. Their axes and chisels were made of copper hardened by hammering." Having worked with copper on numerous occasions, and having hardened it in the manner suggested above, *I was struck that this statement was entirely ridiculous. (Author statement* – Beryllium copper is the hardest alloyed copper known to mankind. That said, beryllium copper is not hard enough to cut granite.)

P – 81 Although the ancient Egyptians were not given credit for having the wheel, the fact is that *archaeological evidence*, when evaluated with a machinist's eye, *proves that they not only had the wheel, but they used it in very sophisticated ways.*

P – 83 Egyptian artifacts representing tubular drilling are clearly the most astounding and conclusive evidence yet presented to indicate the extent to which machining knowledge and technology were practiced in prehistory.

P – 84 For those who may still believe in the "official" chronology of the historical development of metals, identifying copper as they metal the ancient Egyptians used for cutting granite is like saying that aluminum could be cut using a chisel fashioned out of butter.

P – 87 in contrast, ultrasonic drilling fully explains how the holes and cores found in the Valley Temple at Giza could have been cut, and it is capable of creating all the details that Petrie and I puzzled over. In my opinion, the application of ultrasonic machining is the only method that completely satisfies logic, from a technical viewpoint, and explains all noted phenomena.

Mr. Dunn's book I rate as five stars. He is consistent and persistent in his dogged pursuit for empirical evidence…. and he found it! Sections of this book I have read and reread. I will keep this book in my personal library as reference material, his excellent work, explanations, and specific technical revelations will always be an important and respected source of information for me.

P – 91 When I was asked by Egyptologists how the ancients could have produced this work with mere copper tools, I told them they were crazy and that they were using at least state of art techniques

Sincerely,
Roger Hopkins

P – 93 While there, I came across and measured some artifacts produced by the ancient pyramid builders that *prove beyond a shadow of a doubt* that highly advanced and sophisticated tools and methods are employed by this ancient civilization. (Author's italics)

P – 103 In the Great Pyramid alone there are an estimated 2,300,000 blocks of stone, both limestone, and granite, weighing between 2 ½ and 270 tons each. This is a mountain of *evidence, and there are no tools surviving to explain even this one pyramids creation.* (Author's italics)

P – 253 However, we can no longer ignore the factual evidence that a prehistoric civilization capable of developing advanced machining techniques once existed on this planet. (Notice that Mr. Dunn does not attribute this factual evidence to ancient Egyptians or today's Egyptologists.)

Chapter 18: Technological Advancement

THOTHS' RAY GUN   The Emerald Tablets of Thoth

Then raised my staff and directed a Ray of vibration,

Striking them still in their tracks as fragments of stone of the mountain.

Cowed I them by my display of magic- science,

Until at my feet they groveled, Then I relented them.

TRIGONOMETRY ON A 3,700-YEAR-OLD BABYLONIAN TABLET – PLIMPTON 322

Two Australian mathematicians assert that an ancient clay tablet was a tool for working out trigonometry problems, possibly adding to the many techniques that Babylonian mathematicians had mastered.

"It's a trigonometric table, which is 3, 000 years ahead of its time," said Daniel F. Mansfield of the University of New South Wales. Mansfield and his colleague Norman J Wildberger reported their findings in the journal *Historia Mathematica*.

The tablet, known as Clinton 322, was discovered in the early 1900s in southern Iraq and has long been of interest to scholars. It contains 60 numbers organized into 15 rows and four columns inscribed on a piece of clay about 5 inches wide and 3.5 inches tall. Based on the style of cuneiform script used for the numbers, Clinton 322 has been dated to between 1822 in 1762 BC.

One of the columns on Plimpton 322 is just a numbering of the Rows from 1 to 15. The other three columns are much more intriguing. In the 1940s, Otto E. Neugebauer and Abraham J. Sachs, mathematics historians, pointed out that the other three columns were essentially Pythagorean triples – sets of integers, or whole numbers, that satisfy the equation "A squared+ B squared= C squared."

This equation – the Pythagorean Theorem – also represents a fundamental property of right triangles, that the square of the longest side, or hypotenuse, is the sum of the squares of the other two shorter sides.

That by itself was remarkable given the Greek mathematician Pythagoras would not be born for another thousand years.

Wildberger, who once had proposed teaching trigonometry in terms of ratios rather than angles, wondered if Babylonians took a similar angle- less approach to trigonometry. "You don't make a trigonometric table by accident," Mansfield said. "Just having a list of Pythagorean triples doesn't help you much. That's just a list of numbers. But when you arrange it in such a way so that you can use any known ratio of a triangle to find the other sides of a triangle, then it becomes trigonometry. That is what we can use this fragment for."

A Babylonian faced with a word problem may have found it easy to set up: a right angle with the long side, or hypotenuse, 56 cubits long and one of the shorter sides 45 cubits. Next, the problem solver could have calculated the ratio 56/45, or about 1.244 and then looked up the closest entry on the table, which is line 11, which lists the ratio 1.25.

From that line, it is then a straight forward calculation to produce an answer of 33.6 cubits. In their paper, Mansfield and Wildberger show that this is better than what would be calculated using a trigonometric table from the Indian mathematician Madhava 3000 years later.

Kenneth Chang, New York Times Sunday, September 10, 2017

PRECESSION

From an early age I knew that Earth's axis tilts 23.5° from the perpendicular and until probably four decades ago I knew almost nothing about Precession and for a better understanding of the subject matter, let me define it:

Axial precession – Wikipedia: The precession of the Earth's axis has a number of observable effects. First, the positions of the south and north celestial poles appear to move in circles against the space-fixed backdrop of stars, completing one circuit in approximately 26,000 years.

Precession Wikipedia – Earth goes through one such complete precession all cycle in a period of approximately 26,000 years or 1° every 72 years, during which the positions of stars will slowly change in both equatorial coordinates an ecliptic longitude.

Precession of the Earth's Axis – The Earth Axis Rotates (Processes) just as a spinning top does. The period of Precession is about 26,000

Years. Therefore the North Celestial Pole will not always be point towards the same starfield.

Astronomy: precession of Earth – The phenomenon we call "precession" was discovered by Greek astronomer Hipparchus when he compared to his own circa 200 BC records with older charts. What he saw was that the equinoxes in his day (when the sun's path crosses the celestial equator) are in a different position among the stars.

I discuss Precession here for the purpose of showing, you the reader, approximately when this scientific information was known and who knew it. Moreover who would have the need millennia ago to have the need to define or the ability to calculate precision.... millennia past.

I have to disagree with the statement above, that the Greek astronomer Hipparchus discovered precession. It was the Anunnaki who presented us with the knowledge of precession. No one could explain this more comprehensively than Mr. Zechariah Sitchin, the Godfather of the ancient text. From his book, "When Time Began," Pages 23 through 25.

But it was not Man who had first grouped the myriads of stars into recognizable constellations, defined and named those that spanned the ecliptic, and that divided them into 12 to create the 12 houses of the zodiac. *It was the Anunnaki* who had conceived of that for their own needs; Man adopted that as his link, his means of ascent, to the heavens from the mortality of life on Earth.

For someone arriving from Niburu with this vast orbital "year" on a fast orbiting planet (Earth, the "seventh planet" as the Anunnaki had called it) whose year is but one part of 3600 of theirs, timekeeping had to pose a great problem. It is evident from the Samarian Kings Lists and other texts dealing with the affairs of the Anunnaki that for a long time – certainly until the Deluge – they retained the *sar,* the 3600 Earth years of Niburu, *as the divine unit of time. But what could they do somehow to create a reasonable relationship, other than 1:3600, between that Divine Time and Earthly Time?*

The solution was provided by a phenomenon called precession. Because of this wobble, the Earth's orbit around the sun is slightly retarded each year; the retardation or precession amounts to 1° and 72 years. Devising the division of the ecliptic (the plane of planetary orbits around the Sun) into 12 – to conform to the 12 member composition of the Solar System – the Anunnaki invented the 12 houses of the zodiac; that allotted to each zodiac house 30°, in consequence of which the retardation per house added up to 2, 160 years (72×30 = 2, 160) and the complete Precessional Cycle or "Great Year" to 25,920 years (2, 160 × 2 = 25,920) in *Genesis Revisited* we have suggested that by relating 2, 160 years to 3, 600 the Anunnaki arrived at the Golden Ratio of 6:10 and, more importantly, at the sexagesimal system of mathematics which multiplied 6 x 10 x 6 x 10 and so on and on.

"By a miracle that I have found no one to interpret," the pathologist Joseph Campbell wrote in *The Masks of God: Oriental Mythology* (1962), "the arithmetic that was developed in Sumer as early as circuit 3200 B. C . whether by coincidence or by intuitive induction, so matched the celestial order as to amount itself to a revelation." The "miracle," as we have since shown, was *provided by the advanced knowledge of the Anunnaki.*

Modern astronomy, as well as modern exact sciences, owes much to the Sumerian "firsts." Among them, the division of the skies tells us and all other circles into 360 portions ("degrees") is the most basic. Hugo Winckler, who with but a few others, combined, at the turn-of-the-century, mastery of "Assyriology" with knowledge of astronomy, realize that the number 72 was fundamental as a link between "Heaven, Calendar and Myth." It was through the *Hameshtu, the "fiver" or "times five,"* he wrote, *creating the fundamental number 360 by multiplying the celestial 72 (the processional shift of 1°) by the human five of an Earthlings hand.* His insight, understandably for his time, did not lead him to envision the role of the Anunnaki, whose science was needed to know of Earth's retardation to begin with.

Among the thousands of mathematical tables discovered in Mesopotamia, many that served as ready-made tables of division begin with the astronomical number 12,960,000 and with 60 as the 216,000th part of 12,960,000. HV Hilprecht (*The Babylonian Expedition of the University Of Pennsylvania*), Who Studied Thousands of Mathematical Tablets from the Library of the Assyrian King Ashurbanipal in Nineveh, concluded that the number 12,960,000 was literally astronomical, stemming from the enigmatic Great Cycle of 500 Great Years of complete precessional shifts (500 × 25,920 = 12,960,000). He and others had no doubt that **the phenomenon of precession,** presumably first mention by the Greek Hipparchus in the second century BC, **was already known and followed in Sumerian times.**

As described in Zechariah Sitchin's 1976 book, *"The 12th Planet,"* he points out that the Sumerians had described Uranus as MASH.SIG or as he had translated it "bright greenish." When we look at others who are knowledgeable in translating Sumerian, Akkadian, Ugaritic, etc. they give us the Samarian, EN.TI.MASH.SIG translated as *Planet of the Bright Greenish Life.*

In January 1986, Voyager 2 reached its flyby point of Uranus, which was shown on national television. The expectations, of our scientists and astronomers, were that Uranus would be a totally "gaseous" planet like the giants Jupiter and Saturn. From here I will let Mr. Sitchin describe what he wrote in his book *Genesis Revisited,* as the event happened:

As the images of Uranus grew bigger on the TV screen the closer Voyager 2 neared the planet, the moderator at the Jet Propulsion Laboratory drew attention to its usual green-blue color. I could not help but cry out, **"Oh, my God, it is exactly as the Sumerian's had described it!"** I hurried to my study, picked up a copy of *The 12th Planet,* and with unsteady hands looked up page 269 (in the Avon paperback edition). I read, again and again, the lines quoting the ancient texts. Yes, there was no doubt: though they had no telescopes, the Sumerians had described Uranus as MASH.SIG "bright greenish."

A few days later came the results of the analysts of Voyager 2's data, and the Samarian reference to water on Uranus was also corroborated. This abundance or even the mere presence of water on the supposed "gaseous" planets and their satellites at the edges of the Solar System is totally unexpected.

Yet here we had the evidence, presented in *The 12th Planet,* in their **texts from millennia ago the ancient Sumerians had not only known of the existence of Uranus but had accurately described it as greenish-blue and watery!**

All of the planets in our solar system are named and described in the ancient text. Uranus for example, in Akkadian, is called *Kakkab shanamma and is translated as "Planet Which Is the Double" (of Neptune.)* So the question is, is the ancient text scientifically accurate in their description of the planets comparing the similarities between Uranus and Neptune? The answer is a definitive, undeniable yes! And I will let Mr. Sitchin describe the comparison and similarities in his own words as he had earned this recognition. Taken from Genesis revisited page 13:

"An unexpected similarity has been found regarding the two planets' magnetic fields: both have been unusually extreme inclination relative to the planets' axis of rotation – 58° on Uranus, 50° on Neptune. "Neptune appears to be almost a magnetic when of Uranus," John Noble Wilford reported in *The New York Times*. The two planets are also similar in the links of their days: each about 16 to 17 hours long."

"The ferocious winds on Neptune in the water ice slurry layer on its surface attest to the great internal heat it degenerates, like that of Uranus. In fact, the reports from JPL state that initial temperature readings indicated that "Neptune's temperatures are similar to those of Uranus, which is more than 1 billion miles closer to the Sun." Therefore, the scientist assumed "that Neptune somehow is generating more of its internal heat then Uranus does" – somehow compensating for its greater distance from the Sun to attain the same temperatures as Uranus generates, resulting in similar temperatures on both planets – and thus adding one more feature "to the size and other characteristics that make Uranus a near twin of Neptune. "

"Planet which is the double," the Sumerians said of Uranus in comparing it to Neptune. "Size and other characteristics that make Uranus a near twin of Neptune," NASA's scientists announced. Not only described characteristics but even the terminology – "planet which is the double," a near twin of Neptune" – is similar. But one statement, **the Sumerian one, was made circa 4000 BC, and the other, by NASA in A.D. 1989, NEARLY 6000 YEARS LATER..."**

There have been many scientific discoveries that have been corroborated previously, millennia ago, by the ancient text. I have found nothing in the ancient text, and let me repeat that, I have found nothing in the ancient text that I can prove to be scientifically false. And realize each time Mr. Zechariah Sitchin points out the current scientific substantiation and corroboration of the millennia-old ancient text , he puts his reputation on the line. I make it a point to read everything that Mr. Sitchin refers to in his books, in his interpretation of the Sumerian Texts and in his writings. His profound works have always proved him right, both in meaning and reference.

Chapter 19: Orbiting Gold Dust to Save Planet

Niburu is its name.

A great planet, reddish in radiance; around the Sun an elongated circuit Niburu makes.

For a time in the cold is Niburu engulfed; for part of its circuit by the Sun strongly Is It heated.

A thick atmosphere Niburu envelops, by volcanic eruptions constantly fed.

All manner of life this atmosphere sustains; without it there would be only perishing!

In the cold period the inner heat of Niburu it keeps about the planet, like a warm coat that is constantly renewed.

In the hot period it shields Niburu from the Sun's scorching rays.

Comment: The above-written portion of the ancient text answers the question, "How can a planet in its apogee being so far from the Sun, maintain a source of heat. The twin planets, so-referred to in the Ancient Text, (Kishar and Ashar) Jupiter and Saturn, carry with them more than a few similarities. Saturn maintains an atmosphere similar to Jupiter, although Saturn is more than 1 million miles further from the Sun.

The Lost Book of Enki- Page 86
The atmosphere around the planet Nibiru was seriously depleting. The ancient texts relate to us that the Anunnaki needed to stimulate the volcanic activity on the planet. They did what they could to stimulate volcanic activity. With little to no success, the Anunnaki resorted to atomic weapons to push the ash into their atmosphere.

When the planet Nibiru, headed toward its Perigee, the Anunnaki could not tolerate the heat from the Sun due to its dwindling atmosphere. They finally decided to use gold. They would grind into fine dust, then launch into orbit around their planet to create a more protective atmosphere. We all know now and the Anunnaki knew millennia ago, that gold does not deteriorate. The following describes Abgal, bringing the first cargo of gold being sent from Earth to Nibiru.

He opened the hatch; a multitude of populace was there assembled!

Anu toward him stepped forward, locked arms, warm greetings uttered.

Heroes into the chariot rushed, the gold bearing baskets they brought out.

High above their heads they the baskets held,

To the assembled, words of victory Anu shouted: Salvation is here! To them he was saying.

The gold, a site most dazzling, by the savants was quickly taken;

To make of it the *finest dust, to skyward launch* it was called away.

A Shar did the fashioning last, a Shar (3600 years) did this testing continue.

With rockets was the dust heavenward carried, by crystals' beams was it dispersed.

Where there was a breach, now there was a healing!

Joy the palace filled, abundance in the land that was expected.

To Earth Anu good words was beaming: Gold gives salvation! The obtaining of gold to continue!

When Nibiru near the Sun came, the gold dust was by its rays disturbed;

The healing in the atmosphere was dwindled, the breach to bigness returned.

Anu the return of Algal to earth then commanded; in the chariot more heroes travel,

In its bowels more That Which the Waters Suck in and Thrusts out were Provided;

Great joy there was when   Abgal to Eridu (first establishment on Earth) returned;

Ea and Alalu words exchanged, that which was known they reconsidered:

Where were the golden veins from Earth enters protruding?

In the sky chamber Ea over mountains and valleys traveled,

The lands by oceans separated he with the Scanner examined.

Where dry land from dry land apart was torn, Earth's innards were revealed;

Where the landmass the shape of a heart was given, in the lower part thereof,

Golden veins from Earth's innards were abundant.

Comment: The one and only reason why the Anunnaki came to Earth was for the sole purpose of finding gold. They evidently knew how to get the finely ground gold dust into orbit around their planet for protection. They mined gold for millennia after millennia.

Dr. Edward Teller and other reputable scientists have long argued, to repair the ozone holes in our atmosphere we could put pulverized particles of gold in the upper atmosphere. Gold, being very conductive, would provide a heat shield reflecting the ultraviolet rays, holding down the warming of the planets.

That Which the Water Sucks in and Thrusts Out was evidently a machine that they used to mine gold from local areas of water. That changed when they discovered huge quantities of gold in the Abzu, and we recognize today as South Africa. The mines there had been located and *some of them date back to more than 250,000 years!*

Chapter 20: It's the Anunnaki Stupid!

It is quite bemusing, frustrating and almost incomprehensible to this author that there is a concerted effort, in most cases, consciously and in a few cases subconsciously, to avoid, sidestep, ignore, deviate, fabricate, and intentionally not recognize the empirical information that is so poignantly revealed to the world through the Ancient Texts. Authors and Ancient Astronaut theorists, National Geographic, the History Channel, the Ancient Astronauts series, Science Channel, PBS and others clearly demonstrate their intentions to avoid at all cost, the pregnant elephant in the room, and that is to almost never mention the word, or attribute anything to the **ANUNNAKI!** Instead, we use the word god, god's, Extraterrestrial, Ancient Astronauts, or otherworldly beings. My very favorite, in order to, `avoid the word Anunnaki at all costs,' is the words used by William Bramley in his book, "The Gods of Eden," and that word is *"Custodial Masters."* In my opinion, using those words, are worse than being intentionally ambiguous. I would have to call it, feigned ignorance, that being explained as having knowledge of a given subject but intentionally ignoring it. Too many of the experts are trying to walk across a lake that is not frozen.

James Carville a Democratic strategist gave us the well-known quote, **"It's the economy stupid!"** It was not a sarcastic statement, but it was a statement, boiling down some of the difficult ideas and concepts in a political campaign to a simplistic, yet encompassing statement, highlighting the importance of the economy as a prime issue. So I will borrow that phrase from Mr. Carville to rightfully highlight the importance and significance of the **Anunnaki.**

The question then becomes, why is this being done? And why the almost total avoidance of mentioning the word Anunnaki, and outright ignoring the decade's long work of Zechariah Sitchin and his "Earth Chronicles." I believe the answer to be, that if the Anunnaki and/or the Ancient Texts and/or the dogged research and brilliant effort of Zechariah Sitchin were "excepted" in any way as empirical evidence, as it most certainly should be, then they would no longer be able to write/sell their books, do their, "paid for " personal presentations, appear as an expert in any given area on National Geographic, the History Channel, the Ancient Astronaut Series, etc.

If they and they being the Ancient Astronaut Theorists experts, recognize the Ancient Texts; those being the Sumerian, Akkadian, Babylonian, Ugaritic, Assyrian, Canaanite, Phoenician Texts, etc., most of their book writing days and appearances on television, as an expert in any given area: in short, their ability to make money, would be greatly curtailed. The reason being that the **Ancient Texts can answer 95% of all the questions asked!** The answer is, **"It's the Anunnaki stupid!"**

To many of the books that have been written, along with the programs on the national networks, intentionally avoid pointing out to the reader, and the viewer, that the characters that they are using to tell their millennia-old stories i.e. Enlil, Enki, Thoth Murdoch, Adad, Nergal, or Inanna, for example, **are all ANUNNAKI!** Additionally important is for the reader to be able to recognize that many of the Anunnaki have more than one name or epithet, depending upon their geographical location and/ or a specific function that they are administrating. Below you will find a listing of nothing but the Anunnaki; their primary names followed by their Ancient Text epithets.

Anu/ An, Antu, – Enlil/Zeus, – Enki, (a.k.a. E.a, Ptah, Poseidon, Khnum, Khnemu, Nudimmud, Oannes) – Thoth, (a.k.a. Ningishzid-da, Hermes/ Hermes Trismetgistus, Kukulcan, Queztalcoatl, Tehuti – Marduk, (a.k.a. Ra, Amen, Amon, Asar, Bel, Aten), – Adad, (a.k.a. Hadad, Ish.kur, Ba'al, Teshub, Viracocha, Nannar/Sin, Pachacamac, Rimac, Yerah) – Zu/ An.zu, Alalu, – Ninurta/ Nikkal, (a.k.a.Ashur, Ishum, Nin.gal, Nin.girsu, Nini.urta, Hathor – Ba.u/Gula, Berossus, Dagan, – Ziusudra /Uta-Napishtim,-- Dumu.zi, Inanna/Ishtar, Yam, Mot, Enheduanna,-- Nin.lil/Sud, Ninharsag/ Nin.mah,-- Enoch, En.sag/ Nabu, Eresh.ki.gal, Nergal/Erra, Etana,-- Utu (a.k.a. Shamash, Shalem-- Gabriel, Geb, Gibil, (a.k.a. Ephaestus, Vulcan, -- Gilgamesh, Ninsun, Gudea, Gula,-- Hatshepsut, Hebat,-- Ningal, Kumarbi, Manetho, Nanshe, Naram-Sin, Nidaba/Nisba, Nin.a.gal, Nin.kashi, --Ninki/ Dam.ki.na,-- Nut, Set, Shu, Shu-Sin,-- Ubartutu, Ur-Nam-mu .

As an example of an intended (?) inaccuracy, one of the ancient astronaut theorists, on an Ancient Aliens program, clearly stated that Ptah was from Phalides. To step back that " inaccuracy" looking at the last paragraph, you will notice that Ptah has seven other epithets i.e.

Enki/Ea and the ancient texts repeatedly tell us that *all* of the Anunna-ki including, Mr.Ptah *are from the planet Nibiru.*

To point out another intentional ambiguity, Phalides is not a place, it's a named (by the Anunnaki) constellation. To say that Ptah was from Phalides would be like me saying that I'm from the constellation Capricorn.

The reader of this book, and the general public, interested in the Ancient Texts and the 14 books of Zechariah Sitchin, should be made aware that there are certain groups and organizations, whose sole purpose is to propagate their specific form of nationalism. I see it more and more in the writings of some authors, commentators, Ancient Alien theorists, Egyptologist, etc., that 6, 7, 8, 10, 12 YEARS AGO, PROFFERED TO THE PUBLIC, VIA BOOKS, ARTICLES, SPEECHES AND APPEARANCES ON NATIONAL TELEVISION PROGRAMS, BEING CONVINCED AND ADAMANT IN WHAT THEY HAVE LEARNED ABOUT OUR ANCIENT CIVILIZATIONS; NOW PROFFER TO THE PUBLIC, NOT A DICHOTOMY OF THEIR THOUGHTS AND WRITINGS, BUT A COMPLETE ANTITHESIS OF THEIR THOUGHT AND WRITINGS. To express that in more colloquial terms, that is what most of us would call, "doin a 180."

To point a finger in the right direction, one group would be the Egyptian Minister of State of Antiquities," whose current Minister of Antiquities is none other than Mr. Zahi,-- (You had better believe that the indigenous population of Egypt built all the 155 pyramids in Egypt!) –Hawass. This person, Zahi, (Mr. dogma,) Hawass, through the years, has done whatever he could to obstruct anything and everything from being published or spoken about, relating to denying that the Egyptians built the Great Pyramid. I will give `*Hawas*'credit for the other 152 pyramids built in Egypt by the then indigenous Egyptians, just which are in fact have crumbled and have disintegrated into an unsafe state, where no tourists are allowed. The Ancient Texts repeatedly tell us *specifically by name*, it was the Anunnaki who built the Great Pyramid and the two adjutant pyramids, which form the same geographical positioning as the astrological positioning of the belt in the constellation Orion.` *Hawass*' that statement Mr.Zahi!?

THE GIZA POWER PLANT **VERSUS** LOST TECHNOLO-
GIES OF ANCIENT EGYPT: BY CHRISTOPHER DUNN

This book by Mr. Dunn was published in 1998. It is a five-star
book whereby, in my opinion, is looking for and finds empirical evidence which clearly points out that the Egyptians could not have built
the Great Pyramid This is supported by the statements in his book.

"Having that experience myself, I have some very strong opinions
regarding the level of manufacturing expertise practiced by the ancient
Egyptians. They were not primitive by any means, and their craftsmanship and precision would be an extreme challenge to duplicate today."

Quoting in his book, a respected builder and architect James Hagan: "The Egyptians, *or whoever built the pyramid, he said earnestly in
his southern drawl,* "they could build anything they wanted to!" "His
comment becomes more significant when it is understood within the
context he set forth, admitting that **it would be impossible to build a
Great Pyramid today using modern building methods, and, therefore, impossible by primitive methods."**

Mr. Dunn continues referring to the above paragraph by Mr. Hagan: His hands-on, real-world experience is bolstered by innocent sin-
cerity and respect that transcends the plethora of amateurs (compared
to him) who profess to "know " how the pyramids of Egypt were built."

Merle Booker, technical director of the Indiana Limestone Institute of America was asked, "to prepare a time study of what it would
take to quarry, fabricate, and ship enough limestone to duplicate the
Great Pyramid. Using the most modern quarrying equipment available
for cutting, lifting, and transporting the stone, Booker estimated that
the present-day Indiana limestone industry would need to triple its
output, and it would take the entire industry, which I have said includes 33 quarries, *27* years to fill the order for 131,467,940 cubic ft.
of stone."

"When I informed him of the minute variation in the foundation
of the great pyramid, (.02 inch) he expressed disbelief and agreed with
me that in this particular phase of construction, the builders of the
pyramid exhibited a state of the art that would be *considered advanced
by modern standards. "* (authors italics)
"

The quantity of stone that had to be quarried, hauled, and hoisted into place in the Great Pyramid becomes even more impressive when it is compared to other civil engineering feats, whether real or imagined. It has been stated that it contains more stone than that used in all of the churches, cathedrals, and chapels built in England since the time of Christ. 30 Empire State Buildings could be built with the estimated 2,300,000 stones. A wall 3 foot high and 1 foot thick could be built across the United States and the back using the amount of masonry contained in the Grand Pyramid."

"It is oriented within three minutes of a degree from true North."
"The Great Pyramid was the most accurately aligned structure in the world until the building of the Paris Observatory."

Quoting Max Toth from his book "Pyramid Prophecies:" "Once cut into approximate 1-ton blocks, the stones could not be barged across the River Nile. Flotation apparently was not the simple answer, as has been suggested. The blocks finally had to be ferried across by steamboat."

"Then, teams of 100 workers each tried to move the stones over the sand--- and they could not move them even an inch! Modern construction equipment had to be resorted to and once again, when the blocks of stone were finally brought to the building site, the teams could not lift their individual stones more than a foot or so. In the final construction step, a crane and a helicopter were used to position the blocks."

Now Mr. Dunn lets the 'Egyptologists' get their two cents in, specifically I.E.S. Edwards, who states, "moving a 1 ton block of limestone was not as difficult as the Japanese made it out to be:" " the experimenter soon found that *one man with no difficulty, could push the ton of stone along the wet mud.*" "In ancient records we see Egyptian crews dragging great weights on sleds while water bearers wet down the surface ahead."

Mr. Dunn rejected the noted Egyptologist's remarks, and my comments to Mr. Edwards would be, "Don't try to park that car in my garage!"

"Considering the immense size of the Great Pyramid, the precision with which it was built, the materials that were used, and the uniqueness of its interior passages and chambers, *we are faced with a structure that has no parallel in modern times." (Authors italics)*

"Meanwhile, the credibility of the old theories has been undermined by highly questionable armchair speculations that are passed on as facts – such as the idea that the Egyptians used copper chisels to shape hard, Ignatius rock."

"There is no way to ignore the accuracy of the stone cutting, despite Egyptologists' interpretations of the inscriptions found in pyramids or temples in Egypt."

"When told that giant limestone casing stones, which were cut to within 1/100 of an inch, were cut with hammer and chisel, a typical response was a shake of the head." (Authors comment: To be sure that shake of the head was not up and down.)

Mr. Dunn quotes Graham Hancock from a documentary. "The builders of the pyramids speak to us across the centuries and say 'We are not fools…. Take us seriously!'" "His comments sum up exactly the conclusions I had reached in 1977: The pyramid builders were as intelligent as we are today." "How they applied their knowledge may have been difficult, but it is obvious that they possessed sufficient knowledge to create an artifact having a distinct feature that, so far, *we have not been able to repeat." (Authors italics")*

"I have noticed many inconsistencies between what Egyptologists have taught regarding the tools that were supposedly used in the evidence that can be drawn from the masonry itself. In other words, the stones of the Great Pyramid tell me a different story than they have other observers the stones tell me that they were cut using *machine power*, not manpower as Orthodox Egyptologists theorize."

"The tools displayed by Egyptologists as instruments for the creation of many of these incredible artifacts are physically incapable of producing them." "So why do modern Egyptologists insist that this work was accomplished with a few primitive copper instruments."

"It is shocking that Petrie's studies of those fragments have not attracted greater attention, for there is unmistakable evidence of machine tooling methods.." "Evidence proving that the ancient Egyptians used tools such as straight saws, circular saws, and even lathes *have been recognized for over a century.*"

"I. E. S. Edwards, British Egyptologist and the worlds foremost expert on pyramids, said, "There axes and chisels were made of copper hardened by hammering." Mr. Dunn replies to that statement by saying, "I was struck that this statement was entirely ridiculous.""

"It is quite remarkable that a culture that possessed sufficient technical ability to make a lathe and progressed from there to develop a technique that enables them to machine radii in hard diorite would not have thought of the wheel by then." (Machine radii hard diorite vases have been found inside the Great Pyramid.)

"Egyptian artifacts representing tubular drilling are clearly the most astonishing and conclusive evidence yet presented to indicate the extent to which machining knowledge and technology were practiced in prehistory."

"For those who may still believe in the "official" chronology of the historical development of metals, identifying copper as the metal the ancient Egyptians used for cutting granite is like saying that aluminum could be cut using a chisel fashioned out of butter."

"When I was asked by the Egyptologists how the ancients could have produced this work with mere copper tools, I told them they were crazy and that they were using at least state-of-the-art techniques."

Sincerely,
Roger Hopkins

"In February 1995, I joined Graham Hancock and Robert Bauval in Cairo to participate in a documentary, while there I came across and measured some artifacts produced by the ancient pyramid builders that prove beyond a shadow of a doubt that highly advanced and sophisticated tools and methods were employed by this ancient civilization."

"Much of our ignorance of ancient cultures can be placed at the feet of closed-minded theorists, WHO IGNORE EVIDENCE THAT DOES NOT FIT THEIR THEORIES OR FALL WITHIN THE PROVINCE OF THEIR EXPERTISE."

The above statement is the most accurate, descriptive, sincere, honest and profound statement *ever made by anyone, in or out of Mr. Dunn's field of expertise, and I would have that stamped on any of the subject matter covered in this book!*

LOST TECHNOLOGIES OF ANCIENT EGYPT
BY CHRISTOPHER DUNN

My purpose here is to use a syllogistic approach to make obvious the difference of opinion espoused by Christopher Dunn between his first book, "Giza Power Plant," copyright 1998 and a book he wrote, copyright 2010 entitled, "Lost Technologies of Ancient Egypt."

I hope this will provide a solid example as to what has been, and is currently happening, specifically the pressure that is being placed on different authors, who write anything that deviates from the pseudo-propagandized dogma, relating to who built the Grand Pyramid and in general, Egyptology! I know that authors, Graham Hancock, and Robert Bouval, along with some others have stood tall and resisted being pressured or dictated too, as to how they should write their books. I commend them for that.

I think most anyone being exposed to the difference of Mr. Dunn's books, written 12 years apart will find it, to say the least, surprising. I personally would have to describe the difference between the two books as stupefying. Not only are the two books revelations, opinions, and findings, the antithesis of each other, I find them to be literally oxymoronic. Judge for yourself.

From, Shifting Paradigms, the forward written by Arlen Andrews Sr., ScD for Mr. Dunn's book.

"Large saw blades and other machine tools, if **not secreted away from armies, earthquakes, floods, and mobs,** would not endure very long. Over the millennia, few metal objects from our time would survive or be recognizable. *Life After People,* a popular cable television show that debuted in 2009, shows example after example of the deterioration of man-made objects after years, mainly because of lack of maintenance. In 5000 years, approximately the time span estimated in *Lost Technologies of Ancient Egypt,* almost nothing of today's technology would be left. In a world of resourceful (and destructive) human beings, the devastation would be much worse than Mother Nature alone could cause; **marauding bandits and nomads** would reuse, recycle or otherwise destroy even our ubiquitous automobile engine blocks and our porcelain toilet bowls cremation points.

"It may be that future archaeologists will one day uncover an untouched ancient factory or workshop under the sands or in the caves of Egypt."

Comment: I wish I had thunk of that.

"With centuries of experiment and the practice, those who worked in stone **could have kept their knowledge secret,** offering their finished products to leaders, priests, and the wealthy." "In ancient times the impulse to secrecy may have been even more necessary for survival."

Comment: Right! Just like they kept the Great Pyramid, 'secret.' Don't put that ink in my pen!

Mr. Dunn writes The article ("Advanced Machining in Ancient Egypt?" In the 1984 Analog magazine,) proposed that the ancient Egyptians were more advanced than previously believed and that they used advanced tools and methods to cut granite diorite and other difficult to work stone. It does not seem credible that brilliant architects and engineers would continue to use stone tools and copper chisels for three millennia.

Comment: The Egyptians did continue to use stone tools and copper chisels to build their collapsing, deteriorated, and crumbling pyramids for millennia. It was the **Anunnaki** who did the machining and built the Great Pyramid.

"The ancient *Egyptians who built the pyramids and the temples,* who crafted monumental statues out of the igneous rock, was thinking with the minds of architects, engineers, and craftspeople." (Authors italics)

"I have proposed in the past that higher levels of technology were used by the ancient Egyptians, but *you will find in this book that I have* rejected some ideas and **cast doubt on all my previous assertions as to the level of technology they enjoyed.**"

Comment: I could not describe, "Lost Technologies of Ancient Egypt," any better.

"Nobody can claim that they know what was in the minds of the ancient Egyptians. All we have by their works: "By their works, ye shall know them."*

Comment: Let me provide this impromptu quote: "By the **Anunnaki's** works ye shall know them."

"For an engineer or artisan, to walk through the Temple of Luxor is an exercise in humility."
"----- The experience of seeing these temples is suffused with profound sadness for a civilization that had risen to great heights and then suffered a cyclic decline."
"In exploring what is left – the mere skeletons of the Egyptians' achievements – and then going beyond, a veil is lifted to reveal the incredible material loss of a *people who created perfectly crafted buildings* and statues from the hardest stones known to mankind."

Comment: Mr. Dunn's book, "The Giza Power Plant," he attributes the ability and knowledge of building the Great Pyramid, and those who "created perfectly crafted buildings and statues from the hardest stones in the world.........too no one. In the above paragraph, he attributes all of that to "Egyptians' achievements." If so, with all those magnificent scientific achievements, which were, as he describes in "The Giza Power Plant," technology and scientific know-how that we cannot match today-- known to the Egyptians----- then why the decline!?

"Perfection was the goal, and the ancient *Egyptians' stoneworking craft*, as we shall see, was perfected to the extent that exactness was achieved."

"As I hope to demonstrate here, these statues of Ramses challenge the Giza Pyramids themselves as the most perfectly engineered artifacts of ancient Egypt – and perhaps of human history."

"While there are over one hundred known Ramses statues in Egypt, it is astonishing to learn that Amenophis 111, also known as Amenhotep, had more than two hundred fifty statues crafted in his likeness. Once we see the exacting accuracy on one statue, we can only imagine more than two hundred fifty being created. We can imagine a production assembly line, (all ancient Egyptians of course) with the roofers, finishers, and find detailers; followed up by an army of craftsmen applying deeply etched hieroglyphs and reliefs. Moreover, the execution of the design across Egypt, from Abu Sim Bell in the South to Memphis and Alexandria in the north, implies that a standardized system of measure and production line manufacturing must have existed that would *not be out of place in today's society.*"

"I visited the Seraphim in 1995 with a Canadian researcher named Robert McKenty. I possessed a precision-machined parallel that I had been using to determine the flatness at numerous granite blocks scattered around the Giza Plateau. The edge on the parallel was accurate to within

0.0002 inch (0.005 millimeters) or 1/10 the thickness of a human hair.

Comment: If we examine the 0.0002-inch measurement, that specificity is only required in the manufacturing of our spacecraft and satellites, etc. Here on the other side of the Egyptian spectrum, at the Seraphim, we Egyptians have numerous granite blocks scattered around the Giza Plateau, which we have honed down to 0.0002 inches by banging them by hand using diorite balls. And brother, my arms are tired!

"*The ancient Egyptians were engineering wizards* whose work never fails to impress, regardless of how many times we visit."

Comment: These kinds of statements are very frustrating for people like myself who have read and studied the Ancient Texts, which in plain understandable written language tell us that the **Anunnaki** built three pyramids at the Giza Plateau, **how** the Anunnaki built the three pyramids at the Giza Plateau, and **why** the Anunnaki built the three pyramids at the Giza Plateau. So let me finish this comment by saying something that many people may not be aware of **THE ANUNNA-KI BUILT THE THREE PYRAMIDS AT THE GIZA PLATEAU, STUPID!**

"What is remarkable and important about the Valley Temple contoured block is that it shows *the ancient Egyptians* crafted not only flat surfaces but also contoured surfaces, with uncommon precision."

The focus of this book is the evidence of engineering and engineering's symbolism behind *ancient Egyptian artifacts.* As we have seen there is symbolism behind their design and use of sacred geometry, such as the Pythagorean triangle, the Golden Ratio, and the Fibonacci.)

Comment: Here we are told that the ancient Egyptians are trying to convey abstract 'symbolism' and used 'sacred' geometry. What does that mean to convey engineering symbolism and what is sacred geometry? This *revelation* is coming from the ancient Egyptians whose more primary concern was to find a palm tree to go behind and relieve themselves. Now, there is a symbolism that I can understand!

Referring to the Temple of Hathor: "The winged globe, depicted upon a gigantic scale in the curve of the cornice, seems to hover above the central doorway."

Comment: The "winged globe" depicted above the central doorway is **the iconic symbol of the planet Nibiru.** Did I mention that the planet Nibiru is the home of the **Anunnaki!** And if their planet icon is above the entryway, I would have to at least lean towards thinking that the **Anunnaki** built the Temple of Hathor.

"Before we move away from the columns in the Great Hypostyle Hall, there is another feature associated with Hathor to which we should pay closer attention. Statues of Hathor usually depict her with bovine ears, Hathor was often depicted as a full cow with the sun disk between her horns or as a slender woman wearing horns and a sun disk headdress. Hathor is in the Great Hypostyle Hall at Dendera is seen with cow ears, and it is the location of the ears that give us some indication of the geometric replication of the capitals."

"I have spent a considerable amount of time trying to come to terms with how the temple was assembled. As I think of the structure in the comfort of my study, it appears in my mind as a highly complex assembly of precision parts. Even the reliefs on the architraves appear to conform to a particular pattern. Though there are variations between the anthropomorphic reliefs depicted, their overall shape and dimension are remarkably similar.

These images are just a small example of the vast array of images that cover every square inch of the inside of the temple. There seems to be strong evidence to support the view that the walls were carved after the blocks were placed.

Comment: Relating to the last three paragraphs written by Mr. Dunn, it provides an excellent example of being in the right church but the wrong pew. It is not a question of not seeing the forest for the trees, it is the question of too many authors denying that they are in a forest, yet that forest is an **Anunnaki forest.**

Mr. Dunn writes, "Before we move away from the columns in the Great Hypostyle Hall, there is *another feature associated with Hathor to which we should pay closer attention."* He goes on to tell us that "Hathor is a slender woman wearing horns in the sun disk headdress, as seen with cow ears and it is the location of the ears it gives us some indication the geometric replication of capitals." Now I'm going to reveal what the significance of the name Hathor should convey to anyone who gives a Wham, and what seems to be intentionally avoided by too many people.

From "The Earth Chronicles Handbook," HATHOR (Hat-Hor, `Abode of Horus'): A great early Egyptian goddess whose domain was the Sinai Peninsula--- especially its southern mountainous part, where turquoise mines were located (and thus her epithet,`Lady of the Mines'). She is depicted in Egyptian art with cow's horns flanking a planet as her headdress, and as she grew older she was nicknamed`The Cow'. Zechariah Sitchin has suggested that she was the goddess whom the Sumerians called **Ninmah,** who as a peacemaker between the warring **Anunnaki** clans, was assigned the neutral Fourth Region – the

Sinai Peninsula. There, her son **Ninurta (all Anunnaki)** built her a mountain abode, and she was granted the epithet **Ninharsag** (= `Lady of the Mountain Peak'). As she aged, the Sumerians depicted her with a cowlike head.

That "cow like" head is the icon of Hathor. **Hathor is an Anunnaki!** When you see the anthropomorphic reliefs anywhere in the Egyptian pantheon, i.e. a cow's head atop a human body, that iconically identifies Hathor. If you see a human body with the head of an Ibis bird, that is the icon of Thoth, an **Anunnaki,** etc. etc.

Previously in this chapter, I have given you the names and epithets of many of the **Anunnaki** for the simple purpose of reference. Whenever you hear or read any of these names, it's the **Anunnaki. ubiquitously they are intentionally overlooked and ignored.**

"Although only twenty-nine obelisks survived from the distant past, the ancient Egyptian landscape was at one time dotted what was estimated to be more than one hundred of these enigmatic shafts of pink granite. The obelisk was a focal point that gave the population heart and connection to their solar deity, the god Ra."

Here Ra is identified as a solar deity and the author moves on. But there is more to Ra than meets the written eye:

RA (=` The Pure One `): The son and successor of PTAH (Enki/ **Anunnaki**) as ancient Egypt's leading deity, who at times was called RA-AMEN (or AMON) –`The Unseen'. He was venerated as a great god "of Heaven and Earth," for he had come to earth from the `Planet of Millions of Years'(**Nibiru**) in his `Ben Ben' – a conical `celestial barge' which was In the Holy of Holies of a special Temple in Anu (the later Heliopolis). When expectations of the return of Nibiru into view began, the Unseen RA/Marduk (**Anunnaki**) was also worshiped as the Aten – the planet of the gods, depicted as a Winged Disk. (Iconic symbol of the planet **Nibiru home of the Anunnaki!**

"There should be no doubt by now that *the ancient Egyptians* were exceedingly brilliant in their conception and execution of large scale projects. But what powered the tool and how it was applied against the rock are questions that lead us to the real world of the ancient temple, statue, and obelisk builders. This was a world that engaged in engineering on a massive scale and building a civilization for millennia. Surely such a grand vision that allowed the ancient Egyptians to think in these terms **also 'requires us to grant them the intelligence' to have developed tools that are of similar scale and their grandeur."**

Comment: I totally disagree with that unfounded and disputable statement. That apple ain't going to find no pie!

"Academic historians may argue that modern engineers are overly influenced by their machines, thus all the Egyptians' works are interpreted through the prism of modern technology and there is little respect for the abilities and talents of the ancient Egyptians, who, they believe, may do with simple tools. For their part, engineers argue that the ancient Egyptian toolbox accepted by scholars has no tools in it that are capable of producing what is found in Egypt, and that to advance our understanding of that time in prehistory, *we must assign sensible and workable tools and methods that can physically demonstrate the capacity to create such work.*"

Comment: Let me restate that: We must assign sensible and workable tools and methods that can physically demonstrate the capacity to create such work and *we must assign it to the **Anunnaki** who repeatedly and comprehensively, in translated Sumerian, tell us the specifically named, four **Anunnaki** <u>who</u> built everything of lasting significance at the Giza Plateau, <u>how</u> the **Anunnaki** built those structures and <u>why</u> the **Anunnaki** built those structures.* In my opinion, the Egyptians did not have the "capacity" to build a **granite, two holer outhouse!**

"We, therefore, need have no hesitation in allowing that the graving out of lines in hard stone by jewel points, was a well-known art. And when we find on the surfaces of the *saw cuts in **diorite**,* grooves as deep as 1/100 inch, it appears far more likely that such were produced by **fixed jewel points**, than by any fortuitous rubbing about of a loose powder. And when, further, it is seen that in these deep grooves are almost always regular and uniform in depth and equidistant, **their production by the successive cuts of the jewel teeth appears to be without question."**

Comment: Then a couple of pages later Mr. Dunn writes: " If we apply Stock's data to determine how long it would take to saw the six sides of the granite box in Khafre's pyramid, it would take approximately 6, 270 hours. The total hours given are conservative estimates."

Realize that 6, 270 hours equates to 522.5 days, **working 24 hours a day**, for more than one year and a half. Now if we apply that same labor rate to produce (and not place into position) one four-ton granite block, and if there were let us say at least 100,000 granite blocks used in building the Great Pyramid, which contains an estimated total of 2.4 million blocks, based on the production of 100,000 granite blocks it would've taken the "Egyptians" **more than 150,000 years to build the Great Pyramid Alone!** My advice to those who keep perpetuating the ridiculous, absurd, and asinine and obtuse thinking that the Egyptians built any structure of difficulty in Egypt, – *GAVE IT UP!*

"As we consider the mega saw at Abu Roash, it might be useful to consider machines with similar dimensions that are in use today. Between 1987 and 1994, mega machines that were thought of as marvels of modern technology chewed through 31.6 miles (51 km) of calk marble beneath the English Channel at a rate of 482 feet (150 m) per week. Hardened steel and carbide bits at predetermined placements around the cutting face of a Tunnel Boring Machine (TBM) traveled around and 84-foot circumference, creating a tunnel that was 27 feet (8.2 m) in diameter. These were monster machines designed for a mammoth project in which size truly mattered."

•"objective evidence shows that **the ancient Egyptians used mega saws** for cutting granite, limestone, and basalt **that exceeded that diameter.**"

"One of the more widely known debates of the modern era was a contentious disagreement at the American Association for the Advancement of Science Convention in Chicago in 1992 between Egyptologist Dr. Mark Lehner of the Oriental Institute and geologist Dr. Robert Schoch of Boston University. Schoch became involved with the ancient Egyptian studies when he was persuaded by John Anthony West to write an opinion on West's claim, after Schwaller de Lubicz, that water weathering on the Great Sphinx, and especially on the Sphinx enclosure wall, was indicative of a much earlier than excepted date for his carving. After performing an on-site analysis, Schoch reported that the Great Sphinx is thousands of years older than scholars generally believe. Lehner called the findings "pseudoscience," and the normal cool politeness of academic debate was thrown on the sacrificial fire is heated voices continued past the time allotted and on into the hallway after the presentation."

"Lehner argued: "You don't overthrow Egyptian history based on one phenomenon like a weathering profile "and "that is how pseudoscience is done, not real science."

"Schoch, however, held to his evaluation, which was based on the science in which he was trained – geology – and he reiterated his studies of the Sphinx erosion. He used soundwaves, which suggested that the monuments crevices were carved sometime between 7000 and 5000 BCE.

"Scholars of Egyptian history have been scornful of Schoch's science because it is contrary to the research that generations of Egyptologists and archaeologists have developed."

Comment: My critique here is directed solely at the methodology of the argument presented between the two individuals, Mr. Lerner and Mr. Schoch. The above four paragraphs are typical of the extreme hubris attitude displayed by Egyptologists, The Antiquities Authorities of Egypt and people like Dr. Mark Lehner. If Dr. Lehner was open-minded enough and really looking for that which is empirical, he could have recommended that we had another individual with Mr. Schoch's geological credentials provide another study for them to look evaluate. There's absolutely nothing wrong and using a syllogistic approach to any problem, but no Dr. Lehner was not going to allow his professional opinion to be impugned by what he might later refer to as a Gee-ologist.

Mr. Schoch has science on his side and just as important, if not more so, the Ancient Texts. In reference to Dr. Lehner's statement, "You don't overthrow Egyptian history based on one phenomenon like a weathering profile." A weather profile conducted with the latest scientific instruments using soundwaves and duly applied knowledge can be described as a "phenomenon." A fact or event they can be scientifically described which is the definition of the phenomenon, however, Dr. Lehner is using another part of the definition of a phenomenon which is, "anything perceived by the `senses' as a fact:"

Dr. Lehner's hubris stands out like a crumbling pyramid. And the hubristic ideology practiced by too many scientists tells the world, we are at the apex of scientific knowledge. We know it all! My opinion is right, and anyone who wants to provide an opposing opinion or thought is wrong. Who is anyone, not in my specific scientific field, to tell me that they know more than I do?

Then we have this statement, "Scholars of Egyptian history have been scornful of Schoch's science." And I will put this quite bluntly, if you haven't read the Ancient Texts, to any degree, *you have little knowledge of Egyptian history!*

"If I consider all the evidence within the same engineering context without regard to the time each example was built, I am compelled to suggest that the ancient Egyptians had to have used sophisticated machines that cut diorite and granite with little difficulty. The evidence suggests that they had lathes and that lathes were built with precise bearings that regulated the rotation of the spindle. The contoured blocks on the Giza Plateau suggest and that they have that machine move that cut the exact, three-dimensional shapes on three axes.

Comment: I would simply change the word Egyptian to the word Anunnaki.

Stories of an older civilization have long been maintained in traditions of indigenous peoples who refer to them refer to them as a time when gods ruled the earth.

Comment: When the gods ruled the earth, those gods were the Anunnaki gods.

Perhaps it would turn its genius and industry into leaving a message that would survive the coming cataclysm and provide a technological imprint to say to future generations, "We were here. This is who we are and what we are capable of doing."

Comment: That is exactly what the Anunnaki tells us, in no uncertain terms, in all of the different ancient texts. All one has to do is **read them!**

The reason I chose Christopher Dunn's two books, "The Giza Power Plant" and "The Lost

Technologies of Ancient Egypt" is that they clearly demonstrated how one author's scientific findings after years of research can come to two different antithetical conclusions. Not a dichotomy of conclusion but the complete antithesis of conclusion.

In his first book's acknowledgment he gives thanks and credit to people like Robert Bauval, David Hatcher Childress, James Hagan, Graham Hancock, Roger Hopkins; Laura Lee, Robert McKenty, Tom Miller, Richard Noone, and others. And rightfully so, because they all agreed that Mr. Dunn did a brilliant job of applying his knowledge and expertise to the subject matter. If asked, I would add my name to that list with pride.

. Now let's look at the acknowledgment and credits from his second book, "Lost Technologies of Ancient Egypt: " Cecilia El Nadi, Bahgat El Nadi, Mohamed El Nadi, Semir Gharib, and Sharzhad Awyan. He also thanks Steven Mehler and Teresa Carter, who have been "invaluable supporters and have shined their own bright light on the true heritage of the ancient Khemitians (Egyptians)."

Robert Buval, J.J. Hurtak Ph.D., Michael S. Schneider, and John Desalvo Ph.D., none of which attribute the building of the Great Pyramid or any other large structures to the Egyptians. Then there is this:

"If you want to see the precise high technologies ancient Egyptian really had, read this book. It is a serious donation to the Egyptian legacy an opus for the future of this planet."

Antone Gigal, author, researcher,
And president of Giza for Humanity

"I believe, as Chris Dunn superbly details in this book, that ancient Egyptian sculptors and architects were so precise and that their works so monumental that they must have used sophisticated technology, probably hidden in their time and now lost to ours."

Mike Leckie, stone sculptor

The last two creditors attribute everything to the ancient Egyptians. Then there is the most disappointing thank you of all: "Special thanks going to Dr. Zahi Hawass for his Egyptian hospitality and helpfulness in providing permission to the worker's village, to the Great Pyramid, and the search field."

I use the word disappointed because if there is an individual who has fought, being obstinate using threats and intimidation against all who seek truth through scientific knowledge relating to Egypt and Egyptology, it is Zahi Hawass and the Egypt based Minister of State for Antiquities Affairs.

Mr. Hawass is also denied permission for DNA testing of Egyptian mummies. In December 2000, Waseda University in Japan and Cairo's Ain Shams University tried to obtain permission for DNA testing of Egyptian mummies and Mr. Hawass and the Egyptian government said no! Mr. Hawass's refusal of the DNA testing was because "DNA analysis was out of the question because it would not lead to anything."

Further according to Wikipedia-- "Hawass has been a long-standing opponent of normalized relations between Israel and Egypt. In January 2009 Hawass wrote in Al-Sharq Al-Awsat that "The concept of killing women, children, and elderly people.... seems to run in the blood of the Jews of Palestine" and that "the only thing that the Jews have learned from history's methods of tyranny and torment – so much so that they have become artist in this field." When confronted with this revealed information, Hawass replied, "He was not referring to the Jews." When you use the word Jews twice in the same sentence, who else could he be possibly referring too? In my opinion, Mr. Hawass is a 'bad actor, 'and if you want to find out how bad he and the Egyptian Minister of Antiquities are, read the last section in the chapter, "Who built the pyramids." Zahi Hawass is one of the last individuals on this earth that I would give a "special thanks" to! Perhaps Mr. Hawass had some influence over giving the Nobel peace prize to Barack Obama. They were both about equally deserving.

According to Wikipedia: "Hawass has been accused of domineering behavior, forbidding archaeologists to announce their own findings, and courting the media for his own gain after they were denied access to archaeological sights because, according to Hawass, they were too amateurish. Hawass has typically ignored or dismissed his critics, and when asked about it he indicated what he does is for the sake of Egypt and the preservation of antiquities."

Donald M. Blackwell

THE "LANDING PLACE"

"Having been the son of the goddess Ninsun and the highest priest of Uric, Gilgamesh was considered not just a demigod but "two-thirds Divine." This, he asserted, entitled him to avoid the death of a mortal. Yes, his mother told him-but to attain our longevity you have to go to our planet, Nibiru (where one year equals 3600 Earth years). So Gilgamesh journeyed from Sumer (now southern Iraq) to "The Landing Place" in the Cedar Mountains (Lebanon) where the rocket ships of the gods were lofted.

"*The Epic of Gilgamesh,* a text found inscribed on clay tablets, actually describes how Gilgamesh witnessed a rocket ship being launched from the Landing Place. A later Phoenician coin depicted such a rocket standing on a launching pad."

"The depiction shows, the launch facility was located on a great platform; and indeed, the truly ancient site of Baalbek encompassed a paved stone platform of about five million square feet!"

The Colossal Stone Blocks

"The most important section of that ancient Landing Place was its northwestern corner, where the remains of the Jupiter Temple are located. It runs stand atop a platform that rose even higher by rows of perfectly shaped stone blocks weighing some 600 tons each. (Fig. 3); this is a weight that no existing modern equipment can lift." (By comparison, the stone blocks of the great pyramid in Giza Egypt weigh about 25 tons each).

"These are far from being the largest stone blocks there. As described in my latest illustrated books *The Earth Chronicles Expeditions,* the ever-rising layers of the stone blocks form, in the North-Western corner, a funnel-like stone tower. The Western Wall of that tower-like structure has been reinforced with rows ("courses") of stone blocks weighing 900 tons each. On top of them, another higher course is made up of three unique stone blocks weighing 1, 100 tons each. Known as the Trilithon, these are the largest cut and shaped construction stone blocks in the world!

The Quarry

"The enigmas surrounding the site and the colossal stone blocks do not include one puzzle-- where were those stone blocks quarried; because at a stone quarry about 2 miles away from the site, one of these 1100 ton blocks is still there-- it's quarrying unfinished."

"To show it, and give an idea of its size, I had my group stand shoulder to shoulder at the foot of the stone block."

"The quarry is in a valley, a couple of miles from the site of the "ruins." This means that in antiquity, someone had the capability and technology needed for quarrying, cutting and shaping colossal stone blocks in the quarry-- then lifting the stone blocks up and carrying them to the construction site, and there, not just let go and drop the stone block, but place it precisely in the designated course. And there they have remained, intact and unshaken in spite of the passage of time and frequent earthquakes-- held together and in place without any mortar...."

Built before the Flood

"Who was that "someone?" What technology was used for the incredible feat? When and why was it done?"

"The Maronite Christians who for generations deemed themselves custodians of the site (before they were displaced by the Shiite Muslims) told legends of the "giants" who had built the colossal platform I found the answers in the ancient Sumerian texts and related them in *The Stairway to Heaven and the Wars of Gods and Men.*"

"The great stone platform was indeed the first **LANDING PLACE OF THE ANUNNAKI GODS ON EARTH,** built by them before they established a proper spaceport. It was the only structure that had survived the Flood, and was **USED BY ENKI AND ENLIL AS THE**

POST-DILUVIAL HEADQUARTERS FOR THE CONSTRUC-TION OF THE DEVASTATED EARTH."

C- Z. Sitchin 2006

Comment: There are those who can continue to kick Zechariah Sitchin's' "The Earth Chronicles" and the Sumerian texts can, down the road, but I have no intentions of letting them kick it out of sight or out of mind! It all boils down to the application of common sense and one simple sentence and explanation, **IT'S THE ANUNNAKI STUPID!**

Chapter 21: End of Book Synopsys

In 1994, although I did not recognize it at the time, was when my book writing odyssey began. I stopped by a yard sale that had literally several thousand books for sale. Being an avid reader of books relating to ancient times and archaeology, I purchased approximately six books. As I was paying the gentleman who was having the book yard sale, said to me, "Based on the kind of books that you have purchased, I'm sure you would be interested In A Book written by Zechariah Sitchin, entitled The 12th Planet." I asked him if the book was listed as fiction, as I do not read much fiction anymore. He said yes, it is listed as fiction but if you read it, I'm sure you will determine, as I did, it is not fiction. (Several Years ago, all of Mr. Sitchins' books were reclassified from fiction to New Age)

Months went by. The gentleman's words, "It is listed as fiction but it is not fiction", kept going through my mind. The title of the book, "The 12th Planet," seemed anything but intriguing to me. We have nine planets in our solar system, and I was surmising the author was going to do try to convince someone that there are actually 12? Finally, I went to the Hudson library, the first week in January 1994 and checked out Mr. Sitchin's, "The 12th Planet." I read the first 100 or so pages with a healthy dose of cynicism. Chapter six was very interesting, particularly the information pertaining to precession. I was vaguely familiar with precession and I immediately went to the computer and dictionary to acquire a better understanding.... it read: precession of the equinoxes: The earlier occurrence of the equinoxes in each successive sidereal year, because of a slow retrograde motion of the equinoctial points along the ecliptic, caused by the gravitational force of the Sun and Moon upon the earth and by the gravitational force of the planet's upon the earth's orbit: a complete revolution of the equinoxes requires about 26,000 years. Known as a Platonic year, (which is exactly 25,920 years.)

I then went on the computer, researching the Nippurian calendar and the library of Ashur Banipal in Nineveh, along with the Sumerian tablet in the British Museum (VAT.7847) as mentioned on page 181. It showed the mathematical calculations done by the Sumerians, in particular, the number 1,2960,000, the conclusion by professor H.V.

Hilprecht and others who have studied the ancient tablets that that number directly pertains only to the phenomenon of precession. My curiosity was enhanced.

On page 189, I found a diagram of VA 243 depicting a solar system, known to the Sumerians as a solar system consisting of 12 celestial bodies. I expanded the diagram several times with the idea that I would be able to better measure the distance between the planets and then comparing and collating their known distances between each other and the Sun on a horizontal plane.

Although my methodology will certainly not be considered scientific, it was enough to convince me that VA 243, potentially was a valid, scientifically sophisticated diagram and depiction of our solar system depicted in a B.C. Format.

At that time I became totally engrossed, intrigued and yes, even anxious! After finishing The 12th Planet and rereading The 12th Planet, my curiosity was now insatiable! I began reading everything I could find on the computer related to one each Zechariah Sitchin and his books relating to ancient civilizations.

At the beginning of The 12th Planet, I saw listed the other works of Zechariah Sitchin and the fact that The 12th Planets' first printing was in 1976, approximately 17 years ago. I spent days and many hours on the computer looking for any individual or organization that would offer a critique, a refutation, a challenge, a denial, in whole or in part of The 12 Planet'. **I found absolutely nothing of value to challenge Mr. Sitchins "The 12th Planet" or any of the other books he had written to date.**

One gentleman offered this critique, and I'll paraphrase: If the Anunnocki were such an advanced scientific race, why would they still be using a fuel source that bellows flames out the rear of the rocket engine. My answer to him would be, if he had read the ancient texts thoroughly enough he would've found that some of their craft used and described did not bellow flames from the rear of the engine as it had a different kind of propulsion system altogether. That they had helicopters and submarines and other types of craft. In interplanetary and planetary travel the Anunnocki used water as a source of fuel, obviously having the scientific know-how in separating the hydrogen from water. One of the major obstacles just considering our interplanetary travel in our solar system would be a source of fuel. They used water as a source of hydrogen propulsion and as a weapon because water can be found on other planets and moons in our solar system.

One section of the ancient texts describes the Anunnocki spacecraft landing on a planet to refuel. Without getting out of the craft, a circular tube was extended to a source of water which was then brought aboard the craft via the circular tube. The craft was then on its way.

It might be interesting to note that one glass of water provides enough hydrogen when separated to satisfy the entire electrical requirements of New York City for 24 hours.

The only other critique I could find, if you could call his offering a critique, was a gentleman who questioned the conjugation of verbs and words in the Sumerian language that Mr. Sitchin using his books in interpreting the meaning of certain words whether it be in Sumerian, Akkadian, Semitic Hebrew, etc. etc. The reader should be informed that Mr. Sitchin speaks and writes in seven different languages. I would ask the gentleman who questioned Mr. Sitchins linguistic abilities in writing and specific interpretations of the meanings of words, why haven't you put your linguistic interpretation of the meaning of words relating to the languages in question in print? As of this date, I have seen nothing. The above two paragraphs were the **only** critiques of any nature that I found at the time. That tells me much, of what l needed to know in reference to Mr. Sitchins, writings.

I have read every book of every credible author I could find. All books by David Hatcher Childress, Neil Zimmer, Will Hart, Graham Hancock, Robert Buvall, Von Daniken and others. All of these authors have specific themes and subject matter that blend in and complement Sitchin's writings. I say to the reader of this book, if you have an interest in any of the areas of this book, please start your reading with the books of Zechariah Sitchin. There you will find very little opinion, and innumerable condensed and usable, extremely well-researched information using verifiable ancient texts.

In my opinion, Zechariah Sitchin is a brilliant man whose books, to say the least, are profoundly educational and if the reader wants to personally educate themselves, I enthusiastically recommend any and all of Mr. Sitchins' 14 books be read first.

The reader of Mr. Sitchin's and the ancient Sumerian Texts will soon come to realize that Mr. Sitchin is not expressing his opinion in his writings, he is expressing his interpretation of the ancient texts and then presents the reader with the opportunity to read and evaluate for themselves his interpretation of that particular text. For example; Read chapter 7, of the 12th planet which is The Epic of Creation. Then read Enuma Elish, The Seven Tablets of Creation by Leonard William King which was originally published in 1902. One will quickly realize that the ancient texts cannot be read as you would a novel, that they are in most cases a difficult read that needs to be read, reread and seriously studied. Throughout Mr. Sitchin's books, the above-described methodology of writing is repeated throughout each of his 14 books. Then you, the reader, can decide what is empirically written or not!

Bibliography

Allegro, John Margo, – The People of the Dead Sea Scrolls, Double-day and Company Inc., New York, 1958.

Armor, R. A. – *Gods and Myths of Ancient Egypt.* *1986.*

Balfour, M. D. – *Stonehenge, and Its Mysteries.* *1980.*

Barton, George A. The Royal Inscriptions of Sumer and Akkad. 1929.

Breasted, James Henry, – A History of Egypt From the Earliest Times To the Persian Conquest, Charles Scribner's Sons, New York, 1937.

Budge, E. A. W. *The Gods of the Egyptians.* 1904.

Budge, E.A. Wallis, and King, L. W. – Annals of the Kings of Assyria. 1902.

Dalley, S. – *Myths from Mesopotamia.* 1989.

Edwards, I. E. S. – *The Pyramids of Egypt.* *1961.*

Enuma Elish: The Babylonian Epic of Creation. 1923.

Fakhry, Ahmed, – The Pyramids, The University Of Chicago Press, Chicago, 1961.

Goldsmith, Donald and Tobias Owen, – The Search for Life in the Universe, The Benjamin/Cummings Publishing Company., Inc., Menlo Park, 1980.

Guterbock, Hans G. "Hittite Mythology" in Mythologies of the Ancient World.

Hart, Will. *The Genesis Race.* Bear and Company. Rochester, Vermont. 2003.

Hamilton, Tolbert, – The Great Pyramid, Its Importance and Significance in Today's World. Tolbert Hamilton. 1979

Hancock, Graham. *Fingerprints of the Gods. New York: Crown, 1995.*

Hilprecht, Herman V. – Reports of the Babylonian Expedition: Cuneiform Texts. 1893 – 1914

Hilprecht, Herman V. – *Old Babylonian Inscriptions.* *Anniversary Volume.* *1909.*

Jacobson, Thorkild – *The Treasures of Darkness.* Yale University 1976.

King, Leonard W. – Babylonian Magic and Sorcery, being "The Prayers of the Lifting of the Hand." 1896

Babylonian Religion and Mythology. 1899.

The Seven Tablets of Creation. 1902.

Kramer, Samuel M. – *Lamentation over the Destruction of Ur.* *1940.*

From the Tablets of Sumer. 1956.

History Begins at Sumer. 1959.

Sumerian Mythology. 1961.

The Sumerians. 1963.

The Myth of the Pickax.

Kramer, S. N., and Meyer, J. (eds.) – *Myths of Enki, the Crafty God.* *1989.*

Krupp that he gets, E. C. (ed.) – *In Search of Ancient Astronomys.* *1978.*

Lemesurier, Peter. *The Great Pyramid Decoded.* Rockport, Massachusetts: Element Books, 1996

Lambert, W. G., And Millard, A. R. -Atra-Hasis, The Babylonian Story of the Flood. 1970.

Mencken, A. – *Designing and Building the Great Pyramid.* 1963.

Milton, Richard. *Shattering the Myths of Darwinism.* Rochester, Vt.: Park Street Press, 1997.

New G Bauer, Oh. – *Astronomical Cuneiform Texts.* 1935.

Noorbergen, René, – Secrets of the Lost Races, New Discoveries of Advanced all day and I will Technology in Ancient Civilizations, – Merrill Company., Inc., Indianapolis. 1977.

Petrie, Sir W. M. Flinders – The Royal Tombs of the Earliest Dynasties, 1901.

Pinches, Theophilus G. – "Some Mathematical Tables in the British Museum." 1909.

Sanders, N. K., – The Epic of Gilgamesh, Cox, and Wyman, Limited., London, 1964.

SITCHIN, Zechariah – *THE 12TH PLANET*

The Stairway to Heaven

The Wars of Gods and Men

The Lost Realms

When Time Began

The Cosmic Code

The End of Days

The Earth Chronicles Handbook   2009   Bear & Company

Companion Books

Genesis Revisited

Divine Encounters

The Lost Book of Enki

There Were Giants Upon the Earth   2010   Bear & Company

Autobiographical Books

The Earth Chronicles Expeditions

Journeys to the Mystical Past

Janet Sitchin – The Anunnaki Chronicles   2015 Bear & Company

Summer, A. Dupont, – The Essene Writings from Qumran, Basil Blackwell, Oxford, 1961.

Tompkins, Peter. *Secrets of the Great Pyramid.* New York: Harper and Row, 1971.

The Electronic Text Corpus of Sumerian Literature

Atra-Hasis.

Babylonian Table No. 74329 – Sumerian Record of the Line of Ka'in.

Babylonian Text –CT-XU1-44/46.

Book of the Generations of Adam.

A Hymn to Enlil the All Beneficent.

Kadmos Vol. Vl- A. R. Millard Translated by W. G. Lambert

Lamentation for the Destruction of Ur.

Tale of Adapa.

Text of 5001.

The Adam – A Slave Made to Order.

Ea and the Earth.

Enki andNinmah: The Creation of Mankind.

The Attestation of Endubsar.

The Epic of Adapa.

The Epic of Etana.

The Era Epos.

The Eridu Genesis.

Lamentation over the Destruction of Ur.

The Lamentation Texts.

The Lament of Sumer and Urim.

The Legend of King Keret.

Man and His God: Sumerian poem

Deployment of Erra and Ishum: A Babylonian Poet's View of War.

Prophecy Text: Akkadian version.

The Tale of Aqhat.

The Urek Lament

Ancient India text:

The Complete Mahabharata: (Volume 1 of 4) Krishna-Dwaipayana Vyasa – Digireads Publishing copyright 2013.

Mahabarata Book 8 Karna Parva.

Ramayana